The Body in the Mind

THE BODY
IN THE
MIND

The Bodily Basis
of Meaning,
Imagination, and
Reason

Mark Johnson

The University of Chicago Press
Chicago and London

MARK JOHNSON is professor of philosophy at Southern
Illinois University. He is the author, with George Lakoff,
of *Metaphors We Live By,* also published by the University
of Chicago Press, and the editor of *Philosophical Perspectives
on Metaphor.*

Figures 13, 14, 15, and 16 in Chapter 4 originally appeared
in Chapter 1 of Rudolph Arnheim, *Art and Visual
Perception,* as figures 1, 2, 3, and 5. © 1974 The Regents of
the University of California. Used by permission of the
University of California Press.

The University of Chicago Press, Chicago 60637
The University of Chicago Press, Ltd., London

Library of Congress Cataloging-in-Publication Data
Johnson, Mark, 1949–
   The body in the mind.

   Bibliography: p.
   Includes index.
   1. Meaning (Philosophy)   2. Imagination
(Philosophy)   3. Reason.   4. Metaphor.   I. Title.
BI05.M4J64   1987   121'.68   86-25102
ISBN 0-226-40317-3

For Sanders and Paul Michael

Contents

Preface

A Crisis in the Theory of Meaning and Rationality

Without imagination, nothing in the world could be meaningful. Without imagination, we could never make sense of our experience. Without imagination, we could never reason toward knowledge of reality. This book is an elaboration and defense of these three controversial claims. It explores the central role of human imagination in all meaning, understanding, and reasoning.

It is a shocking fact that none of the theories of meaning and rationality dominant today offer any serious treatment of imagination. You will not find it discussed in any of the standard texts on semantics or in any of the most influential studies of rationality. These works will, of course, acknowledge that imagination plays a role in discovery, invention, and creativity, but they never investigate it as essential to the structure of rationality.

The total absence of an adequate study of imagination in our most influential theories of meaning and rationality is symptomatic of a deep problem in our current views of human cognition. The difficulty, as I shall argue, is not a matter of mere oversight, so that we might simply fill in the gap by inserting a chapter on imagination into our theories of mind, language, and knowledge. The problem is far more distressing, for it concerns our entire orientation toward these issues, based as it is upon a widely shared set of presuppositions that deny imagination a central role in the constitution of rationality.

I shall give the name "Objectivism" to the offending cluster of assumptions that has led to this blindness toward imagination. As we shall see, this Objectivist orientation is rooted deeply in the Western philosophical and cultural tradition, and it has recently been elaborated in highly sophisticated ways by philosophers, linguists, psychologists, and computer scientists generally. But Objectivism is not merely an abstruse philosopher's project; it plays an important role in all our lives. In its nonsophisticated manifestation, as a set of shared commonplaces in our culture, it takes the following general form: The world consists of objects that have properties and stand in various relationships independent of human understanding. The world is as it is, no matter what any person happens to believe about it, and there is one correct "God's-Eye-View" about what the world really is like. In other words, there is a rational structure to reality, independent of the beliefs of any particular people, and correct reason mirrors this rational structure.

To describe an objective reality of this sort, we need language that expresses concepts that can map onto the objects, properties, and relations in a literal, univocal, context-independent fashion. Reasoning to gain knowledge of our world is seen as requiring the joining of such concepts into propositions that describe aspects of reality. Reason is thus a purely formal capacity to connect up, and to draw inferences from, these literal concepts according to rules of logic. Words are arbitrary symbols which, though meaningless in themselves, get their meaning by virtue of their capacity to correspond directly to things in the world. And rational thought can be viewed as an algorithmic manipulation of such symbols.

There is nothing about human beings mentioned anywhere in this account—neither their capacity to understand nor their imaginative activity nor their nature as functioning organisms nor anything else about them. Thus, according to recent versions of Objectivism, the *humanness* (the human embodiment) of understanding has no significant bearing on the nature of meaning and rationality. The structure of rationality is regarded as transcending structures of bodily experience. And meaning is regarded as objective, because it consists only in the relation between abstract symbols and things (with their properties and relations) in the world. As a consequence, the way human beings grasp things as meaningful—the way they understand their experience—is held to be incidental to the nature of meaningful thought and reason.

This view of the objective nature of meaning and rationality has been held for centuries by philosophers in the Western tradition, and, in the last several decades, it has come to define *the* dominant research program in a number of related disciplines. In philosophy, linguistics, psychology, computer science, and other disciplines within the new field of "cognitive science," this Objectivist semantics has been developed in a highly technical and logically rigorous fashion.

Within the last decade, a crisis has arisen. This received Objectivist view of meaning and rationality has been seriously questioned, both on logical grounds and on grounds of a wide-ranging collection of empirical studies. The logical argument has been given forceful expression most notably by Hilary Putnam.[1] It concerns the general nature of the relation between systems of abstract symbols and models of the world. Briefly, Putnam demonstrates that any attempt to provide meaning for abstract symbols via their direct and unmediated correspondence to the world, or any model of it, must inevitably violate our most basic understanding of what meaning itself is.

The empirical evidence comes from studies in many different disciplines, all of which share a common concern, namely, they focus on phenomena where human understanding is required for an account of meaning and reason. Among the more important phenomena that have been explored, as challenging Objectivist assumptions, are the following:

Categorization. The classical (Objectivist) view holds that categories are defined by necessary and sufficient conditions which specify the properties shared by all and only members of the category. Recent studies show that, although a few of our categories fit the classical model, most of them differ insofar as they involve imaginative structures of understanding, such as schemata, metaphor, metonymy, and mental imagery. Furthermore, their structures typically depend on the nature of the human body, especially on our perceptual capacities and motor skills. Such categories are formed on the basis of imaginatively structured cognitive models, and their nature is such that they could not correspond directly to anything in reality external to human experience.[2]

Framing of concepts. On the classical view, concepts exist by themselves, objectively. They are characterized only by their relation to states of affairs in the real world, or possible worlds. They are thus independent of any imaginatively structured way of conceiving a domain of human experience. Empirical studies indicate, on the contrary, that most human concepts are defined and understood only within conceptual frameworks that depend on the nature of human experience in given cultures. Such concepts are neither universal nor objective in any sense acceptable within the classical view.[3]

Metaphor. Until recently, metaphors have been regarded as deviant linguistic expressions whose meaning, if any, is reducible to some set of literal propositions. Those propositions, in turn, are understood in terms of the traditional theory of meaning, that is, as characterized by virtue of their ability to fit objective reality. In contrast to this reductionist view, there is a growing body of evidence that metaphor is a pervasive, irreducible, imaginative structure of human understanding that influences the nature of meaning and constrains our rational inferences.[4]

Polysemy. Polysemy is the phenomenon whereby a single word has many meanings that are systematically related (e.g., *newspaper* in "The ad's in the *newspaper*" and "He works for the *newspaper*"). Polysemy is contrasted with homonymy, which involves completely different words that happen to sound (or be written) the same way (e.g., *bank* in "My money's in the *bank*" and *bank* in "Let's go sit by the *bank* of the river"). The traditional account of meaning has never come to grips with the full range of cases of polysemy. Recent studies indicate why this is so: Polysemy involves the extension of a central sense of a word to other senses by devices of the human imagination, such as metaphor and metonymy, and there is no place for this kind of account in the Objectivist view.[5]

Historical semantic change. Standard accounts of semantic change have been overly constricted by the constraints imposed by traditional theories of meaning.[6] They were limited by and large to cases where meanings were either expanded, narrowed, or changed to the opposite. However, Sweetser has demonstrated that there is a large class of historical semantic changes within Indo-European that can only be explained via metaphorical projections within the human conceptual system which are motivated by common human experiences.[7] This mode of explanation goes beyond the traditional theory of meaning because it involves imaginative patterns of human understanding that are projected to connect up different cognitive domains.

Non-Western conceptual systems. On the Objectivist account, there are no truly different alternative conceptual systems for grasping aspects of our experience. Apparently different systems are allegedly reducible to one universal set of concepts that map directly onto the objective features of the world. In recent years, there have been studies of the

semantics of non–Western languages done in very great detail—sufficient detail to demonstrate that the conceptual systems underlying
some of them are fundamentally different from, and even incommen-
surable with, our conceptual system. For example, we have found that
the conceptions of space and time upon which certain non–Western
languages are structured is radically different in kind from the conceptions on which familiar Indo–European languages are structured.[8]

Growth of knowledge. The classical Objectivist view of knowledge
assumes that "science" produces successive theories that progress ever
and ever closer to *the* correct description of reality. And, even though
we will never achieve the final, complete account, it is believed that
genuine empirical knowledge involves universal logical structures of
inference whose results can be tested against theory-neutral "objective" data. This foundationalist view of knowledge presupposes an
Objectivist view of both meaning and rationality. As a result of an impressive and mushrooming body of research on the growth of scientific knowledge, this Objectivist view has been turned on its head, at
least in its strong version. We have learned that what counts as knowledge is always a contextually dependent matter—there are no "theory-
neutral data" in the required Objectivist sense, and criteria of rationality are ineliminably evaluative and dependent on our purposes and
interests. Consequently, most versions of Objectivist theories of meaning and rationality have been undermined by our new understanding
of the nature and development of human knowledge.[9]

The studies in any one of these areas are sufficient to radically question Objectivist views of meaning and rationality. Taken together, they
are overwhelming. They create a crisis in the theory of meaning and
rationality by showing us that we cannot preserve our deeply rooted
Objectivist commitments. In particular, this vast network of related
empirical studies, in conjunction with the logical argument voiced by
Putnam, points to one fundamental moral: *any adequate account of meaning and rationality must give a central place to embodied and imaginative structures of understanding by which we grasp our world.* The traditional Objectivist accounts focus on a very restricted set of phenomena, ignoring,
for the most part, just those kinds of phenomena mentioned above,
which have given rise to the "crisis." So, it has become necessary to
open up the field of semantics, and to enrich our account of reason, in
order to comprehend this new range of phenomena that are now being
recognized as central to human understanding.

Putting the Body Back into the Mind

The key to an adequate response to this crisis is to focus on something that has been ignored and undervalued in Objectivist accounts of meaning and rationality—the *human body,* and especially those structures of imagination and understanding that emerge from our embodied experience. The body has been ignored by Objectivism because it has been thought to introduce subjective elements alleged to be irrelevant to the objective nature of meaning. The body has been ignored because reason has been thought to be abstract and transcendent, that is, not tied to any of the bodily aspects of human understanding. The body has been ignored because it seems to have no role in our reasoning about abstract subject matters.

Yet, in all of the empirical studies cited above, which have given rise to the crisis, the embodiment of human meaning and understanding manifests itself over and over, in ways intimately connected to forms of imaginative structuring of experience. The kind of imaginative structuring uncovered in these studies does not involve romantic flights of fancy unfettered by, and transcending, our bodies; rather, they are forms of imagination that grow out of bodily experience, as it contributes to our understanding and guides our reasoning.

To illustrate this important and undervalued notion of embodied, imaginative understanding, let us consider two types of imaginative structure that are central to the present study: image schemata and metaphorical projections. An image schema is a recurring, dynamic pattern of our perceptual interactions and motor programs that gives coherence and structure to our experience. The VERTICALITY schema, for instance, emerges from our tendency to employ an UP-DOWN orientation in picking out meaningful structures of our experience. We grasp this structure of verticality repeatedly in thousands of perceptions and activities we experience every day, such as perceiving a tree, our felt sense of standing upright, the activity of climbing stairs, forming a mental image of a flagpole, measuring our children's heights, and experiencing the level of water rising in the bathtub. The VERTICALITY schema is the abstract structure of these VERTICALITY experiences, images, and perceptions. One of the central arguments of this book is that experientially based, imaginative structures of this image-schematic sort are integral to meaning and rationality.

A second, related type of embodied imaginative structure central to my inquiry is metaphor, conceived as a pervasive mode of understanding by which we project patterns from one domain of experience in order to structure another domain of a different kind. So conceived, metaphor is not merely a linguistic mode of expression; rather, it is one of the chief cognitive structures by which we are able to have coherent, ordered experiences that we can reason about and make sense of. Through metaphor, we make use of patterns that obtain in our physical experience to organize our more abstract understanding. Understanding via metaphorical projection from the concrete to the abstract makes use of physical experience in two ways. First, our bodily movements and interactions in various physical domains of experience are structured (as we saw with image schemata), and that structure can be projected by metaphor onto abstract domains. Second, metaphorical understanding is not merely a matter of arbitrary fanciful projection from anything to anything with no constraints. Concrete bodily experience not only constrains the "input" to the metaphorical projections but also the nature of the projections themselves, that is, the kinds of mappings that can occur across domains.

As an example of this constraint on meaning and reasoning, let us consider a very simple, but pervasive, metaphorical understanding: MORE IS UP. The propositional expression "more is up" is a somewhat misleading shorthand way of naming a complex experiential web of connections that is not itself primarily propositional. It is no accident that we understand QUANTITY in terms of the VERTICALITY schema mentioned above in exactly the way we do. Examples such as *Prices keep going up; The number of books published each year keeps rising; His gross earnings fell; Turn down the heat,* and many others, suggest that we understand MORE (increase) as being oriented UP (involving the VERTICALITY schema). There is a good reason why this metaphorical projection from UP to MORE is natural, and why MORE is not oriented DOWN. The explanation has to do with our most common everyday bodily experiences and the image schemata they involve. If you add more liquid to a container, the level goes up. If you add more objects to a pile, the level goes up. MORE and UP are therefore correlated in our experience in a way that provides a *physical* basis for our *abstract* understanding of quantity.

In this book, then, the term "body" is used as a generic term for the embodied origins of imaginative structures of understanding, such as image schemata and their metaphorical elaborations. An alternative way to state my project is to say that, contrary to Objectivism, I focus on the indispensability of embodied human *understanding* for meaning and rationality. "Understanding," of course, is here regarded as populated with just those kinds of imaginative structures that emerge from our experience as bodily organisms functioning in interaction with an environment. Our understanding, I shall argue, involves many pre-conceptual and nonpropositional structures of experience (such as image schemata) that can be metaphorically projected and proposi-tionally elaborated to constitute our network of meanings.

Finally, in addition to the key terms "body," "imaginative struc-ture," and "understanding," I want to emphasize a notion of "experi-ence" richer than that typically countenanced by Objectivism. Image schemata and metaphorical projections are *experiential* structures of meaning that are essential to most of our abstract understanding and reasoning. The metaphorical projections are not arbitrary but rather are highly constrained by other aspects of our bodily functioning and experience. "Experience," then, is to be understood in a very rich, broad sense as including basic perceptual, motor-program, emotional, historical, social, and linguistic dimensions. I am rejecting the classical empiricist notion of experience as reducible to passively received sense impressions, which are combined to form atomic experiences. By contrast, experience involves everything that makes us human—our bodily, social, linguistic, and intellectual being combined in complex interactions that make up our understanding of our world.

The Body in the Mind is thus an exploration into some of the more important embodied imaginative structures of human understanding that make up our network of meanings and give rise to patterns of in-ference and reflection at all levels of abstraction. My purpose is not only to argue *that* the body is "in" the mind (i.e., that these imagina-tive structures of understanding are crucial to meaning and reason) but also to explore *how* the body is in the mind—how it is possible, and necessary, after all, for abstract meanings, and for reason and imagina-tion, to have a bodily basis.

Acknowledgments

Six years ago, when George Lakoff and I finished *Metaphors We Live By,* we were painfully aware that our inquiries into the central role of metaphor in human understanding raised a number of difficult issues about the nature of meaning, understanding, and rationality. Since then, we have maintained an ongoing dialogue as we each pursued questions related to that initial joint project. I could never express fully my gratitude to George for his deep insights, unfailing support, sustained criticism, and abiding commitment to our shared undertaking.

There are other important people without whom this body of work would never have achieved even a semblance of sense and coherence. These are people who read one or more versions of this book and supplied copious comments, upon which I have depended heavily. During my stay at Berkeley last year, Claudia Brugman and Eve Sweetser were especially generous with their time, effort, and linguistic insight. On the philosophical side, I want to express my appreciation to Robert N. McCauley and George McClure, who have spent untold hours working on my manuscript and trying to educate me through our continued conversations over the last six years. David Clarke, Michele Emanation, Thomas Mitchell, Bob Radtke, and an anonymous reviewer for the University of Chicago Press have also worked hard in supplying criticism and suggestions on earlier versions. Nancy Tuana co-authored the analysis of Hans Selye's metaphorical reasoning (in Chapter 5). I have benefited also from discussions of semantics with David Banach, Geoffrey Nathan, and Margaret Winters.

Much of my work was completed during a sabbatical granted to me by Southern Illinois University at Carbondale. During part of that time I had the good fortune to receive a development award to work at the Institute of Cognitive Studies, University of California, Berkeley. Anyone who has ever been associated with that interdisciplinary community knows what a stimulating and supportive group it is. In addition to people already named above, I want to thank Hubert Dreyfus, John Searle, and Leonard Talmy for lectures and conversations that shaped my views.

My debt to my wife, Sandra McMorris Johnson, is of a different nature. As an artist, she has gone beyond mere discussion of the nature of meaning to create works of art that make palpably present dimensions of meaning that are not propositional in any ordinary sense. To see her work is to begin to glimpse the depths of meaning that emerge through color, line, texture, form, and sheer physical presence.

Another major force on my thinking has been my son, Paul Michael, who grew to age two as I was working out the bulk of my project. Every single day he gurgled, grasped, crawled, sucked, tottered, and groped his way toward a balanced upright posture and the miracle of speech that comes along with it; he reminded me constantly of the obvious centrality of our embodiment in the constitution of our world and of all its possibilities for meaning.

Introduction: The Context and Nature of This Study

The Importance of the Body in Meaning and Reason

We human beings have bodies. We are "*rational* animals," but we are also "rational *animals,*" which means that our rationality is embodied. The centrality of human embodiment directly influences what and how things can be meaningful for us, the ways in which these meanings can be developed and articulated, the ways we are able to comprehend and reason about our experience, and the actions we take. Our reality is shaped by the patterns of our bodily movement, the contours of our spatial and temporal orientation, and the forms of our interaction with objects. It is never merely a matter of abstract conceptualizations and propositional judgments.

In this book I am going to explore some of the more important ways in which structures of our bodily experience work their way up into abstract meanings and patterns of inference. Special attention is devoted to imaginative structuring and projection, as they affect human meaning, understanding, and rationality. My argument begins by showing that human bodily movement, manipulation of objects, and perceptual interactions involve recurring patterns without which our experience would be chaotic and incomprehensible. I call these patterns "image schemata," because they function primarily as abstract structures of images. They are gestalt structures, consisting of parts standing in relations and organized into unified wholes, by means of which our experience manifests discernible order. When we seek to comprehend this order and to reason about it, such bodily based schemata play a central role. For although a given image schema may emerge first as a structure of bodily interactions, it can be figuratively developed and extended as a structure around which meaning is organized at more abstract levels of cognition. This figurative extension and elaboration typically takes the form of metaphorical projection from the realm of physical bodily interactions onto so-called rational processes, such as reflection and the drawing of inferences from premises. I shall try to show that what are often thought of as abstract meanings and inferential patterns actually do depend on schemata derived from our bodily experience and problem-solving.

There are two especially controversial aspects of the view I will be developing concerning the centrality of image schematic structures in the organization of meaning and in the nature of our inferences. *The first is their apparently nonpropositional, analog nature. The second is their figurative character, as structures of embodied imagination.*

I cannot overemphasize the importance of these two aspects. This book consists chiefly in an extended development of these characteristics of image schemata and their radical implications for a theory of human meaning, understanding, and rationality. The key terms to be explicated include: "image schema," "metaphor," "imagination," "nonpropositional," and "embodied." Since my general perspective is partly at odds with the mainstream theories, it is important to guard against assuming that I employ these terms with their standard meanings. Although I intend to keep these key notions connected to their ordinary meanings, it is necessary to extend them beyond their usual scope. For example, I will not be using "metaphor" in the traditional sense as merely a figure of speech; rather, I shall identify it as a pervasive, indispensable structure of human understanding by means of which we figuratively comprehend our world. And I shall argue that "imagination" is a basic image-schematic capacity for ordering our experience; it is not merely a wild, non-rule-governed faculty for fantasy and creativity. Furthermore, I will eventually show that certain image-schematic meaning structures are not "propositional" in the traditional sense, and yet they *are* propositional in a *special sense* that makes them central to our rationality. At the end of my account, I hope to have given these terms meanings that are both connected to standard or ordinary usage but that make better sense of our experience of meaning and reasoning than the received views do.

According to the dominant philosophical views of meaning and rationality, neither of the above two characteristics of image schemata (i.e., their nonpropositional and imaginative character) is considered relevant to the proper conceptual and propositional nature of meaning.

Virtually everyone agrees that human *experience* and *meaning* depend in some way upon the body, for it is our contact with the entire spatio-temporal world that surrounds us. However, the received notion of the role of bodily input (into meaning and inference patterns) does not include a place for nonpropositional, figuratively elaborated schematic structures.

In the Preface I gave the name "Objectivism" to the tradition that treats meaning and rationality as purely conceptual, propositional, and algorithmic, and therefore in no way dependent on metaphorical extensions of nonpropositional image schemata. Since Objectivists think that meaning and rationality transcend the way individuals might happen to grasp meanings or understand reasoning processes, they tend to view reason in abstract and absolute terms, as if it operated in a realm free of bodily constraints and governed only by its own logical rules. In other words, reason is regarded as master of its own autonomous realm, subject only to its own structures, and providing a universally valid basis for rational analysis and criticism. And, as we shall see later, this Objectivist vision of abstract reason lends support to the argument that humans have access to a value-neutral, ahistorical framework for correctly describing reality.

My central purpose is to develop a constructive theory of imagination and understanding that emphasizes our embodiment as the key to dealing adequately with meaning and reason (and which, incidentally, solves or dissolves certain problems intrinsic to Objectivism). I am going to explore a hitherto neglected domain of human cognition—an area in which what is typically regarded as the "bodily" works its way up into the "conceptual" and the "rational" by means of imagination.

Since the view of meaning, understanding, and reason that I will be developing is largely at odds with the dominant Objectivist tradition in Western philosophy, I want to describe this tradition more fully, in order to explain why it neglects just those aspects of understanding that I shall be emphasizing, namely, operations on nonpropositional, figuratively developed schematic structures in the formation of meaning and in the drawing of inferences based on that meaning.

Objectivist Theories of Meaning and Rationality

So far, I have only described Objectivism as a loosely related cluster of assumptions that form a more or less commonsense view of relations among mind, language, and the physical world. It assumes a fixed and determinate mind-independent reality, with arbitrary symbols that get meaning by mapping directly onto that objective reality. Reasoning is a rule-governed manipulation of these symbols that gives us objective knowledge, when it functions correctly.

It is now necessary to get more precise about Objectivist commitments, if we are to see why a theory of imagination is so badly needed. In particular, we need a statement of the chief implications of Objectivism for the theories of meaning and rationality that dominate contemporary cognitive science. What we find is not so much a list of assumptions attributable uniformly to every mainstream theory, but rather a general view that has fixed the context of discussion for these theories. The major framework has the following character.

THE OBJECTIVIST THEORY OF MEANING

1. Meaning is an abstract relation between symbolic representations (either words or mental representations) and objective (i.e., mind-independent) reality. These symbols get their meaning solely by virtue of their capacity to correspond to things, properties, and relations existing objectively "in the world."

2. Concepts are understood as general mental representations (Kant) or as logical entities (Frege)—in either case, highly abstract and well-defined—that can be used to identify what things or objects there are, what properties they have, and what relations they can stand in. Concepts must be relatively "general" in character if they are to contain or present what is common to several particular objects. The concept "chair," for instance, applies to all chairs (specifies what all chairs share in common that makes them "chairs"), and so incidentally is not a particular image of this or that chair.

3. Concepts are "disembodied" in the sense that they are not tied to the particular mind that experiences them in the way that, say, images are. The image I form of a chair is thought to be particular, subjective, and embodied (in me), whereas my concept of a chair can be objective and float free of any given embodiment. It is this shareable, abstract, and general nature of concepts that is supposed to make our knowledge possible, communicable, and objective.

4. The task of a theory of meaning is to be able to explain the meaningfulness of any string of symbols that is not nonsense. This task is usually defined as follows: To give the meaning of a particular utterance is to give the conditions under which it would be true, or the conditions under which it would be "satisfied" by some state of affairs in the world. To give the meaning of an assertion, such as "All our dishes are dirty," would be to specify the circumstances that would

make the sentence true. To give the meaning of a command, such as "Wash the dishes by noon," would be to give the state of affairs in the world that would satisfy the command. The theory of meaning need not perform this massive task of stating conditions of satisfaction for every possible sentence, but it must be able to do so in principle. What is required is a recursive theory that shows how we can build up larger true or satisfied units from smaller true or satisfied units, which are taken as semantic primitives. And, on the assumption that there is a relatively small number of basic logical connectives for relating the semantic primitives, such a recursive theory would not be an impossible task.

5. Any analysis of meaning must be given ultimately in terms of literal concepts. There can be no irreducibly metaphorical or figurative concepts in the final analysis. This restriction is required by the Objectivist thesis that basic concepts pick out objects, properties, and relations in the world completely independent of human beings and their processes of understanding. The argument is simple: the basic concepts into which meaning is analyzed must map definite, discrete, and fixed objects, properties, and relations. This requires concepts that are definite, discrete, and fixed. Such concepts are called "literal." Metaphorical projections are not the sort of structures that could map onto the world so described, for they involve category crossings that do not exist objectively in the world. Objectivists grant that metaphor and other imaginative projections play a role in discovery and invention and that they may even be necessary for our understanding. Nevertheless, any Objectivist analysis of meaning must ultimately be reducible to literal concepts and propositions, and the structure of rationality cannot be irreducibly figurative.

6. It is important to notice that the Objectivist theory of meaning is compatible with, and supports, the epistemological claim that there exists a "God's-Eye" point of view, that is, a perspective that transcends all human limitation and constitutes a universally valid reflective stance. For example, meanings are treated as relations among symbols and objective states of affairs that are independent of how any individual person might understand or grasp those relations. It is alleged that there is a position *outside* this relationship from which the fit of symbol and thing can be judged. Concepts are said to stand in logical relationships as a matter of objective fact, regardless of how humans might comprehend them or organize them into systems. Conceptual structure is thought *not* to be determined by "subjective" processes of cognition on the part of persons trying to grasp the mean-

ing of a concept. It is often claimed that it is the philosopher's exalted task to deal with these "objective" meanings, concepts, and logical connections, while it is left to psychology to study the "subjective" cognitive operations that govern how we grasp concepts and how they "make sense to us."

I am not claiming that every truth-conditional semantics must assume that we can *achieve* such a God's-Eye-View; nevertheless, Objectivism in its strong version is clearly committed to the existence of such a perspective, since it presupposes an objective relation of language to mind-independent reality.

Associated closely with the Objectivist orientation toward meaning is its correlative view of rationality:

THE OBJECTIVIST VIEW OF RATIONALITY

1. Reasoning is a rule-governed manipulation of connections among symbols. It consists in a series of operations in which connections among symbols and rule-governed combinations of symbols are established and traced out according to various logical canons or principles. Such reasoning, for instance, might have the form, "Something X being given, something else Y follows by a rule of deduction."

2. The core of rationality is formal logic. Concepts can be joined together to form propositions of various sorts, and there is a limited number of "logical connectives" (*and, or, if-then,* etc.) that define the possible relations, either of concepts to one another (as in "red *and* blue," "red *or* blue," etc.) or of propositions (as in "It is raining *and* it is cold"; "It is raining *or* it is not raining"; etc.). There are also "rules of inference" for deciding whether the connections between propositions are valid or not.

3. As with the Objectivist view of meaning, so here, too, rationality is essentially disembodied; it consists of pure abstract logical relations and operations independent of subjective processes in the reasoner's mind. It is usually granted that images, metaphorical projections, and analogical leaps may be part of our mental processes in making novel connections, thinking up new arguments, and drawing out conclusions from premises. But such cognitive processes are regarded by Objectivists as mere "psychological" processes irrelevant to the logical reconstruction and evaluation of rational judgments. Thus, a distinction is often drawn between an alleged *context of discovery,* involving psychological processes for generating new ideas or theories, and a *context of justification,* in which we reconstruct the logical relations of a theory in order to show its grounding and certitude. The way in which

the idea or theory was thought up doesn't matter in the context of justification. Reason is regarded as consisting only of operations tracing out formal relations that obtain among symbolic representations (words, mental representations, concepts, propositions), and this is supposed to be independent of any particular content of those representations that is tied to our processing of them. Of course, the content or material that we are reasoning about will affect the nature of the conclusion drawn, but this in no way affects the *structure of rationality as such*.

4. The idea of a transcendent rationality also supports a God's-Eye-View account of knowledge, parallel to the version reinforced by the Objectivist account of meaning. It is assumed that human beings can somehow "plug into" a transcendent, autonomous rationality that stands beyond all historical developments. Reason is what it is at all times and all places, regardless of the person doing the reasoning. This essential, fixed structure of rationality is the basis for claims to transhistorical and a priori truth. It is even more difficult here (than with the theory of meaning) to see how such a picture can avoid a commitment to a God's-Eye-View, since reason is regarded in essentialist and transtemporal terms.

The Philosophical Context of Objectivism

The roots of the Objectivist views of meaning and rationality lie deep within our cultural heritage. Let us explore briefly the way in which these views are reinforced and made to look plausible by certain recurring tendencies in the Western philosophical tradition. In particular, I want to identify a tendency, manifested even by philosophers of radically different persuasions, to insist upon the existence of a certain gap in human experience that gives rise to a series of repeated dichotomies (either ontological, epistemological, semantic, or logical in nature). Roughly, the gap is thought to exist between our cognitive, conceptual, formal, or rational side in contrast with our bodily, perceptual, material, and emotional side. The most significant consequence of this split is that all meaning, logical connection, conceptualization, and reasoning are aligned with the mental or rational dimension, while perception, imagination, and feeling are aligned with the bodily dimension. As a result, both nonpropositional and figuratively elaborated structures of experience are regarded as having no place in meaning and the drawing of rational inferences.

Because my purposes are constructive—to delineate the outline of a

theory of embodied imagination—I do not want to delay this project
with a lengthy historical survey that documents the origin and development of Objectivist thinking.[1] It is important, however, to have
some understanding of the general cultural orientation that has led to
the devaluation of imagination in theories of meaning and rationality.
For our purposes, the two most decisive programs in Western philosophy have been Cartesianism and Kantianism, both of which are built
upon theories of knowledge.

Descartes was obsessed with the idea that, in order to refute skepticism, knowledge must rest on something that is certain. In his *Discourse on Method* (1637) he expresses his concern that, in spite of
centuries of concerted effort, we are no closer to establishing an un-
shakeable foundation for knowledge. He concludes that the problem is
a failure of *method*. What is needed is something like a general mathematical method that could guarantee the certainty that ought to be the
mark of real knowledge.

Descartes argued that there is, in fact, something we can know with
indubitable certainty, namely, *that* we exist as thinking beings. He concludes that what we know most intimately is *not our bodies* but the
structure of our minds (i.e., the nature of our rationality). The world
consists of physical substances (bodies) and mental substances (minds).
We humans are distinguished by our mental capacities; in particular,
by our *rationality*. We realize our true selves best, therefore, when we
are engaged in rational activity.

So far, this is only an articulation of a view of the mind/body split
that is deeply rooted in certain interpretations of the Judeo-Christian
tradition. In some developments of this tradition humans are distinguished as the sole creatures made in the image of God, which means
that they possess the Divine spark of rationality that sets them off from
brute animals. Whenever someone reasons correctly (including correct
willing) they are said to actually *participate in* God's reason, that is, they
transcend their physical embodiment by plugging into a transcendent
rationality. They realize their true nature as a disembodied mind or soul.

This Cartesian picture of mind, body, and knowledge creates two
fundamental gaps or splits in human experience, one ontological, the
other epistemological. First, on a Cartesian account, the body does
not play a crucial role in human reasoning—rationality is essentially
disembodied. Rationality may make use of material presented by the
senses, but it is not itself an attribute of bodily substance. This gives
rise to a basic ontological gulf between mind and body, reason and

sensation. The ontological problem, then, is to find some way to bridge this gap, to connect mind and body.

Second, there is an epistemological commitment that has established a problem for all succeeding discussions of knowledge. For Descartes, what the mind knows are its own representations, or ideas. Knowledge consists in grasping clearly what those ideas involve and how they are related to each other. Descartes' famous "method" for achieving certain knowledge is a "universal mathematics" which would allow us to trace out all of the possible connections among our ideas in an orderly and complete fashion.[2] But this view of knowledge raises a serious difficulty: if what we know are our own ideas, then how can we ever be sure that they do indeed accurately represent what exists in external reality? This is the problem of skepticism, and it is based, in the Cartesian tradition, on the epistemological gap between ideas and aspects of external reality that they are "about." Descartes' answer to this problem—that God is no deceiver and thus guarantees a connection between our ideas and the external world—satisfied almost no one. What was wanted was a nontheologically based account of knowledge that could answer the skeptical challenge.

Kantianism can be seen as an attempt to avoid the skeptical problem confronting Cartesianism. While Kant rejected the notion that one could prove the existence of a substantial soul or mind independent of the body, he still wanted to make sense of the Cartesian distinction between mental and physical attributes. For Kant this dichotomy survives in his rigid separation of the cognitive faculties into two essentially different components: the *formal,* conceptual, and intellectual, on the one hand, and the *material,* perceptual, and sensible, on the other. In Kant's influential account of knowledge, the material component is identified with bodily processes, while the formal component consists of spontaneous organizing activities of our understanding. So, even though there is no commitment to a Cartesian substantial mind, there is still a fundamental Cartesian tension between the two ontologically different sides of our nature: the bodily and the rational.

Kant argued that genuine empirical knowledge must be knowledge of objects that we all can experience, objects subject to universal laws. In order to have such an "objective" experience, there must be some material given from outside us to our senses, and this content must be organized by patterns of thought given by our mind. The bodily capacity for receiving these sense impressions, *sensibility,* supplies us only with "particular" representations (e.g., images, percepts) given to our senses by whatever objects we are experiencing. The capacity for conceptualizing these contents of sensibility, *understanding,* is an intellectual faculty that gives "general" representations (i.e., concepts) under which the particulars of sensation can be organized in a meaningful manner. The result of formal concepts structuring the material of sensation is an experience of objective realities everyone can share, insofar as they share the same general concepts. It is because certain concepts are shareable, Kant insists, that objective knowledge of our physical world is possible.

Kant thus claims to solve the skeptical problem of how we can know that our concepts correspond to objective reality as follows: what we can know of the external world is what we have received from it, as filtered through and structured by our consciousness. We cannot know things as they are in themselves but only as they appear for us, subject to the universal structuring activity of human consciousness.

In answering a certain form of skeptical objection, however, Kant only reinforces a number of Cartesian dichotomies that give rise to a series of fundamental problems. As I have noted, there is an overly rigid dichotomy between the *conceptual* and the *bodily.* Concepts are products of our understanding, which is formal, spontaneous, and rule-governed; sensations are bodily, given through our sensibility, which is material, passive, and lacking in any active principle of combination or synthesis. For Kant the real work of cognition takes place in the formation of concepts, in their conjunction in propositional judgments, and in their employment to create coherent meaning structures. Imaginative, preconceptual processes are given a role in organizing perceptual input, but they are excluded from our *thought.* In short, the rule-governed nature of meaning is the result of conceptualization and propositional judgment; and rationality consists chiefly of logical operations performed upon concepts and propositions.

The problems generated by this strict formal/material dichotomy are especially evident in Kant's frequent blurring of the concept/sensation distinction in his account of *imagination,* which is a capacity to mediate between concepts and sense impressions. Imagination is described as a faculty for combining sense impressions into a unified image that can be "brought under a concept." For example, in my perception of a dog, Kant thought that imagination ordered various sense impressions (e.g., the feel of fur, four legs, a trunk, long teeth, etc.) into a single perceptual experience (e.g., a unified image of a furry creature), such that I can then recognize it (conceptualize it) as a dog. Understood in this way, imagination would appear to be just the bridge needed between the formal and the material sides of cognition. But as we shall see in Chapter 6, Kant could never adequately explain the workings of imagination, for he vacillated between treating it as a formal, conceptual capacity (tied to understanding) and treating it as a material, sensible capacity (tied to sensibility). He seems occasionally to realize that imagination is both *bodily* and *rational,* but his adherence to the previously mentioned dichotomies prevents him from drawing this reasonable conclusion. I shall urge later that only by recognizing this interactional character of imagination can we hope to explain the nature of meaning.

There is a second Cartesian legacy that Kant handed down to his successors, namely, a view of reason as transcending the body. Human rationality consists of the formal element of cognition, distinct from any particular material content of sensation, any set of images, any emotions, or any bodily processes. And, while, contra Descartes, reason does not reside in a substantial mind, it has an autonomous character that insures its independence from any bodily determinations. In short, Kant reinforces an unbridgeable gap between reason and bodily experience.

The central moral of this brief story is that certain Cartesian and Kantian themes have reinforced a recurring set of ontological, epistemological, and logical dichotomies that are profoundly influential on Western ways of thinking; and these rigid dichotomies have made it extremely difficult to find a place in our views of human meaning and rationality for structures of imagination. Imagination seems to exist in a no-man's-land between the clearly demarcated territories of reason and sensation. I have no intention of denying that these dichotomies do capture important distinctions, but I want to urge a less exclusivist interpretation of them, a reading in which imagination plays a central role in both realms.

Objectivist Themes in Recent Theories of Meaning

It is against the background of this general Objectivist orientation that our most influential semantic theories have emerged into prominence. I suspect that none of the programs flourishing in semantics today accepts *all* of the Objectivist tenets in just the form I have expressed them. My contention is rather that Objectivism provides the primary context in which our most popular theories of meaning and rationality are articulated. Because of this, it is no accident that these theories are unable to give proper attention to structures of imagination.

To aid in understanding the limitations imposed by Objectivist assumptions, I will briefly outline four major views that command considerable attention today, which operate on at least *some* of these assumptions. I will indicate how their Objectivist leanings have led them to undervalue, or even ignore, the kinds of semantic phenomena that are the central focus of this book. This will highlight the need for an enriched view of meaning and rationality that goes beyond any currently influential theory.

Frege

Frege's impact on contemporary semantics and philosophy of language cannot be overestimated. All of the major approaches are either elaborations of, or challenges to, Fregean themes. His famous distinction between "sense" (*Sinn*) and "reference" (*Bedeutung*) has come to define an entire Objectivist tradition in the philosophy of language and in linguistics.[3] In Frege's terminology, a *sign* (such as a word) has a public meaning, its *sense,* by means of which it picks out a *reference.* For example, the word "mother" is a sign with a certain sense or meaning (e.g., maternal parent) that can, in a specific context, refer to an object (e.g., my mother). Now, in order to capture this public and universal notion of meaning, Frege thought it necessary to identify three ontologically distinct realms: (i) the physical, consisting of physical objects such as chairs, written words, spoken sounds, and all spatially extended objects; (ii) the mental, containing what he called "ideas," "images," and other mental representations; and (iii) a realm of thought, consisting of objective senses, numbers, propositions, concepts, and functions. Frege thought he needed this strange third realm to insure the objectivity of meaning and the universal character of mathematics and logic. He rejected as "subjectivist" any suggestion that all of these "objective" entities might exist merely at the mental level, which he regarded as peculiar to individual minds.

Thus Frege's search for a purely objective realm takes him even beyond Kant, who is regarded as too subjectivist, too psychological, because he focuses exclusively on structures of human consciousness. In quest of this absolute realm, Frege is forced to distinguish sharply between objective *senses,* on the one hand, and subjective *images* or *ideas,* on the other, which exist only in the mind that conceives them and cannot have universal validity.

The reference and sense of a sign are to be distinguished from the associated idea. If the reference of a sign is an object perceivable by the senses, my idea of it is an internal image, arising from memories of sense impressions which I have had and acts, both internal and external, which I have performed. Such an idea is often saturated with feeling; the clarity of its separate parts varies and oscillates. The same sense is not always connected, even in the same man, with the same idea. The idea is subjective: one man's idea is not that of another. There result, as a matter of course, a variety of differences in the ideas associated with the same sense. A painter, a horseman, and a zoologist will probably connect different ideas with the name "Bucephalus." This constitutes an essential distinction between the idea and the sign's sense, which may be the common property of many and therefore is not a part or a mode of the individual mind.[4]

One centrally important consequence of Frege's rigid separation of the sense and reference of a sign from any "associated ideas" is that the reference relation of a sign to things in the world is completely objective. On Frege's view, we can move *directly* from the sense to its corresponding reference, that is, from public meanings to specific states of affairs in the world. Ideas, images, bodily processes, and acts of imagination are held to be subjective and completely irrelevant to the specification of meaning and reference. It is their subjective character, their existence only in individual minds, that makes them unfit to serve as objective and universally shareable senses and thoughts.

The upshot of this view for our concerns is that Frege treats meaning and rationality as if they were entirely independent of human imagination and structures of bodily experience. There is the sign, the sense, and the reference in a direct linkage from word to world. Human cognition and understanding are bypassed as irrelevant to objective meaning relations. All mental processes (ideas, images, imaginative projections) that might explain how it is that a sign could come to connect up with the world, and with other signs, are excluded from consideration. This is the Objectivist view of meaning in its purest form.

Model-theoretic Semantics

Perhaps the most prominent contemporary elaboration of such Fregean themes is a new program called "model-theoretic semantics." The project of model-theoretic semantics is to give a precise account of how abstract symbols can be made meaningful by virtue of their correspondence to things in the world.

The view takes from mathematics the notion of a model as a set-theoretical structure consisting entirely of entities and sets built out of those entities. Model-theoretic semantics assumes that the actual world (as well as any possible world) can be placed in one-to-one correspondence with such a model. This is made possible by a set of meta-physical assumptions about the nature of reality: the world consists of entities that have properties and stand in definite relations to one another at any given instant; properties are placed in one-to-one correspondence with the set of entities having those properties, and n-place relations are placed in one-to-one correspondence with the set of n-tuples of entities standing in those relations. On these assumptions, there would have to be a correct model *of the actual world* (or any possible worlds) as consisting only of entities and sets of entities.[5]

The problem of meaning in a model-theoretic semantics is the problem of how abstract symbols, which are meaningless in themselves, can come to have meaning. The answer proposed is that they become meaningful by virtue of correspondences to elements of a model.[6] Since the world, given the assumed metaphysics, stands in one-to-one correspondence to such a model, abstract symbols can be given meaning by virtue of the way they correspond to entities and sets in the model of the world.

Model-theoretic semantics thus manifests Objectivist commitments both in its metaphysics and its view of meaning and of reason. Its metaphysics is Objectivist since it postulates a structure of reality that is independent of the way any beings, human or otherwise, come to experience and understand that reality. Its semantics is also Objectivist, since it gives an account of meaning completely independent of any beings, their nature, or their experiences. Meaning consists simply in the relationship between abstract symbols and elements in models of the real world (and, on many accounts, possible worlds). Moreover, its account of reason is Objectivist, since correct reason consists in a manipulation of symbols in a way that accords with the set-theoretical logic of the model, which is taken to be the logic of the world.

Just as we saw with Frege, then, model-theoretic semantics must drive a wedge between objective meaning and those processes by which humans understand language. As David Lewis insists, Objectivist semantics does not concern itself with human understanding and language use:

My proposals will also not conform to the expectations of those who, in analyzing meaning, turn immediately to the psychology and sociology of language users: to intentions, sense-experience, and mental ideas, or to social rules, conventions, and regularities. I distinguish two topics: first, the description of possible languages or grammars as abstract semantic systems whereby symbols are associated with aspects of the world; and second, the description of the psychological and sociological facts whereby a particular one of these abstract semantic systems is the one used by a person or population. Only confusion comes of mixing these two topics.[7]

It is obvious, now, why Lewis, or anyone else attempting to produce a model-theoretic semantics, can never give its rightful place to understanding (as involving imaginative structures that emerge in bodily movement and perception), for that would destroy the objective character of meaning relations. All that is supposed to matter are the one-to-one correspondences between the abstract symbols and entities or sets in the model.

Situation Semantics

It is also worth examining briefly a new program called "Situation Semantics," that claims to offer an account of meaning that includes human understanding and is sensitive to the nature of various cognitive processes excluded from some versions of model-theoretic semantics. The basic idea is that sentences designate situation types, which can be instantiated by an indefinite number of particular situations. Consider, for example, the situation type "Mark chased Paul Michael around the house." There are many particular situations in the world that can fall under this type, because there are many instances of Mark's chasing Paul Michael around the house. In situation semantics sentences get their meanings by being associated with situation types. This strategy looks very promising, for it appears to introduce aspects of understanding into the process by which sentences map onto the world. It seems as though the situation type represents the level at which we grasp patterns and structure in the world. It turns out, however, that the basic structure of situation semantics rests on the same fundamental Objectivist assumptions as model-theoretic views, in the following respects:

1. Meaning is strictly a matter of an objective relation between sentences and objective reality. Barwise and Perry claim that "(t)he leading idea of situation semantics is that the meaning of a simple declarative sentence is a relation between utterances and described situations."[8] This semantic relationship is completely objective, making no mention of mental processes by which the utterance or the situation is understood. Attention is focused exclusively

on the *external* significance of language, on its connection with the described world rather than the describing mind. Sentences are classified not by the ideas they express, but by how they describe things to be. The standard extensional model-theory of first-order logic is usually seen as a development of this strategy.[9]

2. Meaning is treated as conceptual in the Objectivist sense—it does not involve preconceptual elements, nor does it depend on imaginative projections or elaborations of schematic structures. Once again, it is the "externalist" orientation that defines the position. The meaning of a language is an "intricate relation" between utterances and "objective reality."[10] Structures of human intentionality and cognitive processing are replaced by, or translated into, an analysis of external, objective relations. In particular, "the mental significance of language, including the role of sentences embedded in attitude reports, is adequately explained by their external significance, properly understood."[11]

Situation semantics, then, gives a nod in the direction of the nonpropositional and figurative dimensions of human understanding that I shall treat as essential to any adequate theory of meaning. But, as it is presently elaborated, it retains its model-theoretic commitment to an account of meaning in terms of one-to-one correspondences between symbols and entities (or sets of entities).

Davidsonian Semantics

Another program grounded on Fregean assumptions is that of Donald Davidson, whose work on language, meaning, reference, and truth has had tremendous appeal in America, England, and Australia. Very simply, Davidson argues that an adequate theory of meaning *just is* a theory of truth. A definition of truth

works by giving necessary and sufficient conditions for the truth of every sentence, and to give truth conditions is a way of giving the meaning of a sentence. To know the semantic concept of truth for a language is to know what it is for a sentence—any sentence—to be true, and this amounts, in one good sense we can give to the phrase, to understanding the language.[12]

In one powerful move Davidson turns the search for a theory of meaning into the task of constructing an adequate theory of truth. Such a theory would involve a "set of axioms that entail, for every sentence in the language, a statement of the conditions under which it is true."[13] According to Davidson, what is required is a recursive theory that shows how larger truth-preserving units can be built up from the concatenation of smaller units (the parts) that have truth conditions. Davidson's theory is Objectivist in spirit, if not in all its details. It is concerned only with meaning as an abstract relation between sentences and described conditions in the world. That there is such an objective relation is assumed, and no attempt is made to explain how particular meaning units map onto the world.

Once again, the role of embodied structures of imagination in meaning is denied. There is no room for an account of the structures of intentionality by which we experience something as meaningful. Davidson doesn't deny the possibility of theories on these matters, but he thinks that they are irrelevant to semantics, which has only to do with truth conditions. The trouble here, in sum, is that there is no place for an account of how human beings understand anything, or grasp the meaning of a sentence.

The Objectivist Legacy: Problems for Meaning and Reason

The crucial point I have been trying to make by surveying a few of the more influential semantic theories is just this: they do not give a central place to the operations of nonpropositional and figurative structures of embodied imagination. In fact, they don't even mention such structures. And the chief reason for this is their commitment to a general Objectivist orientation. I want to emphasize that I am not claiming that any of the theories discussed holds to each of the Objectivist tenets of meaning and rationality exactly as I have formulated them. It is impossible in a general statement to capture all of the subtleties of each approach. Instead, I am claiming only that certain Objectivist themes constitute a backdrop against which the main theories are elaborated. So, it might be, for example, that Davidson isn't committed to the Objectivist notion of the possibility of a God's-Eye-View of knowledge. But his view is, nevertheless, chiefly Objectivist in its insistence on a truth-conditional semantics that does not involve a theory of understanding.

It might also be argued by defenders of one of these theories that it can assimilate a treatment of the sort I will be developing. Even if this proves to be true, it is still the case that none of the standard theories can be adequate until it addresses the kinds of phenomena that are central to human understanding. However, I would suggest that the view I am developing will be incompatible with at least those theories that deny a role to intentions and structures of intentionality involving imaginative projections.

I have suggested that the Objectivist tradition has generated, at different times and in different contexts, a recurring set of dichotomies that create gaps that make it extremely difficult to construct an adequate overall account of human experience and cognition. Basically, the decisive line is drawn between the mental, conceptual, rational, cognitive, a priori, and theoretical, on the one side, and the physical, perceptual, imaginative, emotional, a posteriori, and practical, on the other side. Again and again, meaning and rationality are shoved up into the former realm (of concepts and propositions) and dissociated from processes in the latter realm (of perception and imagination).

Objectivism asserts a connection between these two realms, but it can never explain that connection without calling upon processes and structures that it must exclude from its treatment of meaning and rationality. We have seen that what I am calling "image schemata," and the figurative, nonpropositional structures that transform them, have no place in an Objectivist theory, for two reasons. (1) On the one hand, figurative projections of image schemata are too bodily and subjective. As a capacity to form unified images and to order sense impressions, imagination is regarded either as merely mechanical (i.e., contributing nothing of cognitive interest) or as too subjective, particular, and variable. The claim is made that concepts are the bearers of meaning, because they are shared general structures. Meaning cannot reside in structures of imagination, because they are too private and idiosyncratic. (2) On the other hand, imagination is sometimes treated as wild and unruly, just because it can be creative. As a creative capacity to reorder representations and to generate novel structures, figurative projections do not seem to be sufficiently "rule-governed" (and in that sense, predictable), in a way that concepts and propositions are. So, once again, the schematizing and figurative structures of human understanding fail to achieve the required Objectivist standard of formal, abstract, and rule-governed structure.

Putting the Body Back into the Mind: Procedure

The problem I have tried to identify in our most influential contemporary theories of meaning (and their attendant theories of rationality) is the absence of an adequate account of the crucial role of understanding in all meaning. I have suggested that this understanding typically involves image-schematic structures of imagination that are extended and figuratively elaborated as abstract structures of meaning and patterns of thought. It is my chief task in this book to explain what this means and how these structures operate.

My epigram for this undertaking is "putting the body back into the mind." Imaginative projection is a principle means by which the body (i.e., physical experience and its structures) works its way up into the mind (i.e., mental operations). By using the term "body" I want to stress the nonpropositional, experiential, and figurative dimensions of meaning and rationality.

My procedure in what follows requires some explanation. In the following chapter I explore a small segment of human discourse to illustrate what I will be meaning by embodied patterns of imagination. The next three chapters provide accounts of typical structures of recurring aspects of human bodily experience, in order to show how they play a crucial role in what we take as meaningful and in how we reason. Chapter 5 explores the pervasiveness of these image schemata and shows how they determine meaning relations and constrain understanding. The final three chapters explore the underlying theories of meaning, understanding, imagination, and knowledge that emerge from this approach.

My project rests heavily on the naturalness and plausibility of my descriptions of various preconceptual structures of our experience. Unless I have given an accurate and reasonably adequate description of these structures, I cannot begin to explain the nature of their figurative extension to abstract understanding and reasoning. The method I employ might be called a form of descriptive or empirical phenomenology, in that I will be attempting a kind of "geography of human experience." Such a geography seeks to identify the chief contours (structures) and connections that our experience and understanding exhibit. It would explore the emergence of comprehensible form and organization in our experience and the means we have of making sense of it. The test of its success is comprehensiveness, coherence, and explanatory power.

Beyond this general orientation, however, I do not intend to align myself with any particular program in the phenomenological tradition that has developed in Europe in the last century. At the same time, it will be obvious that some of my most important claims are anticipated in the work of philosophers who might legitimately claim allegiance to phenomenology of the post-Husserlian varieties. It is an unfortunate fact that most philosophers, linguists, psychologists, and social scientists trained in, or influenced by, Anglo-American analytic philosophy have shown a strong resistance to phenomenology, which they see as obscure, muddle-headed, and inaccessible. I have tried to search for a vocabulary and a mode of presentation that will make sense to analytically minded philosophers, but which yet allows me to take advantage of some of the deep insights of Continental philosophy in the present century.

I want to insist that a phenomenological account (in my loose sense of the term) does not simply terminate with a description of structures of experience and understanding; instead, it uses that description as the basis of a very powerful *explanation* of the process involved in making semantic connections among systematically related meanings. It shows how the nonpropositional image-schematic structures described can be metaphorically projected to structure our abstract reasoning in ongoing problematic situations of life, art, or science.

To sum up: as animals we have bodies connected to the natural world, such that our consciousness and rationality are tied to our bodily orientations and interactions in and with our environment. Our embodiment is essential to who we are, to what meaning is, and to our ability to draw rational inferences and to be creative. My phenomenological description of image-schematic experiential structures and their figurative elaborations and projections onto abstract domains of understanding is the basis for an enriched account of human meaning and rationality. It is a start on a project that would seek to fill in the gaps created by all those theories whose rigid dichotomies force them to compartmentalize and fragment life, and to ignore the centrality and indispensability of embodied imagination in life and thought. I attempt to do this by giving a plausible description of some of the more prominent ways in which meaning and rationality are tied to bodily experience, as it is imaginatively structured. I am exploring the ways in which *the body is in the mind*.

1

The Need for a Richer Account of Meaning and Reason

An Embodied, Nonpropositional Dimension of Meaning

The vast majority of books on linguistics and the philosophy of language assume that meaning is, first and foremost, something *sentences* have. It is held, quite reasonably, that the meaning of words or phrases depends on their roles in sentences. For the most part, I see nothing wrong with this general orientation in and of itself. However, this exclusive focus on sentential structure has unfortunately contributed to the widely held view that an account of meaning as propositional is all that is required for semantics.

Much of this book is a nontraditional inquiry into the nature of meaning. I want to probe beneath the level of propositional content, as it is usually defined, to ask how propositional structure is possible. Such an inquiry, I shall argue, leads us back down into image-schematic structures by which we are able to have coherent experiences that we can comprehend. These structures are nonpropositional (in the traditional sense, to be explained below), preconceptual factors intimately tied up with the meanings we employ.

In the context of my inquiry into the emergence of meaning and rationality in human experience, one of my chief concerns is to examine the question, How can *anything* (an event, object, person, word, sentence, theory, narrative) be meaningful to a person? And I want to treat "linguistic meaning" as a subcase of meaning in this broader sense. The standard strategy in the philosophy of language and in linguistics today is to take linguistic meaning (regarded chiefly as

I

propositional in nature) as primary and to treat other uses of the term
"meaning" as either parasitic upon linguistic meaning, or else as falling
outside the study of semantics altogether.

My strategy is to question the assumption that only words and sentences have meanings and that all of these meanings must be propositional in the traditional sense. There can be no doubt that linguistic
meaning gives rise to elaborations of human intentionality that would
not be possible without the complex structure of propositions and
speech acts; it does not follow from this, however, that all meaning is
merely propositional in nature.

In describing my project I have repeatedly stressed my intention to
explore "nonpropositional" structures of meaning. This key notion is
elaborated progressively in the following chapters. As an introduction
to my analysis, I want to offer a preliminary statement of what I mean
by image schemata that are nonpropositional. I will be arguing later
that image schemata are abstract patterns in our experience and understanding that are not propositional in any of the standard senses of that
term, and yet they are central to meaning and to the inferences we make.

Let me explain this claim in a very crude, tentative fashion that will
be refined and completed in the next few chapters (especially Chapter 2). Consider, first, an *image schema,* which is a dynamic pattern
that functions somewhat like the abstract structure of an image, and
thereby connects up a vast range of different experiences that manifest
this same recurring structure. One such schema, which I describe in
more detail in Chapter 3, is the COMPULSIVE FORCE schema. Its basic
structure can be represented visually as shown below (see fig. 1). An
actual COMPULSION schema exists as a *continuous, analog* pattern of, or
in, a particular experience or cognition that I have of compulsion. It is
present in my perception of a jet airplane being forced down the run-
way, or in my understanding of forces acting on continental plates, or
(metaphorically) in my felt sense of being forced by peer pressure to
join the PTA. The schema proper is not a concrete rich image or mental picture; rather, it is a more abstract pattern that can be manifested in
rich images, perceptions, and events.

I will argue for each of these claims as we proceed; but, for now, let

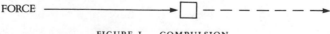

FIGURE 1.   COMPULSION

us ask whether such image-schematic structures are *propositional*. My answer will be that, of the six definitions of "proposition" that follow, only the last one applies to image schemata, and it is not a sense that appears in the dominant theories. The six accounts of "proposition" are:

1. Something proposed—a statement. This is the most general sense, and perhaps the oldest. It is interpreted by philosophers as involving the notion of truth values, that is, a proposition must assert something and thereby be the kind of entity that can be either true or false.

2. A representation using finitary predicate symbols (functions) and a number of argument symbols. Typically, the argument symbols refer to entities, and the predicate symbols represent the properties and relations of those entities.

3. A state of affairs in the world, usually one holding between an entity and its predicates (e.g., properties) or among a number of entities.

4. From model theory: (a) a function from possible worlds to truth values, (b) a function from possible situations to facts (where a "fact" is a property or relation paired with the entities that it holds of).

5. A finitary representation using elements and relational links among those elements. This formulation is offered by Pylyshyn in his argument that images can be propositionally represented.[1] He suggests that any image could be broken into elements or segments whose relations could be completely described in a propositional fashion.

These first five definitions all insist on the finitary character of propositions. Now, I grant that propositional representations of this sort will capture some of the important structural features of any given image schema. But such finitary representations will not capture their analog nature and the crucial role they play in *image-schematic transformations*. By "transformation" I mean such cognitive operations as scanning an image, tracing out the probable trajectory of a force vector, superimposing one schema upon another, and taking a multiplex cluster of entities and contracting it into a homogeneous mass (see Chapter 2). In other words, propositions defined in the senses above will not represent the natural cognitive operations of image schemata.

However, there is a further sense we can give to "proposition" that does properly apply to image schemata and makes sense of their crucial role in meaning and reasoning, namely,

6. A proposition exists as a continuous, analog pattern of experi-

ence or understanding, with sufficient internal structure to permit inferences.

I will argue that, because image schemata and their metaphorical extensions are propositional in this special sense, they constitute much of what we call meaning structure and inferential patterns, although they are not finitary. We will see, for instance, that the COMPULSION schema (fig. 1) has internal structure consisting of a force vector (with a certain magnitude and direction), an entity acted upon by the force, and a potential trajectory the entity will traverse. And this structure constrains the way the schema organizes meaning and influences the drawing of inferences in domains of understanding concerned with forces of a certain kind. The main point is that the internal structure of the image schema exists in a continuous, analog fashion within our understanding, which permits it to enter into transformations and other cognitive operations.

Henceforth, therefore, when I repeatedly describe image schemata as "nonpropositional," I mean this only as that term is understood in Objectivist semantics; and I mean only that Objectivist propositions— in any of senses (1)–(5) above— cannot be the *whole story* about the workings of image schemata and their metaphorical extensions (even though it will often be part of the story).

At this point, I also want to anticipate the standard objection that, since we are bound to talk about preconceptual and nonpropositional aspects of experience always in propositional terms, it must follow that they are themselves propositional in nature. This simply doesn't follow. What *does* follow is that, because of the limitations of our propositional modes of representation, we have a hard time trying to express the full meaning of our experiences. To cite a simple example, my present sense of being balanced upright in space at this moment is surely a nonpropositional awareness that I have, even though all my efforts to communicate its reality to you will involve propositional structures. So, while we must use propositional language to describe these dimensions of experience and understanding, we must not mistake our mode of description for the things described.

Non-Objectivist Metaphorical Meaning and Inference Patterns

With this preliminary definition and its attendant caveat, I want now to introduce the notion of nonpropositional meaning. I shall ease into this notion and avoid any mention of an image schema until the next chapter, where it becomes the central focus. Here I speak of non-propositional meaning and metaphorical structures in only the most general introductory fashion. The first stage in my project is to show the need for an account that centers on the very aspects of understanding that are ignored by Objectivist programs. In the Introduction I noted that Objectivism treats all meaning as conceptually and propositionally expressible in literal terms that can correspond to objective aspects of reality. In the present chapter I want to indicate why this cannot be the whole picture, for two reasons: (1) meaning in natural language begins in figurative, multivalent patterns that cannot typically be reduced to a set of *literal* concepts and propositions; and (2) the patterns and their connections are embodied and cannot be reduced to a set of literal *concepts and propositions.* In other words, meaning typically involves nonliteral (figurative) cognitive structures that are irreducibly tied up with the conceptual or propositional contents attended to exclusively in Objectivist semantics.

To sum up my contention: I am perfectly happy with talk of the conceptual/propositional content of an utterance, *but only insofar as we are aware that this propositional content is possible only by virtue of a complex web of nonpropositional schematic structures that emerge from our bodily experience.* Once meaning is understood in this broader, enriched manner, it will become evident that the structure of rationality is much richer than any set of abstract logical patterns completely independent of the patterns of our physical interactions in and with our environment. Any account of the "logic" of a chain of reasoning thus would have to make reference to such schematic structures and to figurative extensions of them. The inferential structure of our abstract reason is a high refinement upon orderings in our bodily experience, a refinement that ignores much of what goes into our reasoning.

Let us turn, then, to a brief analysis of an actual segment of discourse to suggest some of the dimensions of meaning and rationality not countenanced by Objectivist programs. The Objectivist would try to give the meaning and underlying rationale of the passage solely in terms of literal concepts and propositions, plus the necessary speech act structure (usually regarded as part of pragmatics). I shall argue that this approach neglects the very features that make meaning possible in the first place. I shall show that it is not possible to grasp the logic of the speaker's argument without understanding the basic, irreducible metaphorical structure that holds it together.

The passage to be analyzed is taken from Tim Beneke's *Men on Rape,* a remarkable set of interviews with doctors, lawyers, a rapist, prosecuting attorneys, husbands and lovers of rape victims, and men from other occupations concerning their views of rape. The speaker is a law clerk in the financial district of San Francisco.

Let's say I see a woman and she looks really pretty, and really clean and sexy, and she's giving off very feminine, sexy vibes. I think "Wow, I would love to make love to her," but I know she's not really interested. It's a tease. A lot of times a woman knows that she's looking really good and she'll use that and flaunt it, and it makes me feel like she's laughing at me and I feel *degraded*. I also feel dehumanized, because when I'm being teased I just turn off. I cease to be human. Because if I go with my human emotions I'm going to want to put my arms around her and kiss her, and to do that would be unacceptable. I don't like the feeling that I'm supposed to stand there and take it, and not be able to hug her or kiss her; so I just turn off my emotions. It's a feeling of humiliation, because the woman has forced me to turn off my feelings and react in a way that I really don't want to. If I were actually desperate enough to rape some-body, it would be from wanting the person, but also it would be a very spiteful thing, just being able to say, "I have power over you and I can do anything I want with you"; because really I feel that *they* have power over *me* just by their presence. Just the fact that they can come up to me and just melt me and make me feel like a dummy makes me want revenge. They have power over me so I want power over them.[2]

This interview fragment provides a clear and forceful statement of one individual's view of possible motives for an imagined but unre-alized rape. The passage is fairly straightforward as explanations go, so it is relatively easy to understand what the speaker is trying to express. On an Objectivist account, the meaning of what he is asserting can, in principle, be spelled out in a series of literal concepts and propositions. Setting aside attitudes or moods or emotions expressed by the clerk, there is thought to be a core of publicly accessible meaning reducible to those literal concepts and propositions, together with various func-tions or speech acts performed on those propositions. Whatever else might play a role in our understanding of this text is ignored as not included in the *meaning* of what he says.

But this view completely thwarts our understanding of the real meaning of the discourse. I want to give a reenactment of the logic involved in the clerk's explanation of his view of rape, in order to ex-hibit the increase in our understanding that becomes possible by going beyond standard accounts of meaning.[3] Let us explore some of the connections we must make, or presuppose, in order to grasp this pas-sage as a meaningful whole, that is, to understand what the speaker means. These connections consist partly in our understanding of shared metaphorical projections, partly in "folk" models our culture provides for various aspects of reality, and partly in a broad range of schematic structures that develop in our nonpropositional, embodied experience. These are all part of our understanding of the passage in question—they are part of its meaning. They are not merely background conditions for understanding (such as the necessity of being awake, being able to read, or not being under the influence of mind-altering drugs).

For example, perhaps the dominant metaphorical structure operative in this passage is PHYSICAL APPEARANCE IS A PHYSICAL FORCE, which involves the projection of structure from our experience of interactions of physical objects onto our experience of sexual motivation, activity, and causal interaction. We have a metaphor here, because there is a mapping of structure from a source domain (physical forces) onto the target domain (physical appearance). The proposition "physical appearance is a physical force" is to be regarded as merely a name for the complex web of connections in our experience and understanding formed by this mapping across domains of experience. In other words, the metaphor itself is not reducible to the proposition we use to name it.

The general PHYSICAL APPEARANCE IS A PHYSICAL FORCE metaphorical understanding is reflected in our culture in expressions of the following sort:

PHYSICAL APPEARANCE IS A PHYSICAL FORCE

She's *devastating*. He is *strikingly* handsome. She'll *knock you off* your feet. He *bowled* me *over*. She's *radiant*. I find him so *attractive*. She's a *bombshell*. He was *blown away* by her.

In the rape passage the PHYSICAL APPEARANCE IS A PHYSICAL FORCE metaphor is manifested in the following expressions:

. . . she's *giving off* very feminine, sexy *vibes*.
. . . I'm supposed to stand there and *take it*.
. . . the woman has *forced* me to turn off my feelings and *react* . . .
. . . they have *power over* me just by their presence.
Just the fact that they can come up to me and just *melt me* . . .

Now, given our experience and understanding of PHYSICAL APPEARANCE AS A PHYSICAL FORCE, we can begin to work through the pattern of thought that makes this passage an intelligible narrative. The metaphor involves our understanding of *appearance* as an actual *physical force* that can produce causal effects in the world. The speaker assumes that

A WOMAN IS RESPONSIBLE FOR HER PHYSICAL APPEARANCE

and couples this with the metaphor

PHYSICAL APPEARANCE IS A PHYSICAL FORCE

to get

A WOMAN IS RESPONSIBLE FOR THE FORCE SHE EXERTS ON MEN.

We see this in his assumption that, if she looks sexy ("giving off very feminine, sexy vibes"), she is using her sexy appearance as a force on him ("a woman knows that she's looking really good and she'll use that and flaunt it").

The sexual force the woman exerts is regarded, according to a folk model of sexuality in our culture, as generating certain natural reactions in those affected by that force. Thus we get the connection:

SEXUAL EMOTIONS ARE THE NATURAL RESPONSE TO BEING ACTED UPON
    BY A SEXUAL FORCE

plus

ANYONE USING A FORCE IS RESPONSIBLE FOR THE EFFECTS OF THAT
    FORCE

leads to

A WOMAN WITH A SEXY APPEARANCE IS RESPONSIBLE FOR AROUSING A
    MAN'S SEXUAL EMOTIONS.

As he laments, ". . . they have power over me just by their presence." And where does this sexual arousal lead? The answer is provided by the speaker's acceptance of another folk model in our culture about the relation between sexual emotion and subsequent action or reaction:

SEXUAL EMOTION NATURALLY RESULTS IN SEXUAL ACTIVITY

("because if I go with my human emotions I'm going to want to put my arms around her and kiss her . . ."). This raises a serious problem for him because he shares our moral constraint:

SEXUAL ACTION AGAINST SOMEONE'S WILL IS IMPERMISSIBLE.

(He acknowledges that to act on his desire to kiss her "would be unacceptable.") He concludes from this ethical premise that, in the given case

TO ACT MORALLY, HE MUST AVOID SEXUAL ACTIVITY.

But we know from our previously noted folk model of sexual excitation and response that the natural result of aroused sexual emotions is some form of sexual activity. Therefore, the clerk concludes quite reasonably that his only moral response must be to repress the offending emotions that might lead to immoral sexual activity, or

AVOIDING IMPERMISSIBLE SEXUAL ACTION REQUIRES INHIBITING
SEXUAL EMOTIONS.

(As he says, "I don't like the feeling that I'm supposed to stand there and take it, and not be able to hug her or kiss her; so I just turn off my emotions.")

As a consequence, a woman who looks sexy is responsible for the arousal of his sexual emotions (by natural mechanisms) and for thereby putting him in a position where he must inhibit them if he is to act morally. He explains, "It's a feeling of humiliation, because the woman has forced me to turn off my feelings and react in a way that I really don't want to." The humiliation he now feels is part of his sense that he has become less than human (". . . I feel degraded . . . I also feel dehumanized . . . I cease to be human.") This all makes sense on the earlier assumption that SEXUAL EMOTIONS ARE PART OF HUMAN NATURE so that INHIBITING SEXUAL EMOTIONS MAKES ONE LESS FULLY HUMAN.

It is on the basis of this rationale that the clerk can actually come to contemplate the possibility of rape. As he has already concluded,

A WOMAN WITH A SEXY APPEARANCE MAKES A MAN WHO IS ACTING
MORALLY BECOME LESS THAN HUMAN.

And this is perceived as a definite injury to his full humanity, an unacceptable degradation. The very idea that rape might be justified trades on the biblical eye-for-an-eye folk theory of retributive justice:

ONLY AN INJURY IN LIKE MEASURE AND OF LIKE KIND CAN REDRESS
THE IMBALANCE OF JUSTICE.

Since the alleged injury involved the use of sexual *power*, he sees rape as a possibility for appropriate redress:

If I were actually desperate enough to rape somebody, it would be from wanting the person, but also it would be a very spiteful thing, just being able to say, "I have power over you and I can do anything I want with you"; because really I feel that *they* have power over *me* just by their presence. Just the fact that they can come up to me and just melt me and make me feel like a dummy makes me want revenge. They have power over me so I want power over them.

My analysis of this passage up to this point does, I hope, begin to suggest just how rich our metaphorical understanding is when we make sense of even the most ordinary discourse. So far we have identified an underlying metaphorical assumption and other "folk" knowledge that seems to be operative in our grasp of the rational connections that make this a coherent discourse. Little, if any, of this is ever explicitly entertained by someone reading the passage. But we have re-enacted a certain unnoticed logic that would need to be at work for this to be experienced by us as a reasonable explanation.

There is nothing startling or revolutionary about the idea that there could be so much presupposed for our understanding of even the most simple and straightforward utterances. In fact, a great deal of recent work in cognitive science on language processing focuses directly on the problem of representing the relevant background knowledge that makes it possible for us to comprehend simple literal utterances.[4]

What distinguishes the view of meaning and rationality that I will be developing here is the special emphasis I place on the crucial role of the so-called Background. As I shall explain in Chapter 7, virtually all accounts distinguish between meaning (regarded as conceptual, propositional, representational, intentional) and the Background (regarded as preintentional and nonrepresentational) against which meaning emerges. I want to suggest that there are nonpropositional structures in the Background that play a far more central role in the elaboration of meaning than Objectivism allows. I will question the assumption that the Background can only be part of meaning to the extent that it can be propositionally represented. So, I shall be challenging the exclusive identification of meaning with propositional structure.

In the case at hand, the PHYSICAL APPEARANCE IS A PHYSICAL FORCE metaphor is not just a presupposition, a set of background beliefs, or a cluster of capacities and orientations that allow the meaning of the clerk's explanation to emerge. Instead, the metaphorical structure is part of the clerk's meaning and provides essential connections in his argument. And it involves more than just the propositional structure we use to express it.

Let us consider this central point by exploring in greater detail an important step in the logic of the passage we have been analyzing. The crucial step in the reasoning process involves the following argument:

A WOMAN IS RESPONSIBLE FOR HER PHYSICAL APPEARANCE.
PHYSICAL APPEARANCE IS A PHYSICAL FORCE (exerted on other
    people).
A WOMAN IS RESPONSIBLE FOR THE FORCE SHE EXERTS ON MEN.

This is an inference of the form:

F(A)
A = B
Therefore, F(B).

But the A=B term here is a metaphor: PHYSICAL APPEARANCE IS A PHYSICAL FORCE. In classical logic, metaphors not only don't work in this way, they don't even exist as such. Classical logic can treat metaphor, not as expressing irreducible metaphorical meaning (as is the case here), but only as expressing literal propositional meaning. The best the classical theories could do was to say that metaphors really have the logical form of a similarity statement: A IS LIKE B in having properties X, Y, Z, . . . This view has been shown to be inadequate by Searle, Davidson, and Lakoff and Johnson, among others.[5] But even if the similarity view were correct, the similarity statement for PHYSICAL APPEARANCE IS A PHYSICAL FORCE would not be of the right form to allow for the right inference. People *do,* however, reason in the above manner all the time. And it is not possible to understand the logic of the passage without reference to such an inference pattern, a pattern generalized to include metaphor in the reasoning process.

This point cannot be stressed strongly enough. It is anything but trivial. The key to understanding the passage is this use of metaphor in the inference pattern just described. It is the crucial logical link that makes this passage coherent and meaningful, something that can make sense to us rather than something that doesn't fit together at all.

A classical Objectivist response might be that the passage *isn't rational* and that the reasoning *isn't valid* at all but based on a mistake in logic—a mistake that we have just described. This observation misses the point. We are concerned here with how *real human beings reason* and not with some ideal standard of rationality. We are concerned with *what real human beings grasp as meaningful.* In order to be able to understand the passage, *we, the readers,* must be reasoning that way, too.

Perhaps it will be objected that the view I am proposing confuses "logic" and "reason" and thereby makes it impossible to distinguish valid from invalid reasoning. Someone might insist that my description of how people actually comprehend and reason has no connection to normative validity, to logical correctness, but only to patterns of thought. My approach would be warranted, even if it didn't claim to be about "logic," even if it only gave us more insight into how people actually do make sense of things. This would enrich our view of meaning and rationality in important ways.

But it is also *possible* that our inquiries will help us to understand normative validity much better, too. It may help us to see how our principles of logic are abstract formalizations of more mundane forms of reasoning. Nisbett and Ross, for instance, have explored many forms of reasoning which we have no trouble comprehending but which violate normative standards.[6] And Alvin Goldman has argued that we may shed new light on epistemology by taking seriously the work of cognitive psychologists who are exploring cognitive processes hitherto deemed irrelevant to logical justification.[7] It may well turn out that, as we learn more about human cognition, we will discover that much more is relevant to rationality than classical formal standards of evaluation. It might be that we will expand our notion of logical correctness.

The question is What makes us human? If it is the capacity that human beings have *to reason,* then we need to describe that capacity. It includes reasoning through the use of metaphors and other figurative structures; it is, indeed, one of the chief means we have of making sense of our experience.

But there is more to understanding than just tracing our inference patterns. Even if it were possible to reduce such metaphors as we have discussed to literal, nonfigurative expressions, we would still not have a full and adequate analysis of the passage in question. The reason for this is that grasping the clerk's meaning, and understanding his reasoning, is not merely a matter of grasping concepts and framing propositions (in the Objectivist sense) that constitute the content of his argument. Also essential are various kinds of schematic structures of experience and figurative (nonpropositional) projections that make it possible for us to have coherent, structured, and meaningful experience, and to reason about it.

Non-Objectivist Embodied and Nonpropositional Meaning

Let us return once again to the rape passage to emphasize some of the nonpropositional, preconceptual dimensions of meaning that it exhibits. Consider some of the nonpropositional dimensions of the central metaphor operative in the passage, namely, PHYSICAL APPEARANCE IS A PHYSICAL FORCE. On the face of it, this expression takes a straightforward propositional form. It seems to contain two concepts (that of *physical appearance* and that of *physical force*) which it conjoins propositionally according to certain relations between the two concepts. Moreover, it appears that we could spell out the meaning of each of the two concepts by listing other concepts they "contain." But the fact is that some of the meanings in this passage are based on preconceptual structures of experience. Take the concept of *physical force* as it operates in the PHYSICAL APPEARANCE IS A PHYSICAL FORCE metaphor. Though we forget it so easily, the meaning of "physical force" depends on publicly shared meaning structures that emerge from our *bodily experience* of force. We begin to grasp the meaning of physical force from the day we are born (or even before). We have bodies that are acted upon by "external" and "internal" forces such as gravity, light, heat, wind, bodily processes, and the obtrusion of other physical objects. Such interactions constitute our first encounters with forces, and they reveal patterned recurring relations between ourselves and our environment. Such patterns develop as meaning structures through which our world begins to exhibit a measure of coherence, regularity, and intelligibility.

Soon we begin to realize that we, too, can be sources of force on our bodies and on other objects outside us. We learn to move our bodies and to manipulate objects such that we are centers of force. Above all, we develop patterns for interacting forcefully with our environment— we grab toys, raise the cup to our lips, pull our bodies through space. We encounter obstacles that exert force on us, and we find that we can exert force in going around, over, or through those objects that resist us. Sometimes we are frustrated, defeated, and impotent in our forceful action. Other times we are powerful and successful. Slowly we expand the meaning of "force." In each of these motor activities there are repeatable patterns that come to identify that particular forceful action. These patterns are embodied and give coherent, meaningful structure to our physical experience at a *preconceptual* level, though we are eventually taught names for at least some of these patterns, and can discuss them in the abstract. Of course, we formulate a *concept* of "force," which we can explicate in propositional terms. But its meaning—the meaning it identifies—goes deeper than our conceptual and propositional understanding.

Out of these bodily interactions our sense of force becomes extended and modified. In response to our actions there come the reactions of other objects and persons. We discover that our force has limits and that there is a horizon to the influence we can exert on our surroundings. But then we find out that our force can be amplified and that the horizon of our forcefulness can be extended through the use of tools. One day we find ourselves grappling with the dizzying notion of force at a distance. Later, we go on to learn that there are more ways than one to act forcefully on others. In addition to moving them physically, we can move them in other ways, such as when we force them to perform a certain deed through moral suasion or peer pressure.

What I am describing here in a superficial way is the growth of meaning for our notion of force. I shall take up the nature of our experience of force in greater depth in Chapter 3. For the present, I want to stress that the meaning of "force" as it operates in the PHYSICAL APPEARANCE IS A PHYSICAL FORCE metaphor involves more than a conceptual nugget or a set of associated propositions. It includes also the *sense* of force that we gain through interactions of the sort described above. I use the term "sense" here to indicate that meaning includes patterns of embodied experience and preconceptual structures of our sensibility (i.e., our mode of perception, of orienting ourselves, and of interacting with other objects, events, or persons). These embodied patterns do not remain private or peculiar to the person who experiences them. Our community helps us interpret and codify many of our felt patterns. They become shared cultural modes of experience and help to determine the nature of our meaningful, coherent understanding of our "world."

The public, shared character of this preconceptual dimension of meaning can be seen further in the notion of sexuality that underlies the "logic" of the rape passage. My claim is not that the relevant concept of sexuality employed by the law clerk is too complex and rich to be easily defined. Rather, certain aspects of the meaning of "sexuality" are culturally, and perhaps humanly, shared dimensions of our experience *at the preconceptual level*. Each individual's developing notion of sexuality will be a blend of his or her awareness of bodily rhythms, orientations, moods, desires, interested responses, frustrated impulses, cultural attitudes, mythological influences, language structure, personal history, etc. The reality of *sexual force* emerges meaningfully out of such experiences that are carried up into the meaning of sexuality.

Furthermore, these preconceptual dimensions of the meaning of sexual force cannot be ignored as part of what the Logical Empiricists used to call "emotive meaning." We are not talking about an emotional overlay on, or response to, some core concept of sexuality but rather about bodily and imaginitive structures of attitude, rhythm, pattern of interaction, sense of pressure, and so forth, that are constitutive of sexual force. Neither are these patterns merely my private projections or responses, since they are culturally influenced modes of meaningful interaction with other sexual creatures. Moreover, they are conventionally encoded in language and are immediately understood by hundreds of millions of other people.

Another important point concerns the nature of the metaphors that constitute our understanding of sexuality. I am using the term "metaphor" in a special sense (to be explored in Chapter 4) that highlights its experiential nature. A metaphor is not merely a linguistic expression (a form of words) used for artistic or rhetorical purposes; instead, it is a process of human understanding by which we achieve meaningful experience that we can make sense of. A metaphor, in this "experiential" sense, is a process by which we understand and structure one domain of experience in terms of another domain *of a different kind*. Thus, in the metaphor SEXUAL APPEARANCE IS A PHYSICAL FORCE we project meaningful structure from our experience of forceful interactions of physical objects and events onto the domain of our sexual experience. Many of the connections across these two domains are experiential projections at the preconceptual level of our understanding. We thus come to experience our sexuality by means of these preconceptual structures that are meaningful to us in a *bodily* way.

Finally, I want to mention one of the more abstract notions operative in the law clerk's discourse, the idea of moral responsibility. What, one might ask, could be more a matter of abstract, disembodied conceptual connections than this difficult notion? But even moral responsibility has a nonpropositional dimension in our shared sense of what it means to "respond." Response is not mere reaction, as when my leg jumps when the doctor taps my knee. Response involves my awareness of myself as a center of force capable of action. There is felt sense of spontaneity involved in my responding to some event or causal interaction. My response, then, presupposes an encounter with something prior that elicits it, and this involves my directed action in light of that stimulus. This action, in turn, presupposes my sense of myself as a causally efficacious source of movement and force (e.g., I say, "I made that happen"), as involved in what happens next. The notion of causality here calls for further extensive analysis, but it should be clear that the meaning of causality, too, is grounded in preconceptual structures of experience.

Step-by-step, I begin to acquire the notion of responsibility that is not tied to reflex response alone. I discover that I can sometimes respond to a physical stimulus by means of a self-initiated, purposive action, which I come to experience as very different from mere automatic, or "knee-jerk," reflex reactions. The more I experience my world, the more I come to realize that I am not merely a passive being pushed around by external forces and driven by internal forces over which I have no control. Instead, I learn that I sometimes have a choice as to how I will respond to some force. I may be very hungry, but I learn that I don't necessarily have to cry, as I did when I was an infant. The situations in which I find myself typically offer a range of possible responses, and I feel myself *responsible* for what happens, that is, as personally a causal factor in the outcome. I can even reflect on what has happened to me and consider how I shall respond. In short, *response* is no longer mere reflex reaction. There is often a space of deliberation between a force that affects us and our response in light of that force. We learn to act *in light of our conception of a situation* and not only by means of automatic reactions. In this way, the term "responsible" keeps a certain ambiguity in natural language, pointing both to reflex and to deliberative response, and to their intimate experiential relation.

So, it is now possible to develop an understanding of *moral* responsibility by means of a basic metaphorical projection. The moral realm does not involve *physical* compulsion, and it does not involve only *physical* response to stimuli. The forces acting in the moral realm are not physical. But we project metaphorically from our sense of physical force and interactions onto the more abstract, psychological realm of moral interactions. Our moral responsibility consists in our making commitments and performing (or refraining from) actions that are not physically compelled. So moral responsibility is understood metaphorically on the basis of our experience of more bodily responses. We do not project all of the structure of the experience of automatic, reflex responses onto the moral realm, since choice of alternative bodily responses introduces a crucial gap between the stimulus and our response to it. This gap allows us to be moved by the *force of moral reason* rather than physical forces, such as bodily desires, needs, and interests.

Thus, the law clerk's sense that the woman is responsible for the sexual force she exerts is meaningful and understandable to us, because of our culturally shared experiences of bodily response and causality, which make up part of our metaphorical grasp of moral responsibility. When the clerk later suggests that he must inhibit his emotions if he is to act in a morally responsible manner, he employs just such patterns of physical response interpreted now metaphorically to cover the domain of moral duty. He experiences himself as responsible to *moral* forces that can overpower the physical forces (drives, needs, desires) acting upon him.

My description of the development of some of the meanings of "force" is obviously meant to highlight preconceptual and nonpropositional dimensions. I have no objection to the claim that this analysis is principally a partial explication of a *concept* of force, if "concept" is used broadly to cover any meaning structure whatever. I want only to insist that a central place be given to structures of bodily experience that are meaningful to us, yet not propositional in the standard senses. It is these that have been ignored in our most influential theories of meaning.

My brief analysis of the law clerk's explanation of rape suggests that there is meaning that comes through bodily experience and figurative processes of ordering, all of which are ignored by dominant Objectivist treatments of language, meaning, understanding, and reasoning. In particular, there is the functioning of preconceptually meaningful structures of experience, schematic patterns, and figurative projections by which our experience achieves meaningful organization and connection, such that we can both comprehend and reason about it. In the next several chapters I want to take up the more important types of nonpropositional structure that make meaning, understanding, and reasoning possible.

2

The Emergence of Meaning through Schematic Structure

My brief analysis of the "rape" passage in the previous chapter indicates that Objectivist accounts of meaning and rationality do not tell the whole story. Objectivist approaches treat meaning in a fairly narrow sense, as a relation between symbolic representations and objective (mind–independent) reality. Semantics, so defined, focuses on truth conditions and other conditions of satisfaction for propositions (including their constituent parts, such as words). It is not surprising, therefore, that Objectivist treatments try to analyze meaning, truth, and reason without mentioning nonpropositional structures such as images, schematic patterns, and metaphorical projections (all of which are considered components of understanding, but not essential to meaning in the "proper" sense).

On the account I shall develop, it is just these previously ignored structures that are regarded as central. Though they are nonpropositional in any of the five Objectivist senses listed in Chapter 1, they are intimately tied to propositional contents of sentences and utterances. They play a crucial role in our ability to comprehend anything (an object, person, event) meaningfully; so, they also play a role in the meaning of more abstract objects, such as words, sentences, and narratives. For this reason, I want to try to understand *linguistic* meaning as a special case within the broader notion of *meaningfulness in general*. My investigation thus is oriented toward figuring out how it is that a large range of structures arise out of our bodily experience and provide patterns that are meaningful to us and that influence our reasoning.

In Chapter 1 I began this new kind of investigation with the suggestion that there are irreducibly metaphorical projections and structures of meaning with a nonpropositional dimension. I now want to pursue this claim more thoroughly by focusing chiefly on the nature and operation of "image-schematic" structures of meaning. This requires an exploration of the way in which our perceptual interactions and bodily movements within our environment generate these schematic structures that make it possible for us to experience, understand, and reason about our world.

Embodied Schemata

I want to propose a meaning for the term "schema" that differs in important respects from what has come to be the standard meaning of the term in recent cognitive science. My use of the term derives from its original use as it was first elaborated by Immanuel Kant. He understood schemata as nonpropositional structures of imagination. Today, by contrast, schemata are typically thought of as general knowledge structures, ranging from conceptual networks to scripted activities to narrative structures and even to theoretical frameworks. Since my use of the term focuses on embodied patterns of meaningfully organized experience (such as structures of bodily movements and perceptual interactions), I want to distinguish my view from those that put stress exclusively on propositional structure.

Let us consider briefly the mainstream view. A recent survey of schema theory defines the key notion as

a cluster of knowledge representing a particular generic procedure, object, percept, event, sequence of events, or social situation. This cluster provides a skeleton structure for a concept that can be "instantiated," or filled out, with the detailed properties of the particular instance being represented.[1]

The most popular version of this general view regards schemata as abstract conceptual and propositional event structures. Thus, Rumelhart defines "schema" as "generalized knowledge about a sequence of events."[2] Rumelhart illustrates this interpretation with Schank and Abelson's notion of a scripted activity as a basic knowledge structure.[3] Schank and Abelson argue that we understand many situations by fitting them into structured frameworks or schemata (which they call "scripts") that include characters, settings, sequences of events, causal connections, goals, and so forth, that are the means by which we organize our knowledge of the world. They explain the key idea as follows:

A script is a structure that describes appropriate sequences of events in a particular context. A script is made up of slots and requirements about what can fill those slots. The structure is an interconnected whole, and what is in one slot affects what can be in another. Scripts handle stylized everyday situations. They are not subject to much change, nor do they provide the apparatus for handling totally novel situations. Thus, a script is a predetermined, stereotyped sequence of actions that defines a well-known situation.[4]

As an example, consider the act of buying a new car, an activity that gives rise to a highly structured schema. There are typical participants (salesperson, buyers, managers), props (new cars, a car lot, a showroom), a normal sequence of events (buyers go to car lot, salesperson shows various cars, buyers test-drive cars, participants haggle over merits of cars and fair prices), and standard goals (buyers want good, inexpensive cars, the salesperson wants to maximize profit without alienating the buyer, and so forth). Under this interpretation the schema is a unified, recurring organization of conceptual and propositional knowledge and values that we share about typical situations and events.

Schank, Abelson, Rumelhart, and others are surely correct in stressing that we encounter and understand our world partly by means of general knowledge structures of this sort. But we also need to enrich and complement this popular interpretation of schemata as event structures by exploring the way image schemata operate as organizing structures of our experience and understanding at the level of bodily perception and movement. Ulric Neisser has urged this notion of an embodied schema as tied to perception and motor programs:

A schema is that portion of the entire perceptual cycle which is internal to the perceiver, modifiable by experience, and somehow specific to what is being perceived. The schema accepts information as it becomes available at sensory surfaces and is changed by that information; it directs movements and exploratory activities that make more information available, by which it is further modified.

From the biological point of view, a schema is a part of the nervous system. It is some active array of physiological structures and processes: not a center in the brain, but an entire system that includes receptors and afferents and feed-forward units and efferents.[5]

Neisser emphasizes the role of perceptual and movement capacities in the active organization of our experience. Even our most simple encounters with objects, such as the perception of a cup, involve schemata that make it possible for us to recognize different kinds of things and events as being different *kinds*. Our perceptual schemata are the

various possible structures that our experience must fit if it is to be
coherent and comprehensible. These structures are not rigid or fixed,
however, but are altered in their application to particular situations.
Furthermore, they are not just templates for conceptualizing past experience; some schemata are *plans* of a sort for interacting with objects
and persons. They give expectations and anticipations that influence
our interactions with our environment. "The schema is not only the
plan but also the executor of the plan. It is a pattern *of* action as well as
a pattern *for* action."[6]

Neisser's view is distinctive because of its emphasis on schemata as
malleable structures of perception and motor programs. Such structures do not operate propositionally in the Objectivist sense, though
they may play a role in our propositionally expressed knowledge insofar as they constrain inferences. This use of "schema" shares certain
features with the conception introduced by Kant in the eighteenth century. Kant understood schemata as structures of imagination that connect concepts with percepts. He described them as "procedures for
constructing images" and as thus involving perceptual patterns in our
bodily experience. As we shall see, Kant's interpretation is somewhat
limited by his peculiar view of concepts, but he does recognize the
imaginative and nonpropositional nature of schemata.

To introduce the closely related sense in which I will be using the
term "schema," let us consider briefly an ordinary instance of image-
schematic structure emerging from our experience of physical containment. Our encounter with containment and boundedness is one of the
most pervasive features of our bodily experience. We are intimately
aware of our bodies as three-dimensional containers into which we put
certain things (food, water, air) and out of which other things emerge
(food and water wastes, air, blood, etc.). From the beginning, we experience constant physical containment in our surroundings (those
things that envelop us). We move in and out of rooms, clothes, ve-
hicles, and numerous kinds of bounded spaces. We manipulate objects,
placing them in containers (cups, boxes, cans, bags, etc.). In each of
these cases there are repeatable spatial and temporal organizations. In
other words, there are typical schemata for physical containment.

If we look for common structure in our many experiences of being
in something, or for locating something *within* another thing, we find
recurring organization of structures: the experiential basis for *in-out*
orientation is that of spatial boundedness. The most experientially salient sense of boundedness seems to be that of three-dimensional containment (i.e., being limited or held within some three-dimensional

enclosure, such as a womb, a crib, or a room). If we eliminate one or two of these dimensions, we get equally important two- and one-dimensional containment. In these latter cases, however, the relevant experience is chiefly one of differentiation and separation, such as when a point lies *in* a circle or *in* a line segment. Whether in one, two, or three dimensions, physical *in-out* orientation involves separation, differentiation, and enclosure, which implies restriction and limitation.

There are thus at least five important entailments or consequences of these recurring experiential image-schematic structures for *in-out* orientation. (i) The experience of containment typically involves protection from, or resistance to, external forces. When eyeglasses are *in* a case, they are protected against forceful impacts. (ii) Containment also limits and restricts forces within the container. When I am *in* a room, or *in* a jacket, I am restrained in my forceful movements. (iii) Because of this restraint of forces, the contained object gets a relative fixity of location. For example, the fish gets located *in* the fishbowl. The cup is held *in* the hand. (iv) This relative fixing of location within the container means that the contained object becomes either accessible or inaccessible to the view of some observer. It is either held so that it can be observed, or else the container itself blocks or hides the object from view. (v) Finally, we experience transitivity of containment. If B is *in* A, then whatever is *in* B is also *in* A. If I am *in* bed, and my bed is *in* my room, then I am *in* my room.

What I have just described are five of the most important consequences of the structure of *in-out* schemata. George Lakoff and I have called such consequences "entailments" because they are implications of the internal structure of image schemata.[7] It is a matter of great significance, as I argue later, that patterns such as these, which exist preconceptually in our experience, can give rise to rational entailments (which we describe propositionally).

I am not insisting that there must be only one central schema for all *in-out* orientation that covers all cases of the meaning of "in" used for physical containment; rather, there are a small number of related schematic structures that emerge from our constant and usually unnoticed encounters with physical containment. What is important is that these recurrent patterns are relatively few in number, they are not propositional in the Objectivist sense, and yet they have sufficient internal structure to generate entailments and to constrain inferences (and thus to be propositionally elaborated).

There is a temptation to draw diagrams of the relevant schemata as a way of suggesting intuitively how they operate preconceptually. For

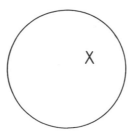

FIGURE 2.   CONTAINMENT

example, we might diagram a typical pattern for physical containment (one that operates for cases such as "The chair is *in* the room") as shown in figure 2. Henceforth, I will employ drawings of this sort as aids in the description of particular image schemata. Such diagrams are particularly helpful in identifying the key structural features of the schemata and in illustrating their internal relationships. It is extremely important, however, to recognize the way in which all diagrams of schemata are misleading; in particular, they tend to make us identify embodied schemata with particular rich images or mental pictures. The distinction between schemata and rich images is crucial and merits considerable attention.

How Embodied Schemata Differ from Images and Propositions

In what follows I shall use the terms "schema," "embodied schema," and "image schema" interchangeably. The last two terms remind us that we are dealing with schematic structures that are constantly operating in our perception, bodily movement through space, and physical manipulation of objects. As embodied in this manner, therefore, *image schemata are not propositional,* in that they are not abstract subject- predicate structures (e.g., "The cat is on the mat") that specify truth conditions or other conditions of satisfaction (e.g., the cat's being on the mat). They exist, rather, in a continuous, analog fashion in our understanding. And, while we may describe features of their structure propositionally using finitary representations, we thereby lose our ability to explain their natural operations and transformations (see below).

On the other hand, *image schemata are not rich, concrete images or mental pictures, either.* They are structures that organize our mental representations at a level more general and abstract than that at which we form particular mental images.

Once again, it was Kant who saw this crucial point most clearly. He argued that a schematic structure cannot be identical with an image, since the image or mental picture will always be of some one particular thing, which may not share all the same features with another thing of the same kind. The schema, by contrast, contains structural features common to many different objects, events, activities, and bodily movements. Kant makes this point in explaining why there must be something besides the image of a triangle that connects up our perception of particular triangles with our abstract concept TRIANGLE.

No image could ever be adequate to the concept of a triangle in general. It would never attain that universality of the concept which renders it valid of all triangles, whether right-angled, obtuse-angled, or acute-angled; it would always be limited to a part only of this sphere. The schema of the triangle can exist nowhere but in thought.[8]

By "thought" here Kant means that schemata are not merely physiological processes but have a reality as structures or patterns of mental representations. The important point for our purposes is that schemata have a generality that raises them a level above the specificity of particular rich images. This can be seen by considering a few simple examples of image schemata as contrasted with rich images or mental pictures. You can easily form an image of a human face that is full of detail—it can have eyes that are wide open, with one pupil larger than another; lips cracked from exposure to the sun; ears that stick out unusually far; a scar running beneath the left eye; a mole just to the right and below the left corner of the mouth; and on and on through one detail after another. Now, in contrast with this "information rich" image, our schema for a face has only a few basic features—lines for eyes, nose, curve of face, etc. This schema can, therefore, be instantiated in a huge number of different images of faces.

There is a growing body of experimental evidence in support of the thesis that there is a distinctive image-schematic level of cognitive processing that must be distinguished from rich images or mental picturing. In a recent summary of this research John Anderson identifies important differences between image schemata (which he calls "images") and my "rich" images (which he calls "mental pictures"):[9]

1. Image schemata are abstract and not limited only to visual properties. Brooks[10] performed experiments in which subjects were shown

a figure that was taken away, whereupon they were required to scan their mental images and to answer questions on the basis of this scanning activity. Brooks discovered, among other things, that properties associated with visual images can derive from tactile (and not just visual) experience. In other words, what I am calling "image schemata" have a certain kinesthetic character—they are not tied to any single perceptual modality, though our visual schemata seem to predominate.

Lakoff cites more recent research with blind subjects[11] that indicates the kinesthetic nature of these mental transformations. When congenitally blind people are asked to perform various operations on mental images, but to do so via touch, they perform these tasks with success similar to that of sighted persons, only with slower performance times. It would seem that image schemata transcend any specific sense modality, though they involve operations that are analogous to spatial manipulation, orientation, and movement.

2. It is no surprise, therefore, that we can perform mental operations on image schemata that are analogs of spatial operations. Shepard and Metzler,[12] for example, studied our ability to rotate mental images. They presented subjects with two-dimensional drawings of pairs of three-dimensional objects. The task was to determine whether the two represented objects were identical except for orientation. Some of the figures required rotation solely within the picture plane, while others required rotation in depth ("into" the page). The general result was that, whether for two- or three-dimensional rotations, subjects seem to rotate the objects mentally at a fixed rate of approximately 60 degrees/second. Further experiments seemed to confirm this phenomenon.[13]

Anderson regards these phenomena as evidence for the thesis that mental operations on image schemata are abstract analogs of physical processes or operations. To illustrate the notion "abstract analog," Anderson suggests the length of a line as an analog for a person's weight. The length of a line would vary with the weight, but there is no detailed correlation between a line and weight. Humans seem to have the ability to scan and transform mental arrays and image structures in a fashion analogous to the scanning and manipulation of physical objects. It is as though we have a "mental space" in which we perform image-schematic operations that may or may not involve visual rich images.

3. A related body of evidence is given by Lakoff[14] who describes a series of "image-schema transformations" that indicate nonproposi-

tional schematic operations a level of abstraction above that of rich images. Consider, for example, our ability to perform the following transformations on basic image schemata:

a) *Path-focus to end-point-focus.* Follow, in imagination, the path of a moving object, and then focus on the point where it comes to rest, or where it will come to rest.

b) *Multiplex to mass.* Imagine a group of several objects. Move away (in your mind) from the group until the cluster of individuals starts to become a single homogeneous mass. Now move back down to the point where the mass turns once again into a cluster.

c) *Following a trajectory.* As we perceive a continuously moving object, we can mentally trace the path it has traversed or the trajectory it is about to traverse.

d) *Superimposition.* Imagine a large sphere and a small cube. Increase the size of the cube until the sphere can fit inside it. Now reduce the size of the cube and put it within the sphere.

In these and myriad other cases of natural image-schema transformations, we make use of our ability to manipulate abstract structure in mental space.

4. Another distinction between mental pictures and image schemata is that the latter are influenced by general knowledge in a way that the former are not. Schemata are more abstract and malleable than mental pictures. A study by Carmichael, Hogan, and Walter[15] suggests that linguistic descriptions used as cues for recall of visual images influenced the subject's drawing of the recalled image. An actual mental picture, however, should remain unchanged. The linguistic description appears to call up certain related schemata that are brought to bear in recalling and drawing the image. Thus, consider the picture of two equal-sized circles connected by a straight line. Shown such a picture, subjects were inclined to draw it differently from memory depending on the recall cue they were given. If the cue was "eyeglasses," they might tend to curve the line between the circles; if the cue was "dumbbells," they might tend to draw a shaft between the two circles. If they only grasped the mental picture, and not some schematic representation, they should be able to reproduce the original drawing exactly.

To summarize: there is a large and growing body of evidence (see also Chapter 5) for the existence of an image-schematic level of cognitive operations. And this evidence supports the distinction between image-schematic structure and the more concrete level of rich images or mental pictures. An image schema, then, is not a particular rich image.

However, there remains another major argument against image schemata and their natural transformations that has proponents in recent artificial intelligence research.[16] This is the "propositional theory" which regards mental imagery as a mere epiphenomenon of underlying propositional representations. Pylyshyn denies any independent mental reality to imagery and thus claims that any mental image, schematic structure, or operation on them can be fully represented in propositional form.[17]

To see just how strong a claim this is, consider what it entails. On this strong propositionalist view, every mental scene will be represented in terms of arbitrary symbols (such as X, Y, Z) which are used to stand for features of the scene, such as points, edges, surfaces, or entire objects. Other completely arbitrary symbols will be used to represent the relations obtaining among these other symbols. Now, the key issue is not whether we can propositionally describe images or image schemata. Of course, we can describe them propositionally. But the real issue concerns the *cognitive reality* of the images and schemata, and this is what the propositional theory denies.

George Lakoff has shown why this strong version will not work. Basically, it fails because it cannot account for what we called "natural image-schematic transformations" above. It claims that only propositional representations are cognitively real. But such representations are only sequences of arbitrary symbols for elements and relations and, thus, are not "natural." Image-schematic transformations, by contrast, are natural recurring operations that are cognitively real. Lakoff explains:

> The names that we have given to image-schemas, and to image-schema transformations, are very much in keeping with the kind of symbolization that might be used in studies of computer vision. But the names are not the things named. This is shown by the naturalness of image-schema transformations relative to visual experience, as opposed to the arbitrariness of the names for those transformations. It seems to me that image-schema transformations are cognitively real; . . . And the naturalness of these transformations relative to our visual experience suggests that image-schema transformations and the schemas they relate are not propositional in character (in the sense of the term used in computer vision studies). Rather, they are truly imagistic in character.[18]

The upshot of this section is that image schemata and their transformations constitute a distinct level of cognitive operations, which is different from both concrete rich images (mental pictures), on the one side, and abstract, finitary propositional representations, on the other.

Image schemata exist at a level of generality and abstraction that allows them to serve repeatedly as identifying patterns in an indefinitely large number of experiences, perceptions, and image formations for objects or events that are similarly structured in the relevant ways. Their most important feature is that they have a few basic elements or components that are related by definite structures, and yet they have a certain flexibility. As a result of this simple structure, they are a chief means for achieving order in our experience so that we can comprehend and reason about it.

Typical schemata will have parts and relations. The parts might consist of a set of entities (such as people, props, events, states, sources, goals). The relations might include causal relations, temporal sequences, part-whole patterns, relative locations, agent-patient structures, or instrumental relations. Normally, however, a given schema will have a small number of parts standing in simple relations.

A good example that shows what is meant by "parts" and "relations" is the FROM–TO or PATH schema (see fig. 3). This image schema consists of three elements (a source point A, a terminal point B, and a vector tracing a path between them) and a relation (specified as a force vector moving from A to B). This FROM–TO schema is a recurrent structure manifested in a number of seemingly different events, such as: (a) walking from one place to another, (b) throwing a baseball to your sister, (c) punching your brother, (d) giving your mother a present, (e) the melting of ice into water. For each of these very different cases, we have the same schema with the *same basic parts and relations*. In (e) the schema must be interpreted metaphorically, with points A and B representing state (e.g., solid and liquid) of a substance (water). So, we see that image schemata are more general, abstract, and malleable than rich images; and they have definite parts and structural relations that emerge chiefly at the level of our physical or bodily perception and movement.

A Definition of an Image Schema

We are now in a position to give a general definition of "embodied" or "image" schemata. On the one hand, they are not Objectivist proposi-

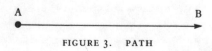

FIGURE 3.   PATH

tions that specify abstract relations between symbols and objective reality. There might be conditions of satisfaction for schemata of a special sort (for which we would need a new account), but not in the sense required for traditional treatments of propositions. On the other hand, they do not have the specificity of rich images or mental pictures. They operate at one level of generality and abstraction above concrete, rich images. A schema consists of a small number of parts and relations, by virtue of which it can structure indefinitely many perceptions, images, and events. In sum, image schemata operate at a level of mental organization that falls between abstract propositional structures, on the one side, and particular concrete images, on the other.

The view I am proposing is this: in order for us to have meaningful, connected experiences that we can comprehend and reason about, there must be pattern and order to our actions, perceptions, and conceptions. *A schema is a recurrent pattern, shape, and regularity in, or of, these ongoing ordering activities.* These patterns emerge as meaningful structures for us chiefly at the level of our bodily movements through space, our manipulation of objects, and our perceptual interactions.

It is important to recognize the dynamic character of image schemata. I conceive of them as *structures for organizing* our experience and comprehension. Kant went so far as to claim (in some passages, at least) that schemata are actually preconceptual structuring *processes* whose structures can "fit" general concepts and can generate particular images, thereby giving our experience meaningful order and organization that we can understand. He also saw schemata as structures of imagination. For the present I have avoided any mention of "imagination," because it tends to suggest, for us, notions of artistic creativity, fantasy, and fiction; whereas, for Kant, imagination is the very means by which we have *any* comprehensible structure in our experience. Since this special Kantian sense of imagination is not commonly acknowledged today, I shall carry on my discussion of schematic structures in this and the next three chapters without mentioning imagination. However, I do take up this important connection between image schemata and imagination in a detailed way in Chapter 6.

In contrast with Kant's view, I have stopped short of his stronger thesis that schemata are procedures for generating images that can fit concepts. Instead, I am identifying the schema as a *continuous structure* *of an organizing activity.* Yet, even though schemata are definite structures, they are dynamic patterns rather than fixed and static images, as their visual diagrams represent them. They are dynamic in two important respects. (1) Schemata are structures *of an activity* by which we organize our experience in ways that we can comprehend. They are a primary means by which we *construct* or *constitute* order and are not mere passive receptacles into which experience is poured. (2) Unlike templates, schemata are flexible in that they can take on any number of specific instantiations in varying contexts. It is somewhat misleading to say that an image schema gets "filled in" by concrete perceptual details; rather, it must be relatively malleable, so that it can be modified to fit many similar, but different, situations that manifest a recurring underlying structure.

This dynamic character of image schemata has important implications for our view of meaning and rationality. Insofar as meanings involve schematic structures, they are relatively fluid patterns that get altered in various contexts. They are not eternally fixed objects, as Objectivism suggests, but they gain a certain relative stability by becoming conventionally located in our network of meaning. So there is a large part of our meaning structure that can be treated as "fixed" most of the time. Such conventionalized meanings are called "literal." It is necessary, however, to remember that even these literal meanings are never wholly context-free—they depend upon a large background of shared schemata, capacities, practices, and knowledge.[19]

We need to correct the popular, but misguided, view that understanding involves only the imposition of static concepts, propositions, schemata, templates, plans, or networks upon some perceptual input. Rather, in addition to propositional comprehension, understanding is an evolving process or activity in which image schemata (as organizing structures) partially order and form our experience and are modified by their embodiment in concrete experiences. This perhaps can be seen more clearly if we focus on an example of *in-out* orientation in more detail to show that it consists of active organization of representations into meaningful, coherent unities.

Nonpropositional Schemata for In-Out Orientation

Consider just a small fraction of the orientational feats you perform constantly and unconsciously in your daily activities. Consider, for example, only a few of the many *in-out* orientations that might occur in the first few minutes of an ordinary day. You wake *out* of a deep sleep and peer *out* from beneath the covers *into* your room. You gradually emerge *out* of your stupor, pull yourself *out* from under the covers, climb *into* your robe, stretch *out* your limbs, and walk *in* a daze *out* of the bedroom and *into* the bathroom. You look *in* the mirror and see your face staring *out* at you. You reach *into* the medicine cabinet, take *out* the toothpaste, squeeze *out* some toothpaste, put the toothbrush *into* your mouth, brush your teeth *in* a hurry, and rinse *out* your mouth. At breakfast you perform a host of further *in-out* moves—pouring *out* the coffee, setting *out* the dishes, putting the toast *in* the toaster, spreading *out* the jam on the toast, and on and on. Once you are more awake you might even get lost *in* the newspaper, might enter *into* a conversation, which leads to your speaking *out* on some topic.

Some of these senses of *in* and *out* involve clear-cut physical orientation in space, while others involve more abstract nonspatial relations, such as entering *into* a conversation. However, they all require some activity of establishing relations, either among physical or among abstract entities or events. In a few ordinary minutes you have performed more orientational feats than you could ever keep track of while they are occurring in rapid-fire fashion. And these are only a fraction of the *in-out* orientations, let alone those for *up-down, near-far, left-right, front-back, toward-away from,* and so forth. What you have just experienced is not meaningful in the Romantic sense of being profoundly moving or significant; but it is meaningful in a more mundane sense, namely, it involves an exceedingly complex interaction with your environment in which you experience significant patterns and employ structured processes that give rise to a coherent world of which you are able to make sense.

Our schemata for spatial and temporal orientation are so pervasive and so constitutive of our ordinary experience that they are taken for granted (and thus overlooked) in standard accounts of meaning and understanding. We thereby miss a large part of the means by which anything can be meaningful for us (whether it is an object, event, word, sentence, or narrative). We need to look more closely, therefore, at the way such schemata operate in our understanding.

Let us ask whether there is any possible connection among the many senses of *out* exemplified above. Is there any meaningful connectedness of these occurrences, or are they discrete and unrelated atoms of meaning? The standard view has been that such words do not operate systematically and that they constitute only a very large number of semantically unrelated and unanalyzable lexical items. Recently, however, a body of empirical work on natural language has developed that challenges this prevailing thesis.[20] This new program, which includes recent work in "cognitive grammar" and "space grammar," denies both that there are autonomous language mechanisms and that language is independent of cognition. Instead, it claims that we have general cognitive and experiential mechanisms or processing capacities that can be specified to language tasks. On this hypothesis, we can better understand syntactic and semantic structure by focusing on patterns of meaningful experience that give rise to image-schematic structures for connecting up our many and varied cognitive activities.

Let us take as our example of schemata those for *in-out* orientation in our experience, understanding, and language. My example is adapted from a small portion of Susan Lindner's study of verb-particle constructions with *up* and *out* in English.[21] Lindner investigated some 600 cases in English of the construction: verb + *out* (e.g., *take out, spread out, throw out, pick out, leave out, shout out, draw out, pass out*), and over 1,100 cases of the construction: verb + *up* (e.g., *raise up, break up, give up, wake up, shake up, think up*). In contrast with the standard view that these represent unrelated semantic atoms, she found a small number of prototypical schematic structures that could be systematically extended to cover nearly all occurrences of the verb-particle construction under study. For the particle *out*, for instance, she identified three basic image schemata (figs. 4, 5, 6).

John went out of the room.
Pump out the air.
Let out your anger.
Pick out the best theory.
Drown out the music.
Harry weasled out of the contract.

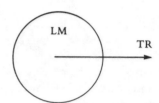

FIGURE 4.   OUT₁

Pour out the beans.
Roll out the red carpet.
Send out the troops.
Hand out the information.
Write out your ideas.

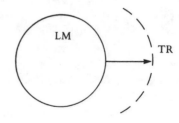

FIGURE 5.   OUT₂

The train started out for Chicago.

FIGURE 6.   OUT₃

In each of the figures for the three schemata the "landmark" (*LM*) is that in relation to which the "trajector" (*TR*) moves, as in a figure-ground relation. The visual diagram is only a distorting image of the actual schema, which is the pattern in some particular experience. Take, for example the OUT₁ schema (fig. 4) operative in "John went out of the room." Here the circle (*LM*) represents the room (as container), and John moves along the arrow (as *TR*) out of the room. Now the actual schema is the repeatable pattern embodied in John's trajectory with respect to the room container. Obviously, the diagram of the OUT₁ schema gives us only one idealized image of the actual schema, since the room needn't be circular, John needn't move along a straight line in leaving the room, there is a break (the door) in the actual boundary, and the schema is a certain structure of typical *out* movements. Furthermore, the schema does not have the finitary propositional form we give it in our linguistic utterance "John went out of the room." It is, rather, a continuous active, dynamic recurring structure of experiences of similar spatial movements of a certain kind.

We can now see that this same OUT₁ schema can represent an enormous number of orientational possibilities, as in:

1(a) Mary got out of the car.
1(b) Spot jumped out of his pen.
1(c) He squeezed out some toothpaste.
1(d) Tear out that cartoon and save it.
1(e) Get out of bed!

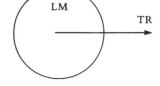

OUT₁

In each of these cases we have fairly straightforward spatial orientation among objects, people, substances, etc. The relevant schema (OUT₁) is the repeatable pattern of *out* movement in each of the specific actions. Notice that in each different case the schema is realized in a different way, though it retains a recognizable form. In other words, there is a recurrence of form in all of these cases, but that form is modified in its realization in each particular instance.

It is also important to observe that our most immediate grasp of the OUT₁ relation in these basic, simple cases is referenced to our *bodies* as they orient themselves spatially, as in "Mary got out of the car." Although nothing crucial rests on this claim, I believe that our sense of *out* orientation is most intimately tied to our experience of *our own* bodily orientation. Our body can be the trajector, as in "Paul walked out of the tunnel," or it can be the landmark, as in "She shoveled the potatoes into her mouth." In other words, the body can take up the role of the "thing contained" or the "container." But, in either case, we seem to develop our sense of *in-out* orientation through a host of bodily movements, manipulations, and experiences.

It seems to me that the projection of *in-out* orientation onto inanimate objects is already a first move beyond the prototypical case of *my* bodily movement. Squeezing out the toothpaste, for instance, seems to involve a projection of *in-out* orientation onto a tube and a substance it contains, on analogy with my prototypical orienting of objects with respect to my body. Whether or not this is correct, the chief point still holds, namely, our IN–OUT schemata emerge first in our *bodily* experience, in our perception and movement.

Another basic type of projection, the one I am most concerned with in this book, is the pervasive act of metaphorically extending a schema from the physical to the nonphysical. In such cases a basic schema, for example, OUT₁, is figuratively elaborated and extended so as to allow the landmark and trajector roles to be filled by entities that are no longer strictly physical or spatial in the prototypical senses. It is a central claim of "cognitive grammar" that metaphorical projections of this sort are one of the chief means for connecting up different senses of a term.

To see what this means, let us consider some of the nonspatial senses of *out*. One such cluster of senses involves the figurative (here metaphorical) extension of the OUT₁ schema as applying to events, states, and abstract entities interpreted as spatially bounded entities. Instances of this type of projection are common, as in

2(a) Tell me your story again, but leave out the minor details. (STORY EVENT AS CONTAINER)

2(b) I give up, I'm getting out of the race. (RACE EVENT AS CONTAINER)

2(c) Whenever I'm in trouble, she always bails me out. (STATE AS CONTAINER)

2(a) is a primitive case of metaphorical extension of the preconceptual OUT₁ schema. The OUT₁ schema, which applies prototypically to spatial orientation, is metaphorically projected onto the cognitive domain where there are processes of choosing, rejecting, separating, differentiating abstract objects, and so forth. Numerous cases, such as *leave out, pick out, take out,* etc., can be either physical bodily actions that involve orientational schemata, or else they can be metaphorically oriented mental actions. What you *pick out* physically are spatially extended objects; what you *pick out* metaphorically are abstract mental or logical entities. But the relevant preconceptual schema is generally the same for both senses of *picking out*.

Cases like *leave out* focus our attention on the close kinship between certain preconceptual schemata and metaphorical interpretations of them. Take, for example,

   3(a) Leave out that big log when you stack the firewood.
   3(b) I don't want to leave any relevant data out of my argument.

Here, in moving from 3(a) to 3(b) we can witness a primitive metaphorical projection at work. 3(a) is a simple case of physical spatial relationships, involving only the minimal projection of *in-out* orientation onto a woodpile. 3(b) is clearly a metaphorical extrapolation in which an abstract entity, an argument, is metaphorically grasped as a container structured partially by means of the OUT₁ schema. In fact, the ARGUMENT IS A CONTAINER metaphor is one of the most common structurings of our concept for argument in Western culture.[22]

Another common type of metaphorical projection treats social or interpersonal agreements, contracts, or obligations as bounded entities. This generates such expressions as,

   4(a) Don't you dare back out of our agreement.
   4(b) If you want out, bow out now, before we go any further.
   4(c) He'll weasel out of the contract, if he can.

Being bound in these cases involves something metaphorically akin to being in a physical space where forces act on and constrain you. If you enter *into* an agreement, you become subject to a (moral or legal) force that acts within the abstract space contained by the agreement. So, to *get out of* such a contract or agreement is to be no longer subject to its force, since you are no longer within the "space" where that force acts upon you. This fact is a consequence of the schema for containment discussed earlier. Where there is a container, there can be forces internal to it that are limited and constrained by the boundaries of the container. Once an object is removed from (taken *out of*) the container, it is no longer influenced by those forces.

As Lindner shows in great detail, there are numerous other relevant kinds of metaphorical elaboration of OUT schemata. Let us consider only one further type of extension that highlights the experientially formative character of these metaphorical extensions.

   5(a) They always get the *Post Dispatch* out on time.
   5(b) Honda just put out its 1986 models.
   5(c) Hand out these flyers to everyone who attends.
   5(d) Were you able to rent out your house?

5(e) It finally came out that he had lied to us.

5(f) When you wear blue, it really brings out your eyes.

In these cases the *out* movement involves a metaphorical bringing into prominence or making public. That which is bounded-in may be hidden, unknown, unavailable, or unnoticed, so that being *out* constitutes being public, known, available for use, or noticed.

The sentences in extension 5 also highlight another feature of many orientational schemata that suggests their preconceptual character, namely, they always presuppose a "viewpoint" from which the movement is observed.[23] Most of the cases in 5 assume a viewpoint outside the landmark, so that making public and open to view consists in bringing something *out* into the open (where the "open" is often a metaphorical mental space). If the *Post Dispatch,* or the new line of Hondas, or the flyers are *out,* they are in the space where we have access to them, they are in the same general space where we are. On the other hand, cases such as

6(a) We kicked him out of the club.

6(b) He bowed out of our agreement.

assume a viewpoint within the landmark. When he gets *out of* our agreement, he is no longer in the same "space" with me, as long as I continue to hold to the agreement.

I want to stress that the assumption of a viewpoint is not typically a matter of entertaining certain concepts or propositions. It is already *part of,* or called up by, our OUT schemata. There can be no orientation (either spatial, temporal, or metaphorical) that does not involve a perspective from which the orientation is viewed. The very structure of orientation is perspectival. And grasping the relevant perspective is not usually a matter of entertaining a proposition, such as "I'm viewing the container from outside"; rather, it is simply a point of view that we take up, *because it is part of the structural relations of the relevant schema.*

I am not claiming that there is one correct perspective correlating with each schema. The movement in "She backed out of the garage" could be viewed either from within the garage, as the car moves away, or from outside the garage, as the car moves toward you. Which perspective is relevant will depend upon the context. But having *some* perspective is part of image schemata, and it is not a reflective or propositional overlay on some nonperspectival pattern. Typically, our ability to assume the proper perspective is a consequence of recurrent perspectival patterns that emerge in ordinary experiences of spatial events. Because we come to understand relevant perspectives in cases of spatial orientation, we have clues to the proper "intellectual" or "epistemic" perspectives in cases of more abstract metaphorical extensions of orientational schemata. Thus, we know that in "She backed out of her moral obligations" there are two possible perspectives to be considered. First, being bound by moral obligations involves being within a metaphorical space where forces of moral constraint act upon you. So, there is one possible perspective from within the space of moral obligation with the woman moving away from you as she backs out of her responsibilities. Second, one might describe this dereliction from a neutral standpoint outside the space of moral obligation. Once again, the proper perspective is context-dependent, but there must be some appropriate perspective.

This brief and highly selective sampling of "verb + *out*" constructions is meant to give some idea of how pervasive, complex, and important image-schematic meaning structures are in our meaningful and coherent experience of the world. We couldn't begin to understand our experience without them. They give comprehensible structure and definiteness to our experience and connect up different experiential domains to establish a measure of coherence and unity in our understanding of our world. Objectivist programs claim that such processes of understanding are irrelevant to semantics, to an account of meaning, which is supposed to consist of objective relations between symbols and objective reality. I am suggesting that we cannot understand meaning without paying attention to such schematic structures as these. On my view, so-called linguistic meaning is treated as a specific case of meaning in a broader sense, namely, meaning as involving our grasp of structures that give definiteness, coherence, order, and connectedness in our esperience of anything. And, as I shall argue below, meaning structures in this broader sense are the basis for human reasoning and inference.

Inference Patterns Based on Containment Schemata

The Objectivist view of rationality is that it consists of abstract logical connections (or inference patterns) among concepts and propositions. No reference whatever is made to embodied structures such as images, image schemata (in my sense), or metaphorical projections of the irreducible, experiential sort I have just described. To "ground" logical inference in this way would, on the Objectivist account, destroy the purity of logic by introducing potentially nonuniversal empirical elements. Such a move is seen as disastrous insofar as it would destroy the possibility of a universal structure of rationality that transcends the different historical contexts in which it manifests itself.

I do not wish to deny the importance of *formal* structures, formal systems, or logical operations. I do not, however, think that they constitute God's-Eye-Rationality as atemporal, universal structures; instead, formal systems with their peculiar logical properties and relations are possible forms for ordering symbols. Many of their properties and relations are simply formalizations of experiential patterns by means of which we organize our experience and understanding. Although we can more or less successfully abstract from particular empirical contents in framing a formal system (and in mathematics do it quite thoroughly), it does not follow that the inferential structures and logical connectives of the system are therefore "pure," "nonempirical," "transcendent" patterns.

I would like to suggest, in this and succeeding chapters, possible experiential bases for some logical connectives and inferential structures. In particular, I want to suggest that image schemata constrain inferences (and thus reasoning) in certain basic and important ways. They can do this because they have definite internal structure that can be figuratively extended to structure our understanding of formal relations among concepts and propositions. It is in this special, non-Objectivist sense only that image schemata can be called "propositional" (=continuous patterns with sufficient internal structure to constrain inferences). Because schemata are so central to meaning structure, they influence the ways in which we can make sense of things and reason about them.

Let us begin with the way we understand formal reasoning. When we reason, we understand ourselves as starting at some point (a proposition or set of premises), from which we proceed in a series of steps to a conclusion (a goal, or stopping point). Metaphorically, we understand the process of reasoning as a form of motion along a path—propositions are the locations (or bounded areas) that we start out from, proceed through, and wind up at. Holding a proposition is understood metaphorically as being located at that point (or in that area). This very general metaphorical system is reflected in our language about reasoning in a large number of ways:

Let us *start out from* the proposition that Hamlet feared his father.
You can't *move to* that conclusion from *where* you are now.

From here I'll proceed to show that humans are slaves of their passions.

Once you *reach that point* in the argument, you've got to *go on to* the conclusion.

The *next step* is to demonstrate that monkeys can make tools.

He *got off the track* of the argument.

That assumption will *lead you astray.*

When we actually move from one place to another, we experience ourselves as traversing a path from one bounded area to another. This experience, together with the metaphorical understanding of propositions as locations, provides a basis for our understanding of negation. To hold a proposition is to be located in a definite bounded space (the space defined by the proposition). Being in such a bounded (mental) space involves being contained within certain boundaries. To hold the negation of that proposition is thus to be located *outside* that bounded space. In this way, the CONTAINER schema enters into our understanding of reasoning.

It follows from the nature of the CONTAINER schema (which marks off a bounded mental space) that something is either *in* or *out* of the container in typical cases. And, if we understand categories metaphorically as containers (where a thing falls within the container, or it does not), then we have the claim that everything is either P (in the category-container) or not-P (outside the container). In logic, this is known as the "Law of the Excluded Middle," that is, there is no third possibility between possessing a property (i.e., falling within a category) or not possessing that property (falling outside the category). In those cases, therefore, where we understand certain phenomena via CONTAINER metaphors (and most of us operate with such simplified models much of the time), the principle "Either P or not-P" has an intuitive basis in our daily experience with containment. We must not forget, however, that it is a principle that holds chiefly for the logic of metaphorical containers, that is, for classical logic.

A second logical relation that is experientially motivated by containment is "transitivity." If a marble is in a small bag, which is placed within a second, larger bag, then we know the *obvious* conclusion: the marble is in the larger bag. This transitivity of containment can be stated formally as follows: if xRy, and yRz, then xRz (if x stands in relation R to y, and if y stands in relation R to z, then x stands in relation R to z). Thus, our experience with containers (and bounded spaces) and their properties is the basis for our understanding of the transitivity of set membership. Sets are understood as containers for their members and their subsets. So, if a set A is a member of (is contained by) set B, and set B is a member of (is contained by) set C, then A is a member of set C.

A third point about logical structure that appears to be tied to CONTAINMENT schemata concerns the nature of negation. We understand our experience as broken up according to basic categories (of objects, events, states, properties, relations, etc.). We understand these categories as abstract containers, so that whatever is *within* the category is *in* the appropriate container. Thus, a negation of some type (or category) of experience is understood as characterizing what is *outside* the category. It makes perfectly good sense, therefore, that model-theoretic semantics should analyze the *not* operator as set complementation, that is, not-X is interpreted as all things falling "outside" the set X.

This basic logic of containment also motivates the elementary equivalence for double negation, $\sim\sim P \equiv P$ (read as: not-(not-P) is equivalent to P). This follows immediately from the CONTAINMENT schema. Not-P places us outside the container, or bounded area, P. But if we then negate this not-P position, we are moved *back into* the original position within the container P. This schematic movement rests, of course, upon the assumption of Classical Logic that the only two options are either being in the container, or being outside it, with no other choice (i.e., the negation of not-P must move you back into the bounded space of P and not into some other part of the space of not-P).[24]

I am suggesting that such inferential patterns (e.g., $Pv\sim P$, $\sim\sim P \equiv P$, transitivity, etc.) arise from our bodily experience of containment. Their use in abstract reasoning is a matter of metaphorical projection upon CONTAINER schemata, in which the inferential structure is preserved by the metaphorical mapping. In succeeding chapters I will identify other schematic bases for so-called logical inference structures. This is not to deny our marvelous human capacity for abstraction and formalization, without which we could not progress in our theorizing about our world. Nor do I deny the possibility that there may exist a priori structures of rationality. But I will suggest that we can go a very long way toward understanding logic by focusing on the properties of certain image schemata. Since we are animals it is only natural that our inferential patterns would emerge from our activities at the embodied level. This is a theme I shall pursue in later chapters, where I stress the amount of *structure* that exists preconceptually and nonpropositionally in our ongoing meaningful organization of our experience, understanding, and reasoning.

3

Gestalt Structure as a Constraint on Meaning

We have begun to explore the way in which image-schematic structures of experience generate complex patterns of meaning. I used as an example one of the most pervasive features of human experience, namely, the experience of containment, boundedness, and differentiation. I argued that there are recurrent patterns in these "containment" experiences and that the patterns could be extended, transformed, and metaphorically projected to give the meaning of *out* for many of its different (but related) senses. In other words, the analysis of *out* highlighted the nonpropositional and embodied nature of the image schemata for containment and boundedness.

I now want to redirect our attention toward the *internal structure* of these experiential schemata. I shall emphasize their *gestalt* characteristics, that is, their nature as coherent, meaningful, unified wholes within our experience and cognition. They are a principle means by which we achieve meaning structure. They generate coherence for, establish unity within, and constrain our network of meaning. Most important, these "experiential gestalts" are neither arbitrary, nor are they "mushy" forms that have no internal structure.

To explain and defend my case, I shall examine a second, ever-present dimension of our experience, that of forceful interaction. The previously described schemata for CONTAINMENT gave prominence to the limitation, restriction, and channeling of forces. By paying more attention to our experience of force as such, we uncover new considerations that did not arise in the analysis of boundedness. These considerations include motion, directedness of action, degree of intensity, and structure of causal interaction (including notions of both agency and patienthood, for animate and inanimate things alike). These new factors constitute further kinds of internal structure that an image schema (as gestalt) might manifest. So, attending to the patterns of our forceful encounters not only enriches our sketch of the contours of experience, it also serves to show just how much structure and constraining form is present in typical image-schematic gestalts.

Preconceptual Gestalts for Force

In order to survive as organisms, we must interact with our environment. All such causal interaction requires the exertion of *force,* either as we act upon other objects, or as we are acted upon by them. Therefore, in our efforts at comprehending our experience, structures of force come to play a central role. Since our experience is held together by forceful activity, our web of meanings is connected by the structures of such activity.

I want to explore the way in which patterns of typical experiences of force work their way up into our system of meaning and into the structure of our expression and communication. The main evidence for the efficacy of these image-schematic gestalt structures will be a demonstration of the way they constrain and limit meaning as well as patterns of inference in our reasoning.

To begin with, let us look at some of the more obvious structures of our forceful encounters with other objects and persons. Because force is *everywhere,* we tend to take it for granted and to overlook the nature of its operation. We easily forget that our bodies are clusters of forces and that *every* event of which we are a part consists, minimally, of forces in interaction. However, a moment's reflection reveals that our daily reality is one massive series of forceful causal sequences. We *do* notice such forces when they are extraordinarily strong, or when they are not balanced off by other forces. For example, I usually pay no attention to the wind, unless it is so strong that it resists my progress as I walk. Only then do I become aware of its force. Likewise, gravity is a force so pervasive that I am seldom aware of it. But we need only encounter a hill in our daily stroll to feel the existence of this force, as if we are suddenly being pulled back.

Even though we do not tend to pay attention to the forces that are everywhere inside us and in our environment, it is clear that these forces manifest structures that are very much a part of our having coherent, meaningful experiences that we can call into consciousness, understand, reason about, and communicate in language. Before I identify the image schemata for some of the more experientially important force structures that bear on semantics and the structure of our conceptual systems, I want to focus briefly on a number of features that typically play a role in our sense of force.

First, force is always experienced through *interaction*. We become aware of force as it affects us or some object in our perceptual field. When you enter an unfamiliar dark room and bump into the edge of a table, you are experiencing the interactional character of force. When you eat too much the ingested food presses outward on your tautly stretched stomach. There is no schema for force that does not involve interaction, or potential interaction.

Second, our experience of force usually involves the movement of some object (mass) through space in some direction. In other words, force has a *vector* quality, a directionality. There may actually be a moving object, or there may be only a force exerted against an object that is not moved or changed. But, in either case, the force is exerted in one or more directions. As the baseball flies through the air, it traces a path that we can describe by a force vector, or series of vectors, leading from the pitcher to the catcher. Or when the baby simply moves its hand to grasp a rattle, there is force exerted in a direction.

Third, there is typically a single *path of motion*. This is tied up with the vector quality of forceful movement. Our prototypical schema would have the force vector moving along a path, or moving an object along a path. The fly traces an agitated path as it buzzes wildly from wall to ceiling to lamp and back to ceiling. The force of gravity pulls a leaf along a path toward the ground, until that path is terminated when another object (e.g., the ground) counteracts the gravitational force. In less prototypical cases, such as explosions, the force moves off in all directions creating a potentially infinite number of paths. We would get a definite path only by focusing on the force as exerted on one object moved by the explosion.

Fourth, forces have *origins* or *sources,* and because they are directional, agents can direct them to *targets.* The cup doesn't just move of its own accord—it moves because something with power moves it from the table to the lips and back to the table. The force that moved the cup came from somewhere and, in this case, moved it to a target or goal.

Fifth, forces have *degrees of power or intensity.* Where there is power there exists the possibility of measuring the force it generates. In some cases, such as physical forces, this can be done rather precisely and quantitatively; in other cases, we may be able to give only a relative ranking, such as saying that force X is stronger than force Y. No matter how mathematically quantifiable a force is, the fact remains that being a force entails having a certain intensity.

Sixth, because we experience force via interaction, there is always a *structure or sequence of causality* involved. The door closes because I, or the wind, or a spring mechanism, acted on it to cause it to shut. Forces are the means by which we achieve causal interactions. The agent of the causal sequence can be either an animate and purposive being, or it can be a mere inanimate object or event; but in either case the relevant forces are always actual or potential forces in an actual or potential sequence of causal interactions. In other words, although we can think of forces abstractly in isolation as bare force vectors, all actual forces are experienced by us in causal sequences.

What I have just described is a general *gestalt structure* for force. I am using the term "gestalt structure" to mean an organized, unified whole within our experience and understanding that manifests a repeatable pattern or structure. Some people use the term "gestalt" to mean a mere form or shape with no internal structure. In contrast to such a view, my entire project rests on showing that experiential gestalts have internal structure that connects up aspects of our experience and leads to inferences in our conceptual system.

What I am calling "image schemata" in this book are all gestalt structures, in the sense just described. Any given schema can, of course, be analyzed and broken down simply because it has parts. But any such reduction will destroy the integrity of the gestalt, that is, will destroy the meaningful unity that makes it the particular gestalt that it is. Throughout this book I am assuming that all image schemata are characterizable as irreducible gestalts. However, I presuppose this with the recognition that there are other kinds of gestalt structure besides schemata. For example, there are gestalts for complex categorical structures, for metaphorical projections, and for unified narrative patterns.

The gestalt I described earlier is a gestalt for forceful interactions. It lays out the elements and their connections that typically hold where some force operates on some object. One of the main claims of this book is that meaning (both in the broad sense that I am using the term and in its more narrow sense, as linguistic meaning) is often carried by gestalt structures of this sort. However, the structure I have described above is too general and a bit too abstract. We need to explore more concretely how forceful bodily experiences give rise to image-schematic

structures of meaning that can be transformed, extended, and elaborated into domains of meaning that are not strictly tied to the body
(such as social interactions, rational argument, and moral deliberation). What I want to do, then, is to identify some more specific image-schematic gestalts for *force* and *force relationships,* to look at particular force schemata in order to see how they can play a role in the
development of meaning and inference patterns. I shall first describe
and diagram several such force schemata and then explore some of
the semantic and speech act domains where these structures play a central role.

The following schemata represent seven of the most common force
structures that operate constantly in our experience:

1. *Compulsion.* Everyone knows the experience of being moved
by external forces, such as wind, water, physical objects, and other
people. When a crowd starts pushing, you are moved along a path you
may not have chosen, by a force you seem unable to resist. Sometimes
the force is irresistible, such as when the crowd gets completely out of
control; other times the force can be counteracted, or modified. In
such cases of compulsion, the force comes from somewhere, has a
given magnitude, moves along a path, and has a direction. We can represent this image-schematic gestalt structure with the visual image below. Here the dark arrow represents an actual force vector and the
broken arrow denotes a potential force vector or trajectory.

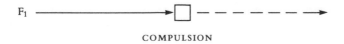

COMPULSION

2. *Blockage.* In our attempts to interact forcefully with objects and
persons in our environment, we often encounter obstacles that block
or resist our force. When a baby learns to crawl, for instance, it encounters a wall that blocks its further progress in some direction. The
baby must either stop, ceasing its exertion of force in the initial direction, or it must redirect its force. It can try to go over the obstacle,
around it, or even through it, where there is sufficient power to do so.
In such a case the child is learning part of the *meaning* of force and of
forceful resistance in the most immediate way. This experience of
blockage involves a pattern that is repeated over and over again throughout our lives. The relevant gestalt can be represented as a force vector
encountering a barrier and then taking any number of possible directions (fig. 7).

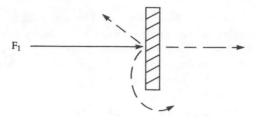

FIGURE 7.   BLOCKAGE

3. _Counterforce_. A third cluster of gestalts focuses on the head–on meetings of forces (fig. 8). Football linemen are most familiar with this force gestalt. Here two equally strong, nasty, and determined force centers collide face-to-face, with the result that neither can go anywhere. Lucky survivors of head–on auto accidents also know the meaning of this particular structure of force.

$$F_1 \longrightarrow \quad \longleftarrow F_2$$

FIGURE 8.   COUNTERFORCE

4. _Diversion_. A variation on the previous gestalt is one in which a force vector is diverted as the result of the causal interaction of two or more vectors. If you have ever tried to row a boat at some angle oblique to the wind, you know that, without compensation in your rowing, your initial force vector is lost before you know it. The appropriate schema shows two colliding forces with a resultant change in force vectors (fig. 9).

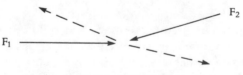

FIGURE 9.   DIVERSION

5. _Removal of restraint_. When the door is opened, we are free to come into the room. When the fence is taken away, the dog can visit its canine neighbors, if it so chooses. The removal of a barrier or the absence of some potential restraint is a structure of experience that we encounter daily. The relevant schema is thus one that suggests an open way or path, which makes possible an exertion of force. In figure 10 the force F_1 is not the source of the removal of the restraining barrier. More properly that would be a special case of the BLOCKAGE schema

described in 3 above. Instead, the diagram is meant to suggest that, either because some actual barrier is removed by another or because a potential barrier is not actually present, the force F_1 can be exerted (i.e., there is nothing blocking it).

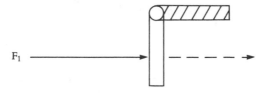

FIGURE 10.   REMOVAL OF RESTRAINT

6. *Enablement*. If you choose to focus on your acts of manipulation and movement, you can become aware of a felt sense of power (or lack of power) to perform some action. You can sense that you have the power to pick up the baby, the groceries, and the broom but not to lift the front end of your car. While there is no actualized force vector here, it is legitimate to include this structure of possibility in our common gestalts for force, since there are potential force vectors present, and there is a definite "directedness" (or potential path of motion) present. That is, you feel able to move the chair *over to the corner,* or to lift the comb *up to your hair.* The gestalt is represented, then, only by a potential force vector and an absence of barriers or blocking counter-forces (fig. 11).

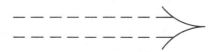

FIGURE 11.   ENABLEMENT

7. *Attraction*. A magnet draws a piece of steel toward itself, a vaccuum cleaner pulls dirt into itself, and the earth pulls us back down when we jump. There is a common schematic structure of attraction shared by these experiences. This same structure is present, too, when we feel ourselves physically attracted to some other person. The force is not gravitational, in the standard sense, but it is a kind of gravitation

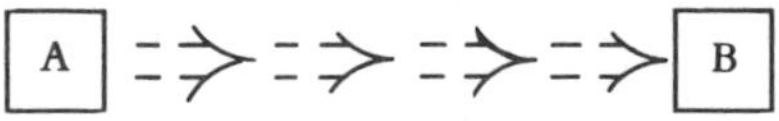

FIGURE 12.   ATTRACTION

toward an object. As such, it shares the same underlying ATTRACTION schema (fig. 12). The vectors here can be either actual or potential, and there might be additional objects added to represent more complex relations of attraction.

The previous list of distinct force gestalts is only a selection of the more important image schemata that play a role in our experience of force. A more complete list, for example, would have to distinguish among schemata for IMPACT versus CONTINUOUS STEADY FORCE versus INTERMITTENT FORCE versus DIMINISHING FORCE, and so on. But this small sample already shows us something extremely important about our experience, namely, that aspects of its meaningfulness and coherence depend upon certain *very definite, highly structured* image-schematic gestalts. Their structure is not elaborate, but it is sufficiently distinct to give comprehensible order to our perceptions, understanding, and actions.

Let us now explore the way in which image schemata of this sort play their indispensable and pervasive role in the development of meaning for us, and in our patterns of understanding and reasoning. In particular, I want to focus on our experience of force and on its structure as it connects up certain parts of our meaning network, our conceptual system, and our language.

Force Gestalts in the Root Senses of Modal Verbs

The experiential (image-schematic) gestalts for force that I have just described are actual repeatable structures of experience that emerge from our forceful interactions in our world. These patterns exist for us prelinguistically, though they can be considerably refined and elaborated as a result of the acquisition of language and the conceptual system that language makes possible. These structures are part of meaning and understanding. They do not merely form a background against which meaning emerges; rather, they *are themselves meaning structures*.

In order to amplify this key point, I am going to discuss a body of recent empirical work on the semantics of modal verbs that has important implications for my account of schemata. Modal verbs, such as *can, may, must, could, might,* are verbs that pertain to our experience of actuality, possibility, and necessity. It might appear that modality is a very abstract and esoteric subject for a study like mine, which claims to focus on basic structures of common human experience. And, if one looks at the massive philosophical literature on modality, this suspicion seems justified. There modality is treated as a purely logical notion, one that concerns logical possibility and necessity. In these logical discussions one finds inquiries into the nature of terms such as "possible" and "necessary" in statements of the following sort: "It is necessary that p = it is impossible that not-p = it is not possible that not-p," and, "It is necessary that not-p = it is impossible that p = it is not possible that p."

In contrast with this logical analysis of modality, there are other senses of modal verbs that are intimately related to our everyday experience, insofar as they represent our pervasive experience of things, events, and relations as being actual, possible, or necessary. To the extent that we experience our world via these three categories of existence, their schemata are crucial to our understanding of our experience. For instance, the modality of possibility is present in our experience of alternative actions open to us in a given situation. We feel the possibility of performing act A, act B, act C, etc., as options that are not necessitated. At other times we experience necessity with all its compelling force, as when shutting off the power causes the motor to stop, or the anesthetic makes us drowsy. Modality is an ineliminable part of our world.

So, the inquiry we are about to undertake into the meaning of certain modal verbs is actually an investigation into a further cluster of extremely significant patterns of experience and understanding. When we inquire into the senses of must, may, and can, we are exploring the image schemata present in situations of the sort we encounter daily: feeling ourselves able to act in certain ways (*can*), permitted to perform actions of our choosing (*may*), and compelled by forces beyond our control (*must*). We will see that there are other major senses of modal verbs besides their logical senses; and we will see that all of these senses are connected and related by virtue of force schemata.

The empirical research I shall be analyzing is taken from a far more extensive, careful, and sophisticated study of modals by Eve Sweetser.[1] Sweetser's treatment of modal verbs is part of a much larger project in which she examines connections among three related dimensions of experience: (1) the *sociophysical* realm that includes physical interactions as well as social relations, practices, and institutions; (2) the *epistemic* realm of rational argument, theorizing, and other activities of reasoning; and (3) the *structure of speech acts*. Sweetser's central thesis is that a pervasive, coherently structured system of metaphors underlies and relates these three realms of experience. The most general metaphorical structure that establishes these connections is one that understands the mental, epistemic, and rational in terms of the physical. This BODY FOR MIND metaphorical structure both guides the course of semantic change through history (diachronically) and provides connections among some senses of polysemous words within a language (synchronically).

What is most relevant to our concerns with schematic structures of meaning is Sweetser's argument that the different senses of modal verbs are related by metaphorical structures, in which the physical becomes a metaphor for the nonphysical (the mental, rational, social). Sweetser distinguishes roughly between two different senses of modal verbs, namely, the *root* and *epistemic* senses:

i) *Root* modals denote ability (*can*), permission (*may*), or obligation (*must*) in our sociophysical world. The origin of the capacity, permission, or obligation has to do either with physical constraints and forces (natural causes) or else with social restrictions or commitments (social forces). Examples of the *root* senses of modals are:

(1) You *must* move your foot, or the car will crush it. (Physical necessity.)

(2) Sally *can* reach the fried eel for you. (She is physically capable of reaching it.)

(3) Paul *must* get a job now, or else his wife will leave him. (Paul is forced, by his wife's threat, to find a job, though the compulsion is not physical.)

(4) You *may* now kiss the bride. (No social or institutional barrier any longer prevents you from kissing her.)

The notion of *root* modality is broader than, and includes, that of *deontic* modality, which tends to be associated by philosophers with the more narrow notion of social or moral obligation alone.

ii) The *epistemic* sense of modality denotes probability, possibility, or necessity in reasoning, as in:

(5) Paul *must* have gotten the job, or else he couldn't be buying that new car. (Read as, "The available evidence forces me to conclude that Paul got the job.")

(6) You *might* be right about her motives, but I'm not convinced. (Read as, "No evidence blocks your conclusion, but neither does the evidence compel me to your conclusion.")

Sweetser's thesis regarding the connection of these two senses is that

root modal meanings are extended to the epistemic domain precisely because we generally use the language of the external world to apply to the internal mental world, which is metaphorically structured as parallel to that external world.[2]

In other words, Sweetser argues that the meanings of verbs such as *can*, *may*, and *might* as applied to the physical (and social) realm are not radically different from their meanings when used in the realm of rational argument and reasoning. This claim to semantic connection stands in contrast to the standard view that the root and epistemic senses are not related in any systematic way.[3] The received opinion is that root meanings of terms like *must*, *may*, *might*, *can*, and so forth, do involve notions of force or obligation, whereas epistemic senses of those terms are seen as involving only combinations of logical operators. In short, the root and epistemic occurrences are taken to be homonymous.

As an alternative to such homonymy approaches, it seems at least reasonable to look for possible connections between different senses that are marked by the *same* word or phrase. Leonard Talmy opened the way for such an interpretation of modals with his argument that root modality can be understood by relating it to our experience of physical forces acting in the presence or absence of barriers.[4]

Sweetser has extended Talmy's analysis to epistemic modals and has focused on the sociophysical level of intentional action as experientially more basic than the purely physical level of causally interacting objects, which Talmy takes as basic. Drawing heavily on Sweetser's analysis, I want to consider three of the most central modal verbs (*must, may, can*), selected from the large range of modals she has examined.[5] My primary contribution will be to suggest that the relevant notions of force needed to explain modal verbs can be best understood as image-schematic FORCE gestalts.

To begin, a brief account of the root senses of *must*, *may*, and *can* is necessary before we can explore their relation to the epistemic senses.

A. *Must*. Sweetser analyzes the root sense of *must* as denoting a compelling force that moves a subject toward an act. But this sense matches precisely the image schema for COMPULSION that I described earlier. Given this image schema, the force can be interpreted in different ways. It may be physical force, as in (1); parental authority, as in (2); "peer pressure," as in (3); or moral authority understood as a universal force acting on the human will, as in (4).

COMPULSION

(1) You *must* cover your eyes, or they'll be burned.
(2) Johnny *must* go to bed; his mother said so.
(3) He *must* help in the blood drive, or his friends won't respect him.
(4) She *must* give blood; it's her duty.

B. *May. May* is understood as absence of external or internal restraint or compulsion. There is no barrier blocking the occurrence or
performance of some action. This root sense is based on the ABSENCE
OR REMOVAL OF RESTRAINT schema. To say that a certain action *may* be
done implies that some potential barrier to the action is absent or has
been removed. We only use *may* regarding actions or events that might
be either blocked or compelled by an external obstacle or force. In (5),
then, an event (a cure) is not blocked by any known state of affairs.

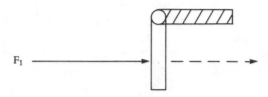

F_1

REMOVAL OF RESTRAINT

(5) We *may* be able to cure his illness.

In (6) an act (opening the window) is permitted that could have been
prohibited, and has previously been prohibited, either by external
physical force or by the force of social or moral authority.

(6) You *may* now open the window, if you like.

C. *Can. Can* is more problematic and controversial. Sweetser explains its difference from *may* as follows: "*Can* denotes positive ability
on the part of the doer; *may* denotes lack of restriction on the part of
someone else."[6] *Can* thus involves a sense of internal power or capacity to act. The agent is a source of energy sufficient to perform some
action. Although *can* tends to assume an absence of restricting barriers, its primary focus is on *potentiality* or *capacity to act. Can* would,
therefore, seem to require its own distinct gestalt, one for ENABLEMENT,
consisting only of a potential force vector. With *may* we emphasize
and focus on the removal of potential or actual barriers, but with *can*
we focus on the potential energy to act. Thus, in (7) the focus is on the
removal of restraint by someone else, but in (8) the focus shifts to the
internal sense of power to act.

ENABLEMENT

(7) You *may* go anytime after the bell rings.
(8) I *can* do anything you *can* do better.

Epistemic Senses for Modal Verbs

The epistemic sense of modals, such as *must, may,* and *can,* find their home in the domain of reasoning, argument, and theorizing. Following Sweetser, I am claiming that the epistemic senses are intimately connected with their root senses and that the basis for this connection is that we understand the mental in terms of the physical, the mind in terms of bodily experience. In particular, we understand mental processes of reasoning as involving forces and barriers analogous to physical and social forces and obstacles. To explore this hypothesis, let us consider whether gestalt structures for force operate in the epistemic domain in ways parallel to their operation in the sociophysical domain.

The key to identifying the connections between the root and epistemic senses is the metaphorical interpretation of *force* and *barrier.* In the domain of social obligations and expectations the relevant forces are exerted upon us either by other people, by institutions, or by what we might call a "universal voice." That voice is typically understood as conscience or moral law. It is this moral sense that is most akin to the voice or permission-granter that operates in the epistemic realm. Sweetser argues that the only possible source of force in the epistemic world is premises (or available evidence); and only premises (or evidence and facts) can constitute barriers capable of blocking the force of a reasoning process. So, Sweetser thinks that there is no genuine "permission-granter" in the epistemic realm in the way there is for the sociophysical realm.

This is surely correct if we hold to our folk theories about reasoning and if we stick to the linguistic evidence. But I would note that there is a philosophical tradition that implies the existence of a permission-granter, even in the epistemic realm. In many Western philosophical treatments of knowledge, rationality, and truth, there is an underlying metaphorical conception of a universal voice that grants permission to move from premises to validly derived conclusions. This is the voice of pure reason. To reason correctly is to speak in agreement with this universal voice. In certain theologically oriented traditions this voice is identified with the "Mind of God," so that reasoning well is being in tune with the Divine Logos. In nontheological traditions this voice is reinterpreted as that of a universal reason, which provides a *logos* to which our reason should conform.

Whether or not there is a permission-granter in the epistemic domain, Sweetser is correct in claiming that it is the *premises* of the argument that do all of the work and that force us along a path toward some conclusion. As Lakoff and I argued concerning the metaphorical structuring of the epistemic domain, one of the chief metaphors for argument and reasoning in our culture involves motion along a path toward some destination (conclusion).[7] Various propositions can block our journey, can help us along our way, can throw us off our path, and so forth. This is not merely a way we can *talk* about argument; rather, it partially structures how we *understand* and *carry on* our reasoning. It is this metaphorical structuring of the epistemic domain that underlies the following force-dynamic interpretation of epistemic modals.

A'. *May.* As in the root case, where *may* denotes the absence of an external barrier, so in the epistemic case there is no barrier to block the forceful movement from the premises to the conclusion. As Sweetser says,

The meaning of epistemic *may* would thus be that there is no barrier to the speaker's process of reasoning from the available premises to the conclusion expressed in the sentence qualified by *may*.[8]

Epistemic *may* may be read as, "There is no available evidence that constitutes a barrier to my moving to the conclusion specified."[9] As with the root sense of *may*, the relevant force schema is that for RE-MOVAL OF RESTRAINT. Thus, we get

(9) You *may* be right. (Read as, "I (We) am (are) not barred by the evidence from drawing that conclusion, based on your premises.")

Saying that someone *may* be correct does not imply that they are. It only claims that no facts or evidence at hand bar the movement to the conclusion. This is not to say that there might not be other evidence, of which we are not now aware, that would bar that very conclusion if it were known. Furthermore, the epistemic *may* frequently connotes that the reasoner, while not barred from drawing a certain conclusion, is still somewhat hesitant and does not feel forced to the conclusion.

B'. *Must*. *Must* denotes an irresistible force that drives me to a conclusion, as in

(10) He *must* be the Scarlet Pimpernel! (Read as, "The available evidence compels me to the conclusion that he is the Scarlet Pimpernel.")

The relevant force gestalt is that for COMPULSION, but here the force is rational rather than physical.

Sweetser notes an interesting asymmetry between the root and epistemic senses of *must*. In the root sense there is usually assumed to be some reluctance to performing the required action, so it is thought that a compelling force is necessary to overcome the resistance. For example, Tommy would rather not clean his room, so it takes the compelling force of parental authority to get him to perform the action. By contrast, in the epistemic domain it is generally assumed that there is *no* reluctance on the part of the person who is supposedly being forced to a conclusion. One may not like, or may be afraid of, the conclusion, but the resistance is not to the act of following out a chain of reasoning as such.

Sweetser has observed (in conversation) that there is a fairly straightforward explanation for this asymmetry. In the sociophysical realm (of root modals) we tend to assume that any restriction on our freedom is undesirable. The more freedom we have, the greater are our options for achieving our purposes. Therefore, we are typically reluctant to be forced, to have our freedom limited. The situation is different, on the other hand, in the epistemic realm. In our reasoning and deliberation, it is preferable that our conclusions be forced and limited. For if there is no limitation, if anything can follow from a set of premises or assumptions, then we could never get any definite knowledge. So it is in our interest to have the premises rationally force us to draw a certain definite conclusion.

C'. *Can*. In the epistemic domain we do not find the positive "*can*" (as in "That *can* be true"). A plausible explanation of this has been offered by George Lakoff (in conversation). Put simply, in the epistemic realm, if we *can* reason to some conclusion, then we *must* reason to it. If there really is sufficient rational force to move us to the conclusion, given the premises, then we are compelled to make the move. Once the barriers are removed, the force becomes irresistible, and we have *must* (i.e., "That *must* be true").

We do, however, find the negative *can* at the epistemic level. We find situations in which some proposition blocks the force along the path leading to the conclusion, as in

(11) She *can't* have gone over to the enemy. (Read as, "Some evidence or proposition [such as knowledge of her character] bars me from concluding that she is a traitor.")

The appropriate force gestalt is ENABLEMENT; but, again, in the epistemic realm it is understood metaphorically as involving rational forces or powers.

To conclude my treatment of the epistemic senses of modal verbs, I shall offer a few representative examples of some of the many additional modals analyzed in Sweetser's study (e.g., *will, shall, might, would, could, should, ought to, have to,* etc.). I offer readings for both the root and epistemic senses to suggest that there is a fairly clear, definite, and regular pattern of analysis possible, according to the hypothesis we have been pursuing.

i) *Ought to:*
    (12a) She *ought to* make her bed. (Root.)
    "Certain forces (family obligation) influence her toward the act of making her bed."
    (12b) That *ought to* work. (Epistemic.)
    "The available evidence influences me to conclude that that will work."

ii) *Have to:*
    (13a) You *have to* do your homework before you watch television.
        (Root.)
    "A force of (parental) authority compels you to do your homework."
    (13b) She *has to* be Sarah's sister—Look at her mouth and eyes.
        (Epistemic.)
    "The available evidence (especially her mouth and eyes) forces me to conclude that they are sisters."

iii) *Need to:*
    (14a) He *needs to* throw a party every month. (Root.)
    "Some internal conditions (his wanting to be liked, etc.) force him to throw parties regularly."
    (14b) She *needn't be* a Communist; not every Pole is a Communist.
        (Epistemic.)
    "The available evidence (her being Polish) doesn't force me to conclude that she is a Communist."

The previous analysis of these epistemic senses of modal verbs suggests an extremely important point about human meaning and reasoning. Note that in each case of an epistemic sense the analysis has the following general form:

"Some set of premises, or available evidence, forces me to conclude (or bars me from concluding) that X is the case."

We see that the modality here is not a property of propositions or connections among propositions in themselves; rather, the modality is a property of the reasoning processes of the *person* drawing, or refraining from drawing, some conclusion. Premises do not lead to conclusions in themselves, independent of reasoners—they lead to conclusions only insofar as their meaning is grasped, and their implications are seen, by a human being situated in the world. Reasoning is something people *do* with propositions, not some abstract relation among propositions.

Speech Act Structure

So far we have examined some root and epistemic modals whose senses are closely connected by means of underlying force-dynamic structures. We saw that in the domain of reasoning there are forces metaphorically related to the kinds and structures of forces operating in our sociophysical experience. The same force schemata appear in both root and epistemic senses, and these schemata are metaphorically elaborated to obtain the different (but related) meanings of the modal verb in question. It should not be surprising, then, to find similar force structures operating in the *structure of speech acts themselves*. After all, speech acts are *actions;* and, since our "physical" and "social" actions are subject to forces, we should expect that our "linguistic" actions are also subject to forces, metaphorically understood.

It might seem as though, in shifting from the *meaning* of modal verbs to the *structure of speech acts,* we jump from semantics to pragmatics and thus disrupt the unity of the previous analysis of force. This is not so, for two reasons. First, the rigid separation of semantics (meaning) from pragmatics (use) cannot be sustained, if we are to understand how meaning works.[10] In many cases, how we use a sentence partially determines its meaning. Second, even if an absolute semantics/pragmatics split is granted (which I do not admit), it would still be valuable to see how our notion of "force" in the realm of speech acts is tied to image-schematic structure metaphorically extended from our bodily experience of force. We could still seek possible connections among the manifestations of force in both the modals and in speech acts.

Ever since J. L. Austin taught us to think of utterances as actions we perform to produce certain effects, it has become standard practice to analyze meaningful utterances into meaningful contents that are presented with one or another standard illocutionary force.[11] In this spirit,

John Searle has argued at length that all speech acts can be represented by the following formula: [12]

(15) F(p)

Here "p" represents the *propositional content* of the utterance, while "F" is the *illocutionary force* with which that content is presented. The utterance "Did John run away?" can be analyzed as a propositional content (*John ran away*) presented with the force of a *question*. We thus see that a single propositional content, such as *the meeting is over*, can be subject to a number of different forces to generate different kinds of speech acts:

(16) The meeting is over. (Force = making an assertion.)
(17) Is the meeting over? (Force = asking a question.)
(18) "The meeting is now over," said by the chairperson. (Force = causing it to be the case that the meeting is over, i.e., adjourning the meeting.)

Based on this model, Searle has constructed a taxonomy of speech act types that lays out the kinds of forces there are and the kinds of conditions that must obtain if the speech act is to be successfully performed. [13]

My only purpose in sketching this shell of speech-act theory is to highlight the fact that there are patterns of force at work in the structure of the speech act itself. So, besides physical force, social force, and epistemic force, there is a level of speech-act force (illocutionary force) dynamics. My central claim, once again, is that the relevant forces at this last level are also based on force gestalts metaphorically elaborated.

To discern these image-schematic structures in the speech act we need only recall that in most speech acts there will be a content presented *under* or *by means of* a given force. One of the relevant gestalts, then, will be that for COMPULSION. We can put some flesh on this skele-

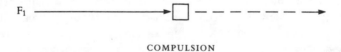

COMPULSION

ton in the following way. As Michael Reddy has reminded us, there is a dominant metaphor that structures the bulk of both our understanding and talk about human communication. [14] He has named this the CONDUIT metaphor, which includes these parts:

1. Ideas or thoughts are objects.
2. Words and sentences are containers for these objects.
3. Communication consists in finding the right word-container for your idea–object, sending this filled container along a conduit or through space to the hearer, who must then take the idea–object out of the word-container.

The metaphor of the CONDUIT is one elaboration of the force gestalt sketched above. There are at least four different kinds of force (metaphorically interpreted) that can operate in a specific speech act situation:

i) First, there is the force that acts on the sentence-container with its idea–object to change the *form* of the expression. This force determines the shape of the utterance (i.e., of the speech-act container). If I am asking a question, then the utterance-container will typically be different from that which I use to make a statement or give a command. "John is home" has a different form or shape than "Is John home?" Thus, there is a force brought to bear by the speaker to adjust the form of their utterance so that it serves the communicative purposes of both speaker and bearer.

ii) Second, there is the force that acts on the hearer to determine how the hearer understands the utterance. This is the "illocutionary force," which determines whether the hearer takes the utterance as a question, assertion, command, or other type of illocutionary act. For example, statements are typically presented by speakers to force the hearers to add some belief to their belief system. Questions force the hearer to try to supply a certain relevant content to fill a gap in some informational structure. Directives exert a force to compel the hearer to realize some state of affairs. And performatives (Searle's "declaratives") constitute forceful changes of the state of the world.

iii) Third, the force with which the word- or utterance-container is sent through the conduit or through the space between speaker and hearer will have a certain magnitude. This means that there can be different "degrees of strength or force" in the making of a speech act. This is principally a matter of emphasis, as we see in (19) and (20).

(19) You might want to be a little careful around the lions.
(20) For God's sake, watch out for those lions!

Both of these are warnings, but the first is rather mild, while the second is obviously much stronger (it is made more forcefully). The difference lies in the force with which the sentence-container is thrust upon the hearer.

iv) Finally, there typically will be some effect(s) brought about as a result of the illocutionary force of an utterance. Your commanding me to spit-shine my shoes might (in addition to my grasping the meaning of your utterance as a command) force me to shine my shoes, or it might cause me to laugh in your face, or to insult you. In speech-act theory these are known as "perlocutionary effects" of a speech act. They were understood by Austin as nonconventional causal effects on a hearer's actions or state as a consequence of the hearer grasping the illocutionary force of an utterance.

So far, I have discussed only the COMPULSION schema in any detail as it operates in the general structure of speech acts. Although I shall not pursue this point, there will be several other relevant force gestalts, besides that for COMPULSION, that make up various speech acts. In particular, one can think of the numerous ways in which certain illocutionary forces can be blocked, either by the content of the utterance itself or else by the context of the utterance.[15] In these cases we would want to analyze, at the very minimum, the role of the gestalts for BLOCKAGE, REMOVAL OF RESTRAINT, DIVERSION, and COUNTERFORCE.

To bring this discussion of force schemata in speech acts to a close, I would like to consider one representative example of phenomena of just this sort, that is, where we can discern tensions in the relations of forces *within the speech act itself*. Another way of stating this is to say that we are focusing on the relation of forces within the domain of the conversational interaction itself. Sweetser offers the following examples to illustrate the existence of forces and barriers in a *conversational* world, in addition to the sociophysical and epistemic worlds. Consider the following two *epistemic* senses of *may:*

(21) He may be a university professor, but I doubt it because he's so dumb.
(22) There may be a six-pack in the fridge, but I'm not sure because Joe had friends over last night.

In both of these cases we have epistemic *may,* to be understood as "I am not barred from concluding that . . ." But now contrast these with (23)–(24), as I have interpreted them:

(23) He may be a university professor, but he sure is dumb. ("I *admit* that he's a university professor, and I nonetheless *insist* that he's dumb.")
(24) There may be a six-pack in the fridge, but we have work to do. ("I *acknowledge* your offer of beer, and I nonetheless *refuse* it.")

As Sweetser points out, given the above readings, these are not cases of epistemic *may.* Her suggestion is that we are here dealing with a conversational world in which there are forces and barriers that constrain relationships of illocutionary forces. She reads (23) and (24) as follows:

(23′) I *do not bar* from our (joint) conversational world *the statement* that he is a university professor, but . . .

(24′) I *do not bar* from our conversational world *your offer* of beer, but . . .

In these two cases, we are not in the epistemic realm where forces push us from premises to conclusion; instead, we are in a conversational space where various speech acts (with their attendant forces) are being constrained or permitted by the speaker. Sweetser sums this up:

In [these cases], then, *may* does not indicate the absence of a real (content)-world barrier, nor of an epistemic barrier, but rather the absence of a barrier in the *conversational* world. The interlocutor is being *allowed* by the speaker to treat a certain statement as appropriate or reasonable, or to present an offer.[16]

The phenomenon being highlighted here is the existence of a form of modal operator in the "conversational world" in which we perform various kinds of speech acts. In a sense, the speaker in (23)–(24) is saying, "I *will allow* your statement *to a certain extent,* but I will affirm another statement somewhat in tension with yours." We are dealing in this conversational world with *forces and barriers* metaphorically related to those that exist in the sociophysical and epistemic domains.

Force Gestalts: Unified Nonpropositional Structures

The central topic of this chapter is the nature and operation of experiential schemata that have gestalt structure. The previous chapter emphasized their nonpropositional dimension; the present chapter highlights their internal structure and explores the way that structure determines our network of meanings. I illustrated this structuring of meaning and understanding with examples drawn from one of the most important dimensions of human experience, that of forceful interaction. There are three main points I wish to stress on the basis of this representative case (i.e., of force gestalts as they influence the meaning of modal verbs).

First, I argued that image-schematic gestalts have considerable internal structure—they are not undifferentiated. On the contrary, it is the organization of their structure that makes them experientially basic meaningful patterns in our experience and understanding. The schemata for these gestalts have parts and dimensions that stand in various relationships that allow us to make sense of our experience. For example, even in the simple COMPULSION schema there is significant structure: The actual force moves in some direction. If it interacts with some object, then it causes that object to move in the same direction. The relevant force vector traces out a path of motion. Thus, the moved object can be located at a given time relative to its progress along that projected path. And, in some cases, there is a goal toward which the force or forced object moves and in relation to which the object can be located. For such a minimal gestalt, this is actually quite a bit of structure.

What makes this an identifiable image-schematic gestalt is its repeatable pattern—a pattern that can therefore contribute to the regularity, coherence, and comprehensibility of our experience and understanding. To say that a gestalt is "experientially basic," then, is to say that it constitutes a recurring level of organized unity for an organism acting in its environment. Gestalts, in the sense I am using the term, are not unanalyzable givens or atomistic structures. They can be "analyzed" since they have parts and dimensions. But, any such attempted reduction will destroy the *unity* (the meaningful organization) that made the structure significant in the first place.

There is nothing "rock bottom" or "foundational" about image-schematic gestalt structures. What constitutes an experientially basic level will depend on background knowledge, motivations, interests, values, and previous experiences. Concerning interactions with physical objects, for instance, what is a basic gestalt for a layperson might differ considerably from that for a physicist, who brings a highly developed theory to bear in understanding the nature of the physical world as well as in interacting with it. Experiential basicness is a relative matter. Yet, because our bodies are very much alike with respect to their physiological makeup, we would expect to find commonly shared (if not universal) gestalt structures for many of our physical interactions within our environment.

Second, I argued that our vast network of meaning depends on the nature and relation of image-schematic gestalts. Sweetser's work served to give some elaboration to the claim that meaning involves image schemata. I did not focus, as I might have, on the more obvious fact that the meaning of our word "force" involves all of the schemata I diagrammed, plus others. Instead, I examined the much more subtle way in which the meanings of modal verbs arise from image schemata for FORCE. The projection of definite, and highly articulated, structure was always from the domain of the physical (as it is preconceptually patterned) onto the social, epistemic, and speech-act realms. Such projections of structure from one experiential domain to another domain *of a different kind* are metaphorical processes. The nature of metaphorical projections is taken up in the next chapter. For now, the key point is that much of the structure we find in the social, epistemic, and conversational or speech-act domains is intimately related to parallel structure in our embodied (so-called physical) experience.

Third, I have suggested tentatively that there is an inferential structure in the epistemic domain that is tied to gestalt features of our experience of physical force and barriers. The meaning of *must* in the epistemic realm, as we saw, involves the COMPULSION schema, in which a force moves an object along a path. In the epistemic realm this movement *just is* an inferential pattern, for, if something *must* be true, then we are forced to infer that it *is*—no other conclusion will do.

Thus, we are brought back to where we started, with the more "logical" notion of modality as it bears on inference. Here, too, we can discern important inferential patterns based on FORCE schemata.   *INFERENTAL*

Inferential Patterns for Force Gestalts

At the end of the previous chapter I made a few suggestions as to the way in which certain inference patterns could be grounded experientially in schemata for containment. An exploration of nonpropositional schemata and their metaphorical extensions offers an alternative to the received view that "it just *is* the essence of rationality to have such an a priori formal structure." It might be that there are a priori structures of rationality, but we needn't simply assume this as an unquestionable foundation. To pursue my suggestion further, I want to consider a representative set of equivalences in modal logic that seem to be based on FORCE schemata.

The traditional branches of modal logic include the study of logical, moral, and epistemic necessity and possibility. As we have seen, Talmy and Sweetser have argued that such modal notions are understood in terms of forces as we experience them in our bodily perceptions and actions. Each of the realms of modal logical involves a corresponding kind of force: the force of logic, moral force, and the force of reason. Let us consider logical necessity, as understood in terms of the force of logic.

What stands behind our understanding of logical necessity is that the force of logic is overwhelming. As shown in Chapter 2, propositions are identified with locations. The force of logic moves us from one propositional location to another—forcing us to conclusions. From this, the basic axiom of the logic of logical necessity follows:

□P→P ("If P is logically necessary, then P is true.") If the force of logic operates to move you to a certain "place," then you wind up in that place.

Correspondingly, logical possibility is the absence of any barrier blocking the path to a given location. That is, something is logically possible if there is nothing to stop us from reaching (moving to) that conclusion. Given our understanding of negation in terms of the CONTAINER schema (not-P is located outside the bounded space defining P), the intuitive relation between necessity and possibility follows immediately:

~□~P→ ◊P ("If it is not logically necessary that P is false, then it is logically possible for P to be true.") This is a consequence of our understanding of necessity in terms of overwhelming force and negation as location outside of a bounded space. Consider what □~P means in the physical domain: it corresponds to the bounded area where there is an overwhelming force leading to the area outside of the space defined by P. ~□~P places us outside of the bounded domain where such force operates, and correspondingly leaves us in a place where there is no overwhelming force to stop us from moving to P. This is the area characterized by ◊P.

These logical relations form the foundations of all accounts of logical necessity. Other axioms vary from system to system. Furthermore, axioms will vary when we move from logical to moral or epistemic necessity and possibility. For example, in the moral realm moral force is not overwhelming, and so we do not always do what we ought to do. But whatever the nature of the force for a particular realm, necessity is still understood in terms of force, whether in the logical, moral, or epistemic realms.

In sum, we are now in a position to begin to explain how our notion of abstract (purely logical) rationality might be based on concrete reasoning that makes use of image-schematic patterns and metaphorical extensions of them. Our acts of reasoning and deliberation are not wholly independent of the nonpropositional dimension of our bodily experience. We can, and do, abstract away from this experiential basis, so that it sometimes looks as though we are operating only with a priori structures of pure reason; however, the extent to which we are able to make sense of these extremely abstract structures is the extent to which we can relate them to such schematic structures as connect up our meaningful experiences.

4

Metaphorical Projections of Image Schemata

In the previous two chapters I have given examples of the way in which schematic structures salient in most of our mundane experience (e.g., structures of containment and force) can be extended and elaborated metaphorically to connect up different aspects of meaning, reasoning, and speech acts. By now it should be obvious that I am placing special emphasis on the role of metaphor in the elaboration of meaning and in the drawing of inferences. My use of the term "metaphor" focuses on dimensions of metaphorical structure hitherto ignored or unnoticed in Objectivist accounts. Most traditional theories have treated metaphor chiefly as a rhetorical or artistic figure of speech. More recent theories extend the scope of metaphor to include its role in scientific reasoning. But only a few have ever recognized metaphor as a pervasive principle of human understanding that underlies our vast network of interrelated literal meanings.[1]

In light of the dominance of Objectivist assumptions, it is necessary to devote considerable attention to the amplification and justification of my central claim that there exist figurative extensions of image schemata. Since the received view locates metaphor exclusively at the level of conscious acts of novel figurative projection, I must give further evidence that metaphor operates also at the level of projections and elaborations of image schemata. My argument proceeds in four stages. First, I begin with a summary of the dominant Objectivist view, to show why it denies metaphor any serious cognitive function. Second, I survey the principle theories of metaphor, to identify the problems they encounter in explaining metaphorical creativity and to suggest why it is that they ignore the image-schematic level of metaphorical projection. I also argue that three of the most important contemporary accounts (i.e., those of Black, Searle, and Davidson) do seem to acknowledge a nonpropositional dimension of metaphor, though they have no theory of its operation. This leads into the third stage, in which I outline a theory of metaphorical projections operating on image schemata. Finally, I apply this new view to an actual case; namely, an exploration of the role of metaphorical projections that contribute to the meaning of *balance,* both as an experience and as a polysemous term (i.e., a term with several related meanings).

The Objectivist View of Metaphor

In the last two decades, metaphor has achieved a remarkable prominence as an important problem in philosophy, psychology, linguistics, and other cognitive sciences.[2] This trend stands in sharp contrast to an earlier view of metaphor as a derivative issue of only secondary importance. According to that extremely influential view, when all of the serious work of explaining meaning, truth, and speech-act structure was done, it was supposed that one could then employ the previously developed syntactic, semantic, and pragmatic apparatus to explain the workings of metaphor. Metaphor was thought to be either a deviant form of expression or a nonessential literary figure of speech. In either case, it was not regarded as cognitively fundamental.

This denial of any serious cognitive role for metaphor is principally the result of the long-standing popularity of the Objectivist assumptions about meaning that I listed in the Introduction. The relevant argument about metaphor runs as follows:

1. The most basic or fundamental level of description of reality is that of *literal* terms and propositions. The world consists of objects and events, with their properties and relations. Its basic categories are fixed, definite, and tied to the natures or essences of things in the world. "Literal concepts" or "literal terms" just are, by definition, those entities whose meanings specify truth conditions for the objects and events (with their properties and relations) that exist objectively in the world.

2. It follows that metaphorical statements cannot constitute a basic or fundamental level of description of objective reality for the following reason: metaphorical projections cross categorical boundaries— they cut across experiential domains of different kinds. So, meta-

phorical projections are not the sort of structures that could properly map onto a world that has discrete and definite categorical boundaries. A metaphorical utterance could only describe reality to the extent that it could be reduced to some set of literal propositions, which then fit, or fail to fit the world.

3. Furthermore, if metaphors are not even fundamental, irreducible structures for *describing or reporting independently existing reality,* then they certainly cannot have a role in the *constitution of that reality.* That is, they cannot contribute to the creation of structure in our experience.

To sum up the Objectivist view of metaphor: the objective world has *its* structure, and our concepts and propositions, to be correct, must correspond to that structure. Only literal concepts and propositions can do that, since metaphors assert cross-categorical identities that do not exist objectively in reality. Metaphors may exist as cognitive processes of our understanding, but their meaning must be reducible to some set of literal concepts and propositions.

The Standard Theories of Metaphor

I now want to consider briefly the three most influential types of metaphor theory, as they bear on the issue of metaphorical creativity. I shall argue that in more recent research there is a growing awareness of the existence of a nonpropositional level at which metaphorical projections can be experientially creative.

1. *Literal-core theories.* The most long-standing and commonly held view is that metaphors are cognitively reducible to literal propositions. Objectivist theories of meaning have always assumed that metaphor is deviation from, or a derivative function on, proper literal meaning. Treated as a "literary device," metaphor would seem to be nothing more than a rhetorically powerful or artistically interesting mode of expression without its own unique cognitive content. At best, it can be only a forceful or convincing alternative way of reporting on an independently existing state of affairs, whose proper description would be given by literal concepts and propositions.

What are called "comparison" or "similarity" theories fall into this category.[3] Comparison accounts treat metaphors in the canonical "A is B" form (e.g., Time is money) as elliptical similes equivalent to the assertion that "A is like B in certain definite respects" (e.g., Time is like money in that it can be quantified, saved, wasted, and so forth). Our ability to process the metaphor depends upon our seeing that the A-domain (e.g., temporal relations) shares certain properties and relations with the B-domain (the domain of monetary institutions and practices). Understanding the utterance "Time is money" involves a transfer of these discrete properties and relations from the money domain so that they can be appropriately applied to enrich our concept of time. The distinctive feature of comparison theories is their insistence that the similarities revealed through the metaphorical transfer exist objectively in the world and are expressible in literal propositions (e.g., "Time is like money in being quantifiable"). There is, then, on this view no such thing as an irreducible metaphorical concept or proposition. There are only metaphorical utterances and thought processes whose meaning reduces to sets of *literal* propositions.

The comparison theory is the best exemplar of the Objectivist orientation toward metaphor. It holds that literal concepts and propositions have meaning only insofar as they can map onto mind-independent realities existing objectively in the world. It treats literal meaning as basic and foundational. Thus, whatever meaning a metaphorical expression has must consist of a set of literal similarity statements. It is only via this literal core of meaning that a metaphor has any cognitive function at all. It follows, therefore, that metaphors have no role in the generation of experiential structure; instead, they can, at best, be only secondary devices for indirectly reporting on preexisting objective states of affairs.

2. *Metaphorical proposition theories*. In spite of the dominance of the Objectivist orientation in the Western philosophical tradition, there have been notable voices of opposition who have claimed for metaphor a serious creative and constitutive role. It was chiefly during the nineteenth century that the issue of metaphorical creativity became a central topic in Romantic treatments of language. Coleridge, for example, distinguishes between *fancy* and *imagination,* which we would today regard as two different kinds of metaphorical thought processes. Fancy, on the one hand, is an associative process in which the mind concatenates discrete images from perceptual memory. Coleridge claims that fancy "has no other counters to play with, but fixities and definites. The Fancy is indeed no other than a mode of Memory emancipated from the order of time and space."[4] Imagination, on the other hand, goes beyond the mere associative activity of fancy, to modify an image, "by a sort of *fusion to force many into one.*"[5] The new whole that is created constitutes an entirely novel unity in our experience. A further distinction is made between two types of imagination: "primary imagination," roughly equivalent to Kant's productive imagination; and "secondary imagination," which is the source of art. This secondary

activity of imagination "dissolves, diffuses, dissipates, in order to re-create . . . it struggles to idealise and to unify. It is essentially *vital,* even as all objects (*as* objects) are essentially fixed and dead." [6]

Putting aside the interpretive difficulties of finding a coherent and intelligible theory in the *Biographia Literaria,* we can at least say that Coleridge captured the Romantic, antireductivist view of meaning. Metaphoric imagination was not merely an associative, law-like pro-cess for combining images and memories. Instead, it could also create new unified wholes within our experience rather than merely supply-ing novel perspectives on already interpreted experiences. What Cole-ridge never supplied, however, was an account of the specific nature of this creative, unifying activity of metaphorical imagination.

In the twentieth century it was I. A. Richards who initiated a revival of interest in metaphor by focusing on Coleridge's claims about cre-ativity. Richards argued that *thought* is irreducibly metaphorical and that linguistic metaphors are manifestations of these underlying meta-phoric thought processes. He suggested that our reality is a "projected world" and that

the processes of metaphor in language, the exchanges between the meanings of words which we study in explicit verbal metaphors, are superimposed upon a perceived world which is itself a product of earlier or unwitting metaphor. [7]

Here we find the creativity thesis in its strongest form—metaphors actually structure our perceived world. Unfortunately, Richards did no better than Coleridge in explaining how it is that metaphor can have such a central ontological function.

Richards's view went more or less unnoticed by philosophers until Max Black resurrected it in the mid-1950's in his influential essay, "Metaphor." [8] Black drew attention to the metaphorical creativity issue with his provocative assertion that there is a class of metaphors for which "it would be more illuminating . . . to say that the metaphor *creates* the similarity than to say that it formulates some similarity ante-cedently existing." [9]

Black's "interaction" theory argues that there is a class of metaphors with irreducible meaning above and beyond any statement of literal similarities between two objects. Such metaphors do not work merely by projecting discrete properties of one object or event onto another object or event that shares those properties. For example, both time and money are thought to share the property of being quantifiable over discrete units. But the meaning of TIME IS MONEY is not simply a list of such properties and relations shared by both time and money. Instead, the meaning of the metaphor depends on thought processes in which an entire *system of implications* from the money-domain interacts with the implicative system for the time-domain, in a cognitive act of "seeing-as" or "conceiving-as." As Black emphasized, the crux of the Interaction theory is the notion of implicative *systems*.[10] What the comparison theory allegedly misses is this interactive process by which an emergent structured meaning complex is generated, such that it cannot be broken into atomistic parts without destroying crucial meaning relations. Cases of live, effective metaphor, then, are seen as irreducible thought processes that can stretch and reorganize conceptual boundaries.

Subsequent debate over the interaction theory has tended to confirm Black's claim that comparison theories are too reductionistic and atomistic in their accounts of meaning and cognition. Unfortunately, Black has not yet provided a sufficiently detailed account of how it is that metaphors *can* be creative. I want to suggest the following explanation for the resulting deadlock in the current debate over metaphorical creativity: Black correctly focused attention on a central phenomenon, namely, the sense we have that certain metaphors play a *constitutive* role in structuring our experience. Black expressed this insight by saying that the metaphor actually *creates* similarities in certain cases and does not just report on preexisting objective similarities. However, as I shall argue shortly, in order to give any real punch to this claim, one must treat metaphors as operating in a nonpropositional, image-schematic dimension where structures emerge in our experience. *That* would constitute genuine creativity, in that metaphor would be taken as a mode of activity in the structuring of experience.

I am suggesting that Black pushes us in this direction, but he stops short of the radical claim that there are metaphorical projections on image-schematic structures. Instead, in his most recent discussion of the topic, he avoids the view that metaphors create new *referents,* in favor of the view that they create new *perspectives* on reality that exist only via the metaphor.[11]

Black implies that he does hold the stronger thesis (that metaphors create reality) when he draws the following conclusion:

> For such reasons as this I still wish to contend that some metaphors enable us to see aspects of reality that the metaphor's production helps to constitute. But that is no longer surprising if one believes that the "world" is necessarily a world *under a certain description*—or a world seen from a certain perspective. Some metaphors can create such a perspective.[12]

As far as I can see, however, there is no explanation of the alleged productive activity that is supposed to be constitutive of reality, even
though it is clear that Black thinks that there is such activity. The
only explanation given concerns the *cognitive* activity by which new
"perspectives" are established. Black calls metaphor a "cognitive instrument"—"an instrument for drawing implications grounded in
perceived analogies of structure between two subjects belonging to
different domains."[13] But in all of this talk of cognitive, perspectival
mechanisms, there is no analysis of the actual operation of metaphor at
a level of experience where structure emerges and can be reorganized.
Such an analysis would, I believe, need to examine figurative extensions of the sort of image schemata I have discussed in the previous
chapters.

    3. *The nonpropositional theory.* Donald Davidson has recently put
forth the highly influential and extremely controversial view that there
is no such thing as a distinctive "metaphorical meaning." According to
him, the only meaning (and the only propositional content) a metaphorical statement has is the literal meaning (with its propositional
content) of the sentence used in making the metaphorical utterance.
Metaphor is a special *use* of this literal meaning to "intimate" or "suggest" something that might otherwise have gone unnoticed. Thus,
according to Davidson, if I say "Smith is a pig" I can only *mean* what
that sentence means literally (namely, that Smith is a four-legged,
cloven-hooved, creature with a long snout and a stout body covered
with bristles). But, I can utter this sentence to "intimate" (not *mean*)
certain things about Smith, so that I come to experience him in a certain way. Even though there is no special "metaphorical" meaning or
propositional content, Davidson still grants that some metaphors perform a very important cognitive function—instead of "meaning" *truth*
something, they "intimate" something, which causes us to notice or
see things. Metaphorical seeing-as, however, does not consist in grasping some unique propositional content: "What we notice or see is not,
in general, propositional in character."[14]

    Davidson claims, correctly, that his view challenges the entire tradi-
tion, since both the comparison and interaction theories grant metaphors a propositional content of some kind (either literal or metaphorical). In particular, his position is directed against all theories that
try to defend the irreducibility of metaphor by reference to a special
"metaphorical meaning." A further consequence of his view is that
metaphors, having no propositional content (other than that of the lit-

eral sentence), are not the sort of thing that could have truth values in any interesting sense. So Davidson takes away both the possibility of a unique and irreducible propositional content and the possibility of "metaphorical truth."

Davidson's motivations are Objectivist through and through. Meaning is, at base, literal. To grasp the meaning of an utterance is to know its truth conditions literally interpreted. Since metaphor has no meaning beyond that of the literal sentence used in the utterance, what most people would call the "metaphor's meaning" is no meaning at all. On Davidson's view a metaphorical utterance is essentially a stick (consisting of a literal sentence) that one uses to hit another person, so that they will see or notice something. Davidson has *no account whatever* of how it is that the literal sentence used is in any way connected up with what the hearer comes to notice.

Focusing on the Image-Schematic Dimension of Metaphor

I find Davidson's view interesting primarily because he recognizes that, to the extent that a metaphor has a distinctive cognitive force, we are not going to explain its force merely by reference to lists of propositions. Searle, who thinks Davidson's general view of meaning is wrongheaded, nevertheless agrees that no account of metaphorical creativity can ignore the nonpropositional side of cognition. Searle sees metaphor as a speech act in which someone utters "S is P" metaphorically and means "S is R." [15] The task of a theory of metaphor is to explain, first, how it is that we recognize "S is P" as requiring a metaphorical interpretation, and, second, how it is that we can compute the relevant values of R (in the intended speaker's meaning "S is R"). In line with his general speech-act theory, he needs a set of rules or principles for determining the range of possible values of R and for selecting the actual values of R that are appropriate in a given context.

At first glance, it appears that Searle has a straightforward "literal-core" theory, for both the sentence meaning (of "S is P") and the intended speaker's meaning (of "S is R") are literal. However, Searle makes it very clear that every literal utterance ultimately presupposes a nonrepresentational, nonpropositional, preintentional "Background" of capacities, skills, and stances in order to determine its conditions of satisfaction. The meaning of any metaphor will be determined only against a preintentional background that cannot be represented propositionally.

It is not surprising, therefore, that when Searle tries to state the principles that connect the "P" in "S is P" to the "R" in "S is R" he is ultimately led to say that some metaphors work *because there are non-propositional connections in the Background.* To see this point, consider some of Searle's principles for computing the relevant values of "R":

i) Things which are P are by definition R.

ii) Things which are P are contingently R.

iii) Things which are P are said or believed to be R.

iv) Things which are P are not R, nor are they like R things, nor are they believed to be R; nonetheless it is a *fact about our sensibility,* whether culturally or naturally determined, that we just do perceive a connection[16] (underline mine).

What Searle is saying in this fourth principle is that we just don't have any idea how some metaphors work, but it must be a matter of connections in the Background (in our sensibility). Searle again repeats this same point when he argues that some metaphors, such as those based on taste and temperature, seem not to be grounded on *any similarities at all:*

It just seems to be a fact about our mental capacities that we are able to interpret certain sorts of metaphor without the application of any underlying "rules" or "principles" other than the sheer ability to make certain associations. I don't know any better way to describe these abilities than to say that they are nonrepresentational mental capacities.[17]

Although Searle and Davidson hold very different views of metaphor, they both share the recognition of a nonpropositional operation of metaphorical projection. Neither seems to think that there is much that we can say about this level of experience. I am suggesting that there is quite a bit more that can be said about this metaphorical activity. We can say more about what Davidson calls "intimation" and Searle calls "connections" in the Background. We have already begun this exploration in the previous two chapters by examining the metaphorical elaboration of CONTAINER and FORCE schemata.

I now want to pursue further this *non-Objectivist* inquiry into the way in which metaphorical elaborations of image schemata give rise to form and structure in our experience and understanding. I want to show how it is possible for metaphorical projections to play a *constitutive* role in the structuring of our experience.[18] My argument consists of an analysis of the meaning of *balance,* understood both as an experience and as a concept. I shall begin by showing how the meaning

of balance emerges in bodily experiences in which we orient ourselves
within our environment. These experiences involve preconceptual
schemata that are the basis for the meaning of *balance*. Next, I examine
several cases of visual perception (including works of art) in which balance is present. In each case there are metaphorical elaborations of
basic BALANCE schemata. Finally, I consider other extended senses of
the term "balance," all connected by metaphorical projections.

   What I hope to show is that the several different senses of the term
"balance" are connected by metaphorical extensions of BALANCE schemata, and that we cannot begin to understand the various meanings of
"balance" without focusing on preconceptual gestalt structures within
our network of meanings. The view of metaphor that emerges goes
beyond the purview of traditional theories insofar as it treats metaphor
as a matter of projections and mappings across different domains in the
actual structuring of our experience (and not just in our reflection on
already existing structures).

The Bodily Experience of Balance as an Activity

The experience of balance is so pervasive and so absolutely basic for
our coherent experience of our world, and for our survival in it, that
we are seldom ever aware of its presence. We almost never reflect on the
nature and meaning of balance, and yet without it our physical reality
would be utterly chaotic, like the wildly spinning world of a very in-
toxicated person. The structure of balance is one of the key threads
that holds our physical experience together as a relatively coherent and
meaningful whole. And, as we shall see shortly, balance metaphorically
interpreted also holds together several aspects of our understanding of
our world.

   It is crucially important to see that balancing is an *activity we learn
with our bodies* and not by grasping a set of rules or concepts. First and
foremost, balancing is something we *do*. The baby stands, wobbles, and
drops to the floor. It tries again, and again, and again, until a new
world opens up—the world of the balanced erect posture. There are
those few days when the synapse connections are being established and
then, fairly suddenly, the baby becomes a little *homo erectus*. Balancing
is a preconceptual bodily activity that cannot be described propositionally by rules. As Michael Polanyi has argued, you cannot tell another what steps to take to achieve the balanced riding of a bicycle.[19]
One can give the beginner a few more or less empty rules, but the balancing activity happens when the rules, such as they are, no longer
play any role. For example, in learning the proper balance of forces for

juggling, I might be told to throw the ball in the hand *under* the closest ball in the air, just as it reaches the peak of its trajectory. But the conscious following of rules is an impediment to balancing the forces in juggling. Instead, the juggler knows when the balance is right, knows how to make adjustments, and "has a feel" for the patterns of bodily movement that generate the proper patterns of the balls in motion.

We also come to know the meaning of balance through the closely related experience of bodily equilibrium, or loss of equilibrium. We understand the notion of systemic balance in the most immediate, preconceptual fashion through our bodily experience. There is too much acid in the stomach, the hands are too cold, the head is too hot, the bladder is distended, the sinuses are swollen, the mouth is dry. In these and numerous other ways we learn the meaning of lack of balance or equilibrium. Things are felt as "out of balance." There is "too much" or "not enough" so that the normal, healthy organization of forces, processes, and elements is upset. We respond to such felt imbalance and disequilibrium by adding heat to the hands, giving moisture to the mouth, draining the bladder, and so forth, until the balance is set right again.

The first major point, then, is that the *meaning* of balance begins to emerge through our *acts* of balancing and through our *experience* of systemic processes and states within our bodies. I shall argue that the meaning of balance is tied to such experiences and, in particular, to the image-schematic structures that make those experiences and activities coherent and significant for us (i.e., recognizable as present or absent, even if we have not yet formed concepts or learned words for them). The key word here is "structure," for there can be no meaning without some form of structure or pattern that establishes relationships. We need to explore, therefore, the nature of this alleged preconceptual structure.

Already, in the previous two chapters, we have developed the notion of preconceptual gestalt (or schematic) structures that operate in our bodily movements, perceptual acts, and orientational awareness. As I stressed earlier, the image schema is *not* an image. It is, instead, a means of structuring particular experiences schematically, so as to give order and connectedness to our perceptions and conceptions. Let us explore this notion in greater depth. Consider an event that takes you out of your ordinary state of consciousness (where you are not aware of your balance) and focuses your attention on the structure of your experience and action. Take, for example, the loss of balance. As you stumble, and fall, balance becomes conspicuous by its absence. You right yourself by rising back to your typical upright posture. That is, you reestablish a prior distribution of forces and weight relative to an imaginary vertical axis. You are balancing out, once more, the relevant physical forces. If you observe a one-year-old learning to walk, you see its initial clumsy attempts to distribute mass and forces properly around this axis, and you will often see the toddler's arms held out to form a balancing horizontal axis relative to the vertical axis.

Now just what *is* this "imaginary" axis, or point, or center around which the forces get distributed? It is not any physical object we can touch or see. It is not an image the toddler forms in its mind as it tries to walk. Nor is it a propositional structure, or a rule, the baby entertains conceptually. Still, it *is* a recurrent pattern in the experience of balancing.

Let us consider another case of this alleged type of experiential structure. Rudolf Arnheim has studied the role of such structures in our visual perception.[20] For instance, in figure 13 shown below he asks us to consider the experience of balance or lack of balance that it gives us. As Arnheim notes, we do not have to measure or calculate to see that the black disk is "off center"—we *see* that immediately. Furthermore, there is a sensed tension in the placement of the disk on the white square. The disk seems to seek out, or to be pulled toward, the imagined center of the square. This center, toward which the disk strives, is not any actual physical presence in the picture. Yet it is still very much present in our perceptual experience, as a hidden landmark.

Arnheim suggests that there is a large "hidden structure" of tensions and forces present in all visual perception. In figure 13 it might seem that the only hidden structure would be an imagined center point, one that could be identified by exact measurement. But this does not begin to capture the relevant patterns of force operating in our perception of balance (or imbalance) in such a simple figure. To see

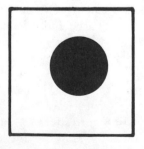

FIGURE 13

FIGURE 14

just how much hidden structure is present, Arnheim experimented with subjects by moving the disk to various placements and asking whether the disk was solidly at rest, pulled in a certain direction, repelled by some contour of the square, and so on. Thus, in figure 14, subjects experienced the disk, as drawn toward the right edge of the square; but if the disk is moved ever closer to that edge, there is a point at which it gets "too close" and is repelled by the right boundary.

What Arnheim discovered was an underlying "structural skeleton" in terms of which he could explain the dynamic forces at work in our perception of such figures. The main contours of this "skeleton" are sketched in figure 15. Arnheim explains the relevant interpretation of this skeleton as follows:

Wherever the disk is located, it will be affected by the forces of all the hidden structural factors. The relative strength and distance of these factors will determine their effect in the total configuration. At the center all the forces balance one another, and therefore the central position makes for rest. Another comparatively restful position can be found, for example, by moving the disk along a diagonal. . . . In general, any location that coincides with a feature of the structural skeleton introduces an element of stability, which of course may be counteracted by other forces.[21]

One further example from Arnheim's study is useful in beginning to suggest how complex the experience of balance can become as we introduce more and more elements into our experience. Consider what happens if we add just one more disk, as in figure 16. In 16*a,* if there were only one of the two disks, it would look unbalanced. But the addition of the second disk at the appropriate place perfectly balances off the first disk. Equal forces are balanced to produce a sense of rest. If, however, we place the same-sized disks the same distance apart, but in a different place on the square, as in 16*b,* they become unbalanced. Arnheim explains this experience:

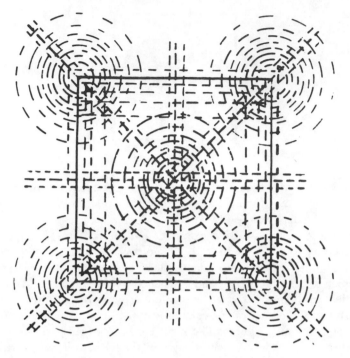

FIGURE 15

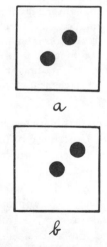

a

b

FIGURE 16

The two disks form a pair because of their closeness and their similarity in size and shape, and also because they are the only "content" of the square. As members of a pair they tend to be seen as symmetrical; that is, they are given equal value and function in the whole. This perceptual judgment, however, conflicts with another, deriving from the location of the pair. The lower disk lies in the prominent and stable position of the center. The upper one is at a less stable location. Thus location creates a distinction between the two that conflicts with their symmetrical pairness.[22]

Once again, the balance (or lack thereof) is a balance of forces in my perceptual activity. The appropriate "hidden structure" specifies the relation of these psychological forces of perception. To the extent that there is a pattern to these force relations, there is a schema.

Now, there are two extremely important points that I want to emphasize about Arnheim's figures. First, while it is true that we say that the *disk*(s) is (are) balanced or unbalanced, the balance does not exist objectively *in* the figure drawn on the page, as if the balance were just *there* to be passively perceived by anyone. The disk on the white square is only balanced *in our acts of perception.* So Arnheim's "hidden structure" exists only relative to sentient perceivers. However, since all humans have the same perceptual hardware, more or less, it will usually make perfectly good sense to speak of the balance being *in* the perceived object. Whatever schemata there might be for balance, then, will be patterns of bodily or perceptual activity. As I stressed in Chapter 2, schemata are not diagrams on a page; nor are they tied to particular images. If we are to experience our world as a connected and unified place that we can make sense of, then there must be repeatable pattern and structure in our experiences. Image schemata *are* those *recurring structures of, or in, our perceptual interactions, bodily experiences, and cognitive operations.* These schematic structures have a relatively small number of parts or components that stand in very definite relations to one another. So, whenever a single schema is instantiated in a number of different experiences or images, these same parts and relations recur. As we shall see for *balance,* there can be one definite schema that structures a number of different kinds of objects, events, and experiences.

The second major point is that what Arnheim calls the "forces," "tensions," and "hidden structures" active in my perceptual grasp of balance or lack of balance in the figures are clearly *psychological* or *perceptual* forces. They are not gravitational or physical forces of the sort that operate on me when I am balancing my body. We might call them *visual* forces or weights to emphasize this important difference. In these cases, "force" and "weight" are obviously interpreted metaphorically.

On the Metaphorical Elaboration of BALANCE Schemata

In the remainder of this chapter I am going to argue that there exist a few schemata that pertain to balance in our bodies, to our grasp of perceptual configurations as balanced or unbalanced, and to the meaning of "balance" in a large number of more abstract domains of our experience (e.g., psychological states, legal relationships, formal systems, and so forth). I shall claim that one and the same image schema can be instantiated in many different kinds of domains, because the parts, or internal structure, of the single schema can be metaphorically understood.

In the cases of bodily and visual balance I am considering at this point, there seems to be one basic schema consisting of a point or axis around which forces and weights must be distributed, so that they "counteract" or "balance off" one another. I now want to explore further the way in which this single schema is understood metaphorically as we move from the balancing of our bodies to our perception of balance in visual configurations.

Let us examine some additional, more complex visual examples of balance that require us to make metaphorical projections of basic level BALANCE schemata. Consider the *Kifwebe* mask of plate 1. When we speak of the balance of this head, we are not simply asserting that "the head is balanced on analogy with one's bodily balancing." It is true that the head is balanced in a gravitational field in the same way that my body is balanced, namely, neither falls over on its face. But this is not the full meaning, or even the chief meaning, of "balance" as applied to the wood. We are not simply projecting a schematic structure that emerges in our experience of acts of bodily balancing onto some visual configuration (here, the face). There is a further dimension involved, because we no longer have "weight" or "force" in the gravitational and physical sense. Instead, we have some complex *metaphorical* (but very real) experience of *visual* weight and force. "Weight" is used metaphorically here in a standard sense of the term "metaphor": we structure and understand a domain of one kind (here, the psychological/perceptual) in terms of structure projected from a domain *of a different kind* (here, the physical/gravitational). What is unusual (i.e., not recognized by standard theories) about this dimension of metaphorical activity is that it is an actual structuring operation *in our experience.* We may not consciously experience a metaphorical projection, but our experience of balance in the figure presupposes such a projection.

What we are experiencing is similar to what Arnheim observed about our perception of the two disks relative to the white square (fig. 16). We experience our visual space as having parts or elements with different weights and forces of different magnitudes. These visual forces exist only in our acts of perception. As we view the *Kifwebe* mask, these forces give rise to the tensions, movement, rest, and balance that we experience in our active grasp of relations among elements in the face. There are two sides of the face with parts (eyes, ears, scars, etc.) having different visual weights that are, in the total visual gestalt, in balance. The key point here is that there are not physical weights or forces in balance; rather, the shapes, lines, forms, and spatial relationships involve visual weights and forces.

The fact that this *Kifwebe* mask is relatively symmetrical might tend to mislead us in determining the meaning of balance. It might seem that there is some general literal concept of balance that applies equally to all cases—to those of my bodily balancing, to balance in this head, to balancing of mathematical equations. If you imagine a vertical axis splitting the mask, you could see that whatever is on the left of the axis seems to be on the right also, with each element being the same size, and in the same relative position, in relation to its corresponding counterpart on the other side of the axis. In this way it might appear that we have an instance of one universal abstract concept of balance, of the form, "Any X is balanced when it is symmetrical, that is, where there are equal elements, with equal weights, in equal locations, one on each side relative to the axis or center point, or where there is an equal distribution of weight and forces relative to the axis."

Obviously, as I have already shown, if such a concept did exist, it could not cover all of the cases of balance I have considered so far (not to mention *all* the possible senses of "balance") unless its key elements were interpreted metaphorically. But even if metaphorical elaboration wasn't essential, there could still be no such concept, since there is no one core set of features shared by all experiences of balance. Both of these points become more obvious if we turn to an object, such as the Udo bronze in plate 2, where a simple symmetry cannot account for our experience of its balance.

The figure is not perfectly symmetrical. There is a sword in one hand and nothing in the other, for instance. But in spite of this lack of equality, the figure is nicely balanced. Observe the lines formed by the sword in the right hand, the strap across the chest, and the empty left hand and arm. The slight curve of the sword balances off the curve of the left arm, in relation to the angled strap. Part of this balance is the sense of equal lengths of the sword, strap, and arm. The balance here is *visual;* it is not a balance of actual physical weights or masses in the bronze figure. It is a balance of line and of visual forces that can create perceptual motion in an apparently static figure.

Furthermore, there is no longer one single axis around which the weights and forces are distributed; there are two axes: the first is a vertical axis splitting the figure into left and right halves, while the second is formed by the roughly parallel lines created by the two arms and the strap. There seems to be an imposition of this second axis upon the first to produce a complex relation of visual elements. Visual weights and forces distributed in a balanced way around the second axis would not necessarily be balanced relative to the first (vertical) axis. Consequently, there is no central axis in relation to which all of the visual elements are in balance.

Someone who wanted to insist that there is really only one relevant axis would still not succeed in demonstrating the existence of a single abstract, literally interpretable, concept for balance. For they would still need to explain away or reduce the metaphorical components of the concept.

It might seem that there is a special difficulty with the notion of metaphorical projections employed here, in that we are dealing with automatic, typically unconscious, operations that require no effort. But most of our understanding is, in fact, active at a level of which we are seldom reflectively aware. So, there is nothing unique about metaphorical understanding of this sort. We can speak of metaphorical projections at this level of understanding, insofar as we are experiencing a meaningful distribution of *visual* forces. It can only be by a metaphorical extension from our experience of physical weight that the sword and right arm could somehow have "equal weight" with the left arm in the composition. Again, the metaphor consists in the projection of structure from one domain (that of gravitational and other physical forces) onto another domain of a different kind (spatial organization in visual perception). The figurative mappings here do not require deliberation on the perceiver's part. Metaphorical interpretations of various components of image schemata are structures in our *understanding and experience* of the world and, as such, are not ordinarily part of our *self-reflective* awareness, though they are part of our awareness. They can properly be called "structures of understanding" because

understand → world.
ing

they are patterns in terms of which we "have a world," which is what is meant by "understanding" in its broadest sense.[23]

This metaphorical character shows itself even more boldly if we examine an abstract painting. By introducing abstraction, we strip away representational features of the figure that might suggest that the perceived figures are balanced in the same literal sense that our bodies can be balanced. When we moved from the *Kifwebe* mask to the Udo figure, we saw that simple symmetry cannot be the essence of balance. Now, with abstract painting, we see just how complex the relevant metaphorical interpretations of balance schemata can be.

In Kandinsky's *Accompanied Contrast* (plate 3), there is an exquisite balance in the work that can be made sense of only by interpreting "weight," "force," "location," and "value" metaphorically, based on a schema whose structure specifies forces or weights distributed relative to some point or axis.

For such a complex visual configuration I would not presume to give an account of relevant image schemata and forces at work in our perception. Kandinsky is exceptional in that he had very explicit and detailed views about the way color, line, figure, composition, and so forth, produce their effects on the viewer. In *Point and Line to Plane* he claimed that "a *composition* is nothing other than an *exact law-abiding organization* of the vital *forces* which, in the form of tensions, are shut up within the elements."[24] Specifying such alleged laws proved to be an immense task that no one really pretends to have completed. Whether or not there are *laws* in any interesting sense is not important for our purposes. It is enough to get a sense of just how many kinds of factors are involved in our meaningful grasp of the work as balanced, and thus to realize how unlikely it is that there could be any single unified literal concept of balance adequate to all cases. Arnheim gives a brief minimal list of factors that influence force and weight relations in a work and thus determine balance: (1) location in the plane, (2) spatial depth, (3) size, (4) intrinsic interest, (5) isolation, (6) shape, (7) knowledge, and (8) color. Imagine the complex of forces that results from the interaction of these factors for each "element" within the work!

If we consider only *color* alone, we become quickly overwhelmed. Kandinsky held the reasonable view that each color has its own distinctive character that generates specific forces. For example:

If two circles are drawn and painted respectively yellow and blue, a brief contemplation will reveal in the yellow a spreading movement out from the center, and a noticeable approach to the spectator. The blue, on the other hand, moves into itself, like a snail retreating into its shell, and draws away from the spectator. The eye feels stung by the first circle while it is absorbed into the second.[25]

If you try this experiment, you will see that Kandinsky is quite correct. There is actually a movement with yellow. Obviously, however, it is a movement in a perceptual (metaphorical) space. We cannot be talking of a literal movement in a physical fixed picture plane. The "movement" refers to structures in our perceptual interaction, in which we form unified images and trace out relations among the various elements in the work.

Kandinsky gives accounts of the forces operating for each of the colors. Yellow is "brash and importunate"; red has "unbounded warmth" but not the "irresponsible appeal" of yellow. Blue gives us a "call to the infinite" and "a desire for purity and transcendence." The account goes on and on. It is not important, for our purposes, whether or not Kandinsky's particular analysis is correct, or whether the effects of color are universal. The crucial point is that colors do not exist in isolation but in relation, and this sets up complex interactions of forces.

In addition to these relations, there are others established by the nature of the color surface. In *Kandinsky: The Language of the Eye,* Paul Overy has adopted David Katz's division of color types into hard opaque surfaces, translucent films, and cloudy volumes.[26] Different dynamics arise for each type of color. Furthermore, color is effected by the form it takes and by the form it stands in relation to. For example, Kandinsky asserted:

In my view a geometric boundary allows a colour a much greater possibility of arousing a pure vibration than the boundaries of any object whatsoever which always speaks very loudly and very restrictedly in arousing a vibration appropriate to it (horse, goose, cloud . . .).[27]

To sum up my discussion of *color* balance: I have made reference to some of Kandinsky's remarks on color because he is universally recognized as someone who successfully manipulated most of the forces pertaining to color. It does not really matter whether or not his explicit theoretical views about color are correct. What does matter is that he gives us a comprehensive sense of the amazing range of factors that go into our perception of color and color relations.

For our purposes, certain points are quite clear. First, it is obvious that colors do not literally "have weight." Their "weight" and "force" can only be metaphorically related to that of physical objects in a gravitational field or other field of forces. Second, the relevant balance of color forces exists only in our act of perception, as we encounter the painting. What we experience is the result of a balancing of complex psychological forces at work in our perceptual "play" with the relations of line, spaces, contours, and colors. Third, we are dealing here with psychological patterns or schemata that make it possible for us to have structured, coherent experiences that we can make sense of. We are dealing with levels of organization that are on the borderline between bodily processes and conscious or reflective acts that we can focus our attention on, if we choose. We are dealing with preconceptual levels at which structure emerges in our experience via metaphorical extensions of image schemata.

Metaphorical Extensions and Interconnections of BALANCE Schemata

Up to this point, we have dealt only with a few common senses of balance as experienced in bodily movement and perception. But there are several additional senses of balance which are also related to the prototypical BALANCE schema I have been discussing. An Objectivist might deny that there are unifying schemata and insist that the various senses of the word "balance" are simply unrelated concepts. This *homonymy* position would deny that imaginative schemata connect up various senses of *balance* by means of metaphorical elaborations. So, the challenge is to show the relevant connections for a large number of representative senses of *balance*.

In the previous discusison I have assumed that there is a prototypical BALANCE schema, consisting of force vectors (which can represent weight, as a special case) and some point or axis or plane in relation to which those forces are distributed. In every case, balance involves a symmetrical (or proportional) arrangement of forces around a point or axis. The prototypical schema can thus be represented by an axis and force vectors, as in figure 17. In all extended senses of "balance" based on this primary schema, either the axis, the vectors, or both will receive a metaphorical elaboration.

Other schemata for BALANCE can be interpreted as variations on, or modifications of, the prototypical schema. What we might call the "seesaw" or the "twin-pan" balance schema (fig. 18) is merely a limiting case of the prototypical schema. In this case the axis (of the prototypical schema) is reduced to a mere point, which serves as a fulcrum. The many symmetrical force vectors are reduced to two symmetrical vectors, since the equal weights do constitute balancing force vectors meeting at a point, as in figure 19. Actually, it is even somewhat mis-

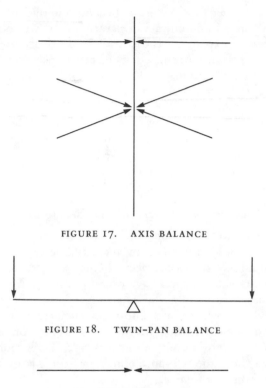

FIGURE 17.   AXIS BALANCE

FIGURE 18.   TWIN-PAN BALANCE

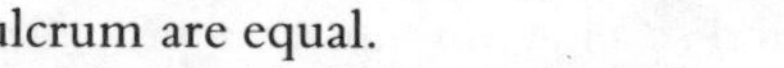

FIGURE 19.   POINT BALANCE

leading to say that there must be equal weights, for that is not true. We can have differing weights, just as long as they are located at the right distances relative to the fulcrum, that is, just as long as the forces on each side of the fulcrum are equal.

A third common schema, the EQUILIBRIUM schema, results from the continuous mapping of symmetrical force vectors meeting at a point onto a curved surface. Consider, for example, figure 20, which represents a closed volume in which the "internal" and "external" forces balance. This schema is simply a complex mapping of balance points onto the surface of the sphere (or other container-surface). Think of the surface of the sphere as made up of points, each of which is the locus of balanced (symmetrical) vectors.

Given these variations of the prototypical schema, coupled with the sense of metaphorical extension elaborated above, we can now explain the relations between several further senses of "balance." My main

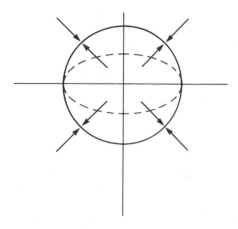

FIGURE 20.   EQUILIBRIUM

claim is that, just as we saw for the senses of *in* and for the modal verbs, the metaphorical projections move from the bodily sense (with its emergent schema) to the mental, epistemic, or logical domains. On this hypothesis, we should be able to see how it is that our experience of bodily balance, and of the perception of balance, is connected to our understanding of balanced personalities, balanced views, balanced systems, balanced equations, the balance of power, the balance of justice, and so on.

   1. *Systemic balance.* A system is an organization of interconnected, interdependent individuals or elements that work together to form a functional unity. The system may be the simplest of functional machines, such as a mousetrap, or it may be an abstract ontological account of the nature of Being, as in a "philosophical system." The system we know best, "from the inside," is the incredibly complex organic unity we call our body. It is an amazing functional system that consists of many component systems, such as the nervous, circulatory, respiratory, and musculo-skeletal systems.

   In all of these systems, there must exist a certain dynamic equilibrium, a proper balance of forces, if the system is to function properly. With respect to our bodies, for example, we know of this requirement in the most immediate way. If there is too much gas in the stomach, we may feel the resultant imbalance in a way that affects our behavior. The relevant schema is that from figure 20, consisting of force, internal and external, related to a three-dimensional container.

The notion of a *system* is so pervasive because functional unities of all sorts, however concrete or abstract, can manifest systemic balance or imbalance. In a purely mechanical system, such as a steam-powered electrical generator, balance can be described entirely in terms of "physical" forces. An ecological system manifests a balance of physical forces also, but its equilibrium consists, in addition, of social forces that are not physical in any literal sense. For instance, in the migrations of animals on the Serengheti Plain, the desired equilibrium requires *both* a balance of forces of nature (e.g., heat, rain, wind, sun, etc.) and a balanced social interaction among the members of the system. These social forces are real, but are understood via metaphorical projections from the schemata for physical force as well as other schemata and their metaphorical extensions (such as "organicism").

2. *Psychological balance.* The experience of physical equilibrium within our bodies gives rise to structures for ordering our experience of so-called psychological realities. The "mental" is understood and experienced in terms of the "physical." The notion of "emotional balance" is a good example here, because our emotional experience is typically thought of as having both a bodily and a mental aspect. We experience our emotions on a homeostatic model in which health depends upon proper balance of emotional forces and pressures. The *buildup* of emotions constitutes a *pressure* in the system, which has physiological and "mental" correlates. George Lakoff and Zoltan Kovecses have argued that emotions like anger are experienced on a model of hot fluid within a container (usually closed).[28] Emotions can *simmer, well up, overflow, boil over, erupt,* and *explode* when the pressure builds up. In such cases an equilibrium must be reestablished. One can *express, release,* or *let out* the emotions (*blow off steam*) to lessen the strain. One can try to *repress, suppress, hold in,* or *put a lid on* one's emotions, but they will not thereby disappear—the forces are still present within the system. In short, we tend to seek a temporary homeostasis where we are emotionally *balanced, stable,* and *on an even keel.* The relevant schema, once again, is that from figure 20, since we are dealing with a form of systemic equilibrium, metaphorically extended to include the "nonphysical" side of emotional experience.

On the other side of the scale of emotional balance, there can be too little emotional pressure. One can be *drained, emotionally bankrupt,* or *exhausted.* The result is lethargy, dullness, lack of energy, and absence of motivation. In such cases we try to *pump up* our emotions, to *stir them up,* to *recharge* them, to *generate some emotional energy.*

In addition to the more specific realm of the emotions, we experience our entire psychic makeup in terms of balance. The ideal is a *balanced* personality. This requires that *sufficient weight* be given to each of the parts or dimensions of our character. The emotions must be sufficiently *under control*. We must find a balance of intellectual, physical, social, religious, and moral activity. If too much *weight* is put on one activity or enterprise, to the exclusion of others, the individual is unbalanced. Furthermore, financial, marital, political, or sexual problems can *weigh on our minds,* throwing us out of balance. In such cases the resulting forces may drive us to ill-advised, or morally improper, behavior.

It is important to see that we are not considering here only how we *talk* about our emotions, nor only how we might *conceptualize* our emotional experience. We are also describing the *structure of our experience* of emotions. When I am emotionally worked-up, I feel myself to be out of balance. My world takes on a different character than it normally has. When I feel emotionally "out of balance" I am not reflecting conceptually on that imbalance; I am merely *experiencing* a sense of psychological distress—I am *feeling* something I cannot quite articulate propositionally.

3. *The balance of rational argument.* When I set out to convince others of my view, I *pile up evidence, amass facts,* and *build up a weighty argument.* Ideally, anyone who listens to my argument will *weigh* its merits. Two arguments may *carry equal weight,* so we then try to *tip the scale* in favor of our view by *adding* further evidence. If we are successful, we feel the *balance tip* in our favor, as we add to our argument. The weights are psychological and epistemic in this domain, and the relevant schema is that represented in figure 18, the "twin-pan balance" structure.

As Jaime Carbonell has pointed out, the notion of *weight* is intimately related to the structure of the BALANCE metaphor.[29] We experience power and force in terms of weight and mass (which is equated with weight in common understanding). Thus we get reports such as,

The Argentine air force launched a *massive* attack on the British fleet. One frigate was *heavily* damaged, but only *light* casualties were suffered by British sailors. The Argentines paid a *heavy* toll in downed aircraft.[30]

We are supposed to decide who won by *weighing* the relative *losses.* And for those who experience ARGUMENT AS WAR, similar calculations would be in order to determine who has been victorious.[31] Whether it be in battle, in politics, in the marketplace, or in rational argument, the structure of our experience is intimately tied to schemata that emerge in our physical experience of balancing.

4. *Legal/moral balance.* The institutions of civil and criminal justice are founded upon a basic notion of balance, as symbolized quaintly by the scale of justice. As we would expect, legal arguments adopt all of the standard features of rational argument in general. The lawyers want the jury to *lean* in their favor, so they employ a confusing *mass* of facts, encourage *weighty* testimony, *pile* one argument upon another, add the *force* of acknowledged authorities, and summon the *weight* of the legal tradition. Justice itself is conceived as the regaining of a proper balance that has been upset by an unlawful action. According to some assumed calculus, the judge must assess the *weight* of the damages and require a penalty somehow equal to the damages as compensation. We have linguistically encoded manifestations of this juridical metaphor, such as "an eye-for-an-eye" and "let the punishment fit the crime."

5. *Mathematical equality.* Equality is a matter of balance. What one side gets, the other must get also. If there are two pounds of potatoes in my right hand, they can only be balanced by two pounds (of something) in my left. To preserve equality, whatever is added to one side must be added to the other. Here the mundane TWIN-PAN BALANCE schema is projected into the highly abstract realm of mathematical computation and equation solution. The basis for this projection is a point-for-point mapping of entities from the physical realm into entities in the abstract mathematical realm, as follows:

   a) Physical objects map onto numbers (abstract entities).
   b) Weights of objects map onto numerical values.
   c) Physical addition of weights to the two sides of the balance-beam becomes mathematical addition (the abstract "adding" of numerical values or numbers).
   d) The fulcrum of the physical balance becomes the equation sign of mathematics.

   Given this mapping of entities and structure, it follows that mathematical knowledge is an abstract correlate of acts of physical addition and subtraction of weights. We *balance* the equation by performing the same operation on each side of the "equals" sign. In one sense, to be "equal" each side must *weigh the same* (=have the same value). The expressions on either side of the "equals" sign need not be identical in sense or meaning, but they must have the same *value* or *weight*.

PLATE I. *Kifwebe* (Luba mask). The Seattle Art Museum, Katherine White Collection, 81.17.869.

PLATE 2. Drawing by Karen Schmitt of a Udo figure after illustration 73 in Philip J. C. Dark, *An Illustrated Catalogue of Benin Art* (London: G. K. Hall and Co., 1982).

PLATE 3. Vasily Kandinsky, *Accompanied Contrast*. March 1935. Collection, Solomon R. Guggenheim Museum, New York. Photo: David Heald.

This same notion of equality and balance can be projected onto our moral and legal experience, as explained in (4) above. Rights, privileges, injuries, penalties, damages, duties, and so forth, all have *weight*. This makes possible a sense of mathematical calculation for the moral and legal realms. If you can sit at the front of the bus (=an action with a specific weight), then I ought to be able to sit in the front of the bus (i.e., to balance your action with mine), insofar as we are considered equals. In short, we have equal rights. It would be an injustice (an imbalance) if you were granted a right (with a certain legal "weight") while I am denied that right, when there is no relevant difference between us.

A particularly unfortunate manifestation of this mathematical structuring of moral experience is the prevalence of what moral theorists call "consequentialist" reasoning. On this view, the morality of an action is determined by a calculation of its consequences. If the sum of the "good" consequences seems to outweigh the "bad" consequences, then the action is regarded as morally permissible, or even obligatory. Utilitarianism, the so-called greatest-good-for-the-greatest-number principle, is the most popular version of consequentialist reasoning today—it is widely accepted by lawyers, judges, social workers, penal authorities, politicians, and mental health workers. It supposes that determining the moral worth of an action is a matter of *calculation* of its effects. The model most often employed is that of *cost-benefit* analysis, in which the costs (economic, political, moral, religious) are weighed against possible benefits to society (or some subgroup) as a whole. Once again, if the benefits outweigh the costs (according to some assumed calculus), then the action is permissible or obligatory.

The chief problem with this mode of *moral mathematics* (moral balancing) is that it can sacrifice justice for individuals in the name of a "greater good" (greater benefit) for a "greater number" (larger group). It assumes that human beings, their actions, and their interests can be given numerical values, that the moral value of each action can be quantitatively assigned, and that the effects of actions can be precisely calculated. In short, consequentialist moral mathematics can sometimes conflict with the notion of moral equality that underlies our sense of justice. In either case, however, the BALANCE schema is essential to the entire framework.

What this brief analysis of various senses of "balance" shows is that there are possible connections between putatively very different uses of the term "balance." We do not find a large number of unrelated concepts (for the systemic, psychological, moral, legal, mathematical domains) that all just happen to make use of the same word "balance" and related terms. Rather, we use the same word for all of these domains for the reason that they are structurally related by the same set of underlying schemata, metaphorically elaborated.

Structures of Inference Based on BALANCE *Schemata*

In the previous two chapters, I suggested that certain abstract inference patterns are the result of metaphorical projections of image schemata for CONTAINMENT and FORCE which arise in our bodily experience. Let us now turn to a third domain, the inferences based on our experience of balance. As we saw earlier, balance involves symmetry. We experience symmetry not only in our perception of symmetrical objects but also in our experience of bodily balance. Symmetry in our perception is understood relative to an axis, such that we can rotate what is on one side of the axis over onto the other side with a good fit. In an object that we perceive as symmetrical, all the sizes, shapes, locations, and relations on, say, the left side, map point-for-point onto those on the right side. With respect to our experience of bodily balance, we also experience a symmetry of weight and forces relative to our own vertical axis.

Balance, in the most elementary sense, involves two symmetrical forces acting with respect to an axis or point. This case is simply a special instance of the prototypical BALANCE schema of figure 17. I have suggested that any appropriate schemata for balance will turn out to be variations on the prototypical schema. What appear to be very different cases of balance are cases of *balance* because they share a common schema in which there is symmetry of forces relative to an axis (or point).

Recall that there are ordinary bodily experiences of balance for each of the three special cases of the BALANCE schema:

1. The pervasive experience of standing upright, or walking, without falling over. (Instance of prototypical schema, fig. 17.)

2. Cases where we carry an equal load in each of our hands. (Instance of TWIN-PAN BALANCE schema, fig. 18.)

3. The experience of homeostasis within our bodily organs. For instance, when there is too much gas in the stomach, we feel discomfort and the attendant sensations of imbalance (the excessive internal pressure). (Instance of EQUILIBRIUM schema, fig. 20.)

In our daily lives we are constantly experiencing symmetries and asymmetries of forces relative to axes and points of various kinds. Despite the different manifestations of balance, there is a single image-schema present in all such experiences: *a symmetrical arrangement of force vectors relative to an axis*. It is because of this shared BALANCE schema that so many different experiences of symemtrical relations are named by the same word, "balance."

Corresponding to this recurring structure, there is a logic to our experiences of balance. The BALANCE schema, as we have seen, has a definite internal structure. This structure has three important properties: symmetry, transitivity, and reflexivity.

1. *Symmetry*. A balances B if and only if B balances A.

If we hold A in the left hand and B in the right hand, and they balance, then interchanging A and B will preserve the balance. This is natural, since our understanding of balance involves a symmetry of forces.

2. *Transitivity*. If A balances B, and B balances C, then A balances C.

Suppose A is in the left hand and B is in the right hand, and they balance. Now suppose I replace A by C and the balance is maintained, that is, B balances C. Then I will know immediately that A and C will balance, even though I have not performed the act of weighing one against the other.

3. *Reflexivity*. A balances A.

Obviously, this is not experienced directly. However, it follows from (a) the understanding of balance in terms of symmetry, and (b) the understanding of symmetry in terms of rotations around an axis to yield a perfect fit. If you could have *exactly the same* element or object on both sides, they would have the same weights and exert the same forces. From an experiential perspective, such a relation never holds, which is why it seems to us such a strange relation. We are, after all, never in a position to balance something with itself. But we know from our understanding of balance in general that this would be true if we could do it.

What we have seen so far is that we have a variety of experiences that are organized by a single schema—the BALANCE schema—and that it has the properties of symmetry, transitivity, and reflexivity. The relevant experiences for each of these properties always involve balance relations among physical objects and weights. However, these *same* relations obtain for *abstract* objects related by the BALANCE schema. It is thus the experience of balance, with its attendant properties, that has given rise to our mathematical concept of the "equality of magnitudes." We would not know what it meant for magnitudes to be equal unless we had a concept of balance, with the properties we have just seen to be inherent in the BALANCE schema.

In considering abstract mathematical properties (such as "equality of magnitudes"), we sometimes forget the mundane bases in experience which are both necessary for comprehending those abstractions and from which the abstractions have developed. The abstract concept of equality of magnitude can only be understood in terms of the experience of balance. It is no accident that the properties of the balance schema are just what mathematicians call the "equivalence relations." The constellation of those abstract relations occurs in our experiences of balance, which are all comprehended in terms of the same image-schematic structure. There is no other category of bodily experience with just that constellation of properties. Balance, therefore, appears to be the bodily basis of the mathematical notion of equivalence.

The Metaphorical Structuring of Experience and Understanding: A Summary

I have been trying to make sense of the claim that metaphors are sometimes creative in giving rise to structure within our experience. That is, they do not merely report preexisting, independent experience; rather, they contribute to the process by which our experience and our understanding (as our way of "having a world") are structured in a coherent and meaningful fashion. In the case of *balance,* for example, we saw how certain very abstract concepts, events, states, institutions, and principles (such as psychological states, arguments, moral rights, and mathematical operations) are metaphorically structured as entities or physical events. And it is by virtue of this metaphorically imposed structure that we can understand and reason about the relevant abstract entities. It is the projection of such structure that I am identifying as the "creative" function of metaphor, for it is one of the chief ways we generate structure in our experience in a way that we can comprehend. The key to seeing how such creativity is possible is the recognition of a dimension of metaphorical projection based on image schemata, such as those for BALANCE.

To describe the nature of these schematic metaphorical projections, I explored some of the intimately related meanings of "balance," as a representative case of figurative projection connecting various senses of a term. Balancing was seen to be an activity, something we do with

a courtroom is not really a weight or a system physically? [handwritten margin note] our bodies. that requires an ordering of forces and weights relative to some point, axis, or plane. I also suggested that our feeling of systemic equilibrium is an equally basic experience of balance. Both of these bodily experiences involve schemata that make them coherent, meaningful, and comprehensible experiences of balance.

We saw next that balance in visual perception already involves a metaphorical projection of schematic structure from the realm of *physical* and gravitational forces and weights to a domain of *visual* forces and weights in "visual space." The balance was not objectively *in* the visual configuration, as a mere set of marks, but existed only in our perceptual grasp of order and figure for those marks. Arnheim's figures showed that the balance exists only in our perceptual activity, and thus that there could not be "force" or "weight" in any literal sense in the figures.

The *Kifwebe* mask, Udo figure, and Kandinsky painting made this metaphorical elaboration of preconceptual schemata even more evident. In particular, we saw that the balance in Kandinsky's *Accompanied Contrast* manifested a complex balance that depended, in part, on color relationships. The image schema of a point, axis, or plane with forces and weights distributed relative to it is still present, but "weight" and "force" can only be metaphorically interpreted. We also saw that no univocal (or literal) concept involving symmetry could account for the range of cases of visual balance we were considering.

I next examined several other prominent senses of "balance" to show how they are metaphorically related to physical balance. In each case (e.g., systemic balance, psychological balance, logical balance, etc.) there was a metaphorical projection from an image schema generated in the experience of physical balance onto the nonphysical, or less clearly structured domain. There is a good reason, therefore, why all of these domains of experience and understanding involve balance in some sense, namely, they all involve BALANCE schemata metaphorically extended.

Finally, I considered three further patterns of logical inference that can be seen to depend on the properties and structures of BALANCE schemata. As in the previous two chapters, the point of this is to provide an alternative to the view that logical structure just exists a priori as the universal essence of rationality. Logical inferences, I am claiming, are not just inexplicable structures of rationality (of *pure* reason). On the contrary, they can be seen to emerge from our embodied, concrete experience and our problem solving in our most mundane affairs. The patterns of our rationality are tied, in part, to the preconceptual schemata that give comprehensible order and connectedness to our experience. In a later chapter I shall take up the reply that it is possible to give a purely formal account of inference patterns that makes no reference to schemata. For the present, I am only suggesting how we might begin to explore the experiential embodied nature of human rationality.

Metaphorical projection is only one way we achieve order and structure in our experience that we can make sense of. Another type of projective structure is metonymy, which deals with part-whole relations. But metaphor proves to be one of the better examples of imaginative schematic operations, because it allows us a glimpse of the creation of meaningful structure via projections and elaborations of image schemata (as we shall see in Chapter 6). The epistemic importance of metaphor is thus seen to rest on its role as an experiential process in which structure is generated and projected in our understanding, construed in the broad sense.

5

How Schemata Constrain Meaning, Understanding, and Rationality

What evidence is there that metaphorically extended image schemata really do structure our understanding and reasoning? Perhaps schemata and metaphors of the sort treated in the previous chapters are only useful, economical ways of describing our understanding, meaning, and reasoning, but are not actually constitutive of it. Furthermore, even if such metaphorical structures do exist, it might be argued that they lack sufficiently definite internal structure to constrain our inferential patterns. It might be objected, for instance, that some metaphors are so open-ended and ambiguous that they don't appear to lead us to any one conclusion rather than to another.

Obviously, the issue of the cognitive reality of image schemata and their metaphorical extensions is central to my project. In this chapter I take up four closely related problems that cluster around this central issue of cognitive reality: (1) Where do image schemata and metaphorical systems exist? That is, what is their ontological status, and why is it so difficult to describe their operations when they are supposed to be pervasive in human meaning and understanding? (2) What kinds of evidence support my claim that we really do make cognitive connections and draw conclusions on the basis of our underlying metaphorical systems? (3) What are the general kinds of constraints that schemata and metaphors impose on our network of meanings and our inferential patterns? (4) And *how* do these constraints operate?

Where Do Image Schemata Exist?

At every turn, our present inquiry into the nature of meaning and rationality is confronted by the same recurring difficulty: How can one describe the embodied, continuous character of an image schema without making it appear to be what it is not, that is, either a rich image or an abstracted finitary proposition, in one of the five Objectivist senses? I have already answered this question implicitly in the earlier chapters, but I now want to take it up explicitly.

To say that a specific image schema (say, the OUT₁ schema) *exists* is to say that some of our experiences have a certain recurring structure by virtue of which we can understand them. For instance, we can understand a certain situation as involving OUT₁ orientation, because it is organized in a specific fashion that manifests the pattern we abstractly call the OUT₁ schema.

A crucial point here is that understanding is not only a matter of reflection, using finitary propositions, on some preexistent, already determinate experience. Rather, *understanding is the way we "have a world," the way we experience our world as a comprehensible reality.* Such understanding, therefore, involves *our whole being*—our bodily capacities and skills, our values, our moods and attitudes, our entire cultural tradition, the way in which we are bound up with a linguistic community, our aesthetic sensibilities, and so forth. In short, our understanding *is* our mode of "being in the world." It is the way we are meaningfully situated in our world through our bodily interactions, our cultural institutions, our linguistic tradition, and our historical context. Our more abstract reflective acts of understanding (which may involve grasping of finitary propositions) are simply an extension of our understanding in this more basic sense of "having a world."

Once we locate image schemata and metaphorical systems as structures of understanding, in this full-blooded, embodied, culturally embedded sense, it becomes quite obvious why it is so difficult to describe them without distortion. The problem is the prevalence of Objectivist views that have overlooked the embodied, image-schematic dimensions of meaning and understanding. For Objectivism, understanding consists in having, and performing operations on, beliefs and other propositional states. Even if image schemata were to be acknowledged, they would only be allowed to influence meaning and understanding insofar as they could be translated into, or reduced to, finitary propositional representations.

By contrast, on the view I am advancing, neither image schemata nor their metaphorical extensions exist *only* as propositions. They can be propositionally represented, but this does not capture their full reality as structures of our embodied understanding. This applies also to metaphors whose target and source domains are partially structured by image schemata. We say, for example, that a certain understanding involves the TIME IS MONEY metaphor, as if the metaphor itself were just the propositional content *time is money*. But what is really involved here is our understanding of a situation by means of connections across domains of our experience (here, the domains of *temporality* and of *monetary transactions*). The metaphorical "proposition" TIME IS MONEY only represents certain discrete and abstractable structures of a complex cross-categorical experience (=our understanding) of temporal relations, and this experience involves bodily orientations, perceptions, and actions that have linguistic and cultural dimensions.

The difficulties we encounter in describing image schemata and their metaphorical elaborations are aggravated by the dominance of Objectivist assumptions, which treat image schemata either as rich images (and thus not part of meaning) or as abstract propositional networks (and thus not imaginative or embodied). Metaphorical projections are regarded either as only propositional (and reducible to literal similarity statements) or as nonpropositional (and not part of meaning). On the Objectivist view, then, we are denied any nonreductionist way of describing the kinds of phenomena that are the central focus of the present study.

The obvious problem here is an unquestioned assumption of all Objectivist orientations, namely, that all meaning is representable entirely by means of finitary propositions. I am suggesting that we submit this foundational bias to criticism, on the hypothesis that propositions might be dependent on embodied, nonpropositional dimensions of meaning. Perhaps if we acknowledge the possibility that there is more to meaning than propositional structure alone (in the Objectivist senses), we may be able to offer more comprehensive and satisfactory explanations of a number of semantic phenomena. On the approach I am urging, we need to extend the more narrow and restrictive Objectivist senses of key terms (e.g., "meaning," "schema," "entailment," "rationality") to encompass the broader range of phenomena treated here. For instance, all standard accounts formulate metaphors in an alleged underlying propositional form (e.g., A is B). But I have described metaphorical projections of image schemata that have a continuous character, which cannot be adequately represented by finitary propositional structure. So I am using the term "metaphor" here in a metaphorically extended sense, not only as a propositional connection of two highly delineated, already determinate domains of experience, but also as a projective structure by means of which many experiential connections and relations are established in the first place.

To sum up: understanding does not consist merely of after-the-fact reflections on prior experiences; it is, more fundamentally, the way (or means by which) we have those experiences in the first place. It is the way our world presents itself to us. And this is a result of the massive complex of our culture, language, history, and bodily mechanisms that blend to make our world what it is. *Image schemata and their metaphorical projections are primary patterns of this "blending."* Our subsequent propositional reflections on our experience are made possible by this more basic mode of understanding.

Evidence for the Reality of Image Schemata and Their Metaphorical Extensions

Having suggested *where* and *how* image schemata exist, I now want to indicate the chief kinds of evidence available to show *that* they exist. The previous chapters have already given arguments for their existence, but it is important to make clear the nature of these arguments. Briefly, there are at least six kinds of evidence for the existence of image schemata and their metaphorical extensions:

1. *Image-schematic transformations.* In Chapter 2 I referred to experiments that reveal a human capacity to manipulate image schemata at a level of generality above that of concrete rich images or mental pictures.[1] As I noted, experiments show that we can perform operations on image schemata that are analogs of spatial operations. For example, we can rotate images through mental space to perform matching operations. We can superimpose one image schema upon another. We can transform schemata (such as "pulling away" from an aggregate of distinct objects until it becomes a single homogeneous mass). In other words, there is a level of image schematic operations more abstract than, and not reducible to, the formation of rich images or mental pictures.

2. *Systematicity of literal expressions.* In *Metaphors We Live By* George Lakoff and I gave evidence for the existence of underlying metaphorical structures of understanding that unify large clusters of literal expressions used to talk about a single concept. For example, we asked

why the following expressions were all perfectly acceptable ways of talking about, and understanding, theory construction. Why is it that we use just these underlined phrases in certain contexts?

> Is that the *foundation* for your theory?
> Quantum theory needs more *support*.
> You'll never *construct* a *strong* theory on those assumptions.
> I haven't figured out yet what *form* our theory will take.
> Here are some more facts to *shore up* your theory.
> Evolutionary theory won't *stand* or *fall* on the *strength* of that argument.
> So far we have only put together the *framework* of the theory.
> He *buttressed* his theory with *solid* arguments.

Lakoff and I argued that all of these (and other) conventional expressions cluster together under one basic metaphorical system of understanding: THEORIES ARE BUILDINGS. We examined several other important metaphors for the concept of ARGUMENT or THEORY CONSTRUCTION, such metaphors as ARGUMENT IS WAR, ARGUMENT IS A JOURNEY, AN ARGUMENT IS A CONTAINER, and so forth. Our central point was that metaphors of this sort are a chief means for understanding, in the rich way I defined it in the previous section. They organize our conventional language about arguments and theories because they constitute our understanding of argument, including how we will experience and carry on rational argument.

Lakoff and I explored a large number of representative domains of human experience (e.g., time, causation, spatial orientation, love, ideas, understanding, etc.) to indicate that the same kind of "conventional" metaphorical systems structure our understanding of virtually all domains of our experience. Numerous other studies have revealed the pervasiveness of metaphorical systems at this level of experience.[2] For my present purposes, the key point here is that human understanding involves metaphorical structures that blend all of the influences (bodily, perceptual, cultural, linguistic, historical, economic) that make up the fabric of our meaningful experience. Metaphor reaches down below the level of propositions into this massive embodied dimension of our being.

One could claim, of course, that there is no underlying reason why our literal expressions cluster in just the way they do, or why they involve terms that relate to underlying conventional metaphors for our culture. But I would reply that it is not an accident, or a lucky coincidence, that we use *support, construct, buttress, reinforce, lay the foundations for,* and other related terms when speaking of arguments and theories.

We do so because our cultural understanding of these realities is structured metaphorically (in this case, by the THEORIES ARE BUILDINGS metaphor). Thus, the hypothesis of underlying metaphorical systems of understanding makes it possible to explain what has hitherto remained unexplained, namely, the systematic clustering of literal expressions associated with a single concept.

Having offered evidence for the existence of such metaphorical systems of understanding, it remains only to show how they are connected up with image schemata. And this we have done by examining a few representative cases of metaphorical elaborations of image schemata. My claim is that, although both image schemata and metaphorical structures can be represented propositionally, no finitary proposition captures their continuous nature as structures of our understanding.

3. *Extensions of conventional metaphors.* In any metaphorical projection (e.g., THEORIES ARE BUILDINGS) only part of the structure of the source-domain (buildings) is typically projected onto the target-domain (theories). Lakoff and I have called this the "used" portion of the metaphor.[3] In THEORIES ARE BUILDINGS, for instance, the used part consists of the foundation and outer shell, from which the typical projected structures are drawn. Expressions such as "construct," "foundation," and "buttress" belong to this used portion, and they are therefore part of our ordinary literal language about theories. However, it is perfectly acceptable to draw on the unused portion of the metaphor by focusing on neglected aspects of the source-domain such as rooms, staircases, facades, and so forth. Thus, we get:

> His theories are Bauhaus in their pseudofunctional simplicity.
> He prefers massive Gothic theories covered with gargoyles.
> Complex theories usually have problems with the plumbing.

Such utilizations of the unused aspects of the source-domain are usually regarded as imaginative expressions rather than straightforward literal utterances. But they are readily comprehensible and fit with our ordinary understanding of theory construction. Lakoff and I suggested that there is a good explanation why such expressions make good sense, while other expressions about theories (e.g., "His theory has lice," "Don't iodize your theory") require the construction of unusual contexts if they are to make sense at all. The reason is that the acceptable expressions are based on the unused part of the source-domain of a pervasive metaphorical understanding in our culture, while the latter expressions are neither part of, nor coherent with, any of the basic metaphors for theories in our cultural understanding.

The fact that only certain expressions are appropriate in talking about theories, and the fact that extensions into the unused part of the source-domain generate permissible imaginative expressions for theory construction give evidence of the existence of such underlying metaphorical systems in our understanding. If there weren't such metaphors, we could not explain the appropriateness of the novel expressions.

4. *Polysemy*. To my mind, some of the strongest evidence for the existence of image schemata and their metaphorical elaborations is the phenomenon of polysemy, by which I mean not just multiple meanings for a single term but multiple *related* meanings. In Chapters 2–4 I examined several typical cases in which a single term (e.g., *out, must, may, can, balance*) has several related meanings, just because *there exists an underlying image schema that is metaphorically extended, typically from the physical domain to a nonphysical or more abstract domain.*

Once again, it is always possible to hold out for the homonymy position, which insists that there are multiple, but *unrelated*, meanings for a single term. But why, then, should we have come to use the *same* term for all of those different meanings. On the view I am supporting, the answer is quite simple: we use the same term because all of the senses are related. They are related because they share some underlying image schema, some extension of that schema, or some metaphorical projection of that schema. The evidence for this type of analysis of polysemy is rather compelling.[4] It points to the reality and indispensability of image-schematic structures that are extended in various figurative ways.

5. *Historical change*. Investigation of the way in which underlying metaphorical systems relate the various senses of polysemous terms has also suggested a new way of explaining diachronic semantic change. Sweetser[5] examined certain cases of semantic change over time to show that the nature and direction of the change can be explained (but not predicted) by means of culturally shared metaphors. In particular, she emphasizes the "general tendency to borrow concepts and vocabulary from the more accessible physical and social world to refer to the less accessible worlds of reasoning, emotion, and conversational structure."[6] If such metaphorical understandings do exist, then it would make sense that semantic change would manifest a general pattern, a movement from the more concrete and physical toward the more abstract and nonphysical.

There is ample evidence of just such a directionality of change. Furthermore, we can also explain why certain words would be used for certain concepts. To cite just one of her examples, consider why we should use chiefly the language of vision to conceptualize and talk about various intellectual activities, as in the following metaphorical system:

UNDERSTANDING IS SEEING
I *see* what you mean. The argument *looks* different from my *point of view*. What's your *outlook* on this project? Let me *point out* something to you in her argument. Tell me no more, I've *got the whole picture*. That's a very *clear* argument.

Sweetser identifies a basic metaphorical understanding of vision which leads to the connection of vision with intellectual activity.

VISION IS PHYSICAL TOUCHING/MANIPULATION
be*hold*, *catch* sight of
per*ceive* (Lat. -*cipio* "seize")
scrutinize (Lat. *scrutari* "pick through trash")
examine (Lat. *ex* + *agmen*- "pull out from a row")
discern (Lat. *dis-cerno* "separate")
see (**sek*ʷ-, which also gives Lat. *sequor* "follow")

Each of these vision terms involves physical perceptions or manipulations that come to have correlates in the domain of intellectual operations. When we *scrutinize an argument,* for example, we "pick through" it to determine its validity and correctness. When we *examine* a theory, we pull it out for special consideration. And when we *discern* the various stages of an argument, we separate off each successive stage in distinction from the others. Sweetser examines several Indo-European roots that originally referred to vision but which eventually developed meanings appropriate to *mental* operations. What emerges is a recurring pattern of metaphorical development from visual seeing to intellectual seeing.

Sweetser suggests three bases for this parallelism between vision and intellection: (i) Vision is our primary source of data about the world. It typically gives us far more information than any of the other senses, and it appears that children rely most heavily on visual features in their early categorization. In other words, vision plays a crucial role in our acquisition of knowledge. (ii) Vision involves the remarkable ability to focus at will on various features of our perceptual array, to pick out one object from a background, or to differentiate fine features. All of these operations have parallels in intellectual acts. (iii) Furthermore, vision is more or less identical for different people who can take up the same viewpoint. It thus seems to provide a basis for shared, public knowledge.

Perceptual phenomena of this sort make vision a primary candidate as a metaphorical basis for intellectual acts in which one must discriminate features, examine details, and perform mental operations that are held in common with other people. There are, of course, other experiential bases for knowledge metaphors (such as touching, hearing, and tasting), but none of these is as dominant as vision.

The assumption of underlying metaphorical systems of understanding allows us to differentiate natural and comprehensible directions of semantic change from those which are unnatural and do not make sense. The "natural" direction of change would be one based upon metaphorical structures of understanding of the sort we have been considering in this book. An example would be the development of new senses of a term by metaphorical extension of earlier senses, typically, with the projection from the more concrete or physical toward the more abstract or nonphysical. We would not be able to *predict* semantic change, but we could show how a certain change was motivated and natural in its direction.

In short, the direction, structure, and details of historical semantic change suggest the existence of shared metaphorical systems (e.g., UNDERSTANDING IS SEEING) in our understanding that are tied up with our bodily experience (perception, manipulation of objects, bodily movement). *If* there is any intelligibility to this change, then we have good reasons to think that metaphorical projections in our experience are central to the whole process.

6. *Metaphorical constraints on reasoning.* Finally, I want to consider experiments performed by Dedre and Donald Gentner to test the hypothesis that there really are analogical thought processes that structure our conceptual system.[7] Their use of the term "analogical model" is somewhat different from the sense of "metaphorical system" I have been exploring, but, for the purposes of their experiment, there are no important differences. Gentner and Gentner claim that in analogical reasoning we map features of the source-domain onto the target-domain via a metaphorical projection. The key issue is to determine *which* features are metaphorically transferred and which are left behind. There are two possible candidates that might be transferred: (a) *attributes,* such as "is wet" or "is cold," which are represented by predicates taking one argument (of the form WET[x]); and (b) *structural rela-*

tions, such as "revolves around," which are represented by predicates taking two arguments (of the form REVOLVES AROUND[x, y]).

Gentner and Gentner argue that in analogical reasoning we map *structural relations* holding among objects in the source domain onto the corresponding objects in the target domain. We do not map the particular *attributes* of those objects, which is the chief difference between metaphor and analogy, as they use the term. For example, in understanding the relation of an electron to its nucleus on analogy with the relation of a planet to its sun, the relevant mapping transfers selected structural features (e.g., ATTRACTS, REVOLVES AROUND, MORE MASSIVE THAN), but not particular attributes (e.g., the sun is *hot, massive,* and *yellow,* while the nucleus presumably has none of these properties).

Given this structure-mapping approach, Gentner and Gentner identified the two most common models that people use to explain electricity. The first is the *water-flow* analogy in which electric current is understood metaphorically as water flowing through a pipe. On this model we get the following common mappings from the base domain (hydraulic system) to the target domain (electrical circuit):

a) *Object mappings:* pipe maps to wire, pump maps to battery, narrow pipe maps to resistor.

b) *Property mappings:* PRESSURE of water maps to VOLTAGE, NARROWNESS of pipe maps to RESISTANCE, FLOW RATE maps to CURRENT OR FLOW RATE of electricity.

c) *Relations imported:* CONNECT (pipe, pump, narrow pipe) maps to CONNECT (wire, battery, resistor); INCREASE WITH (flow rate, pressure) maps to INCREASE WITH (current, voltage); DECREASE WITH (flow rate, narrowness) maps to DECREASE WITH (current, resistance).

The second basic model is the *moving-crowd* analogy, where the flow of electricity is understood as the movement of a crowd of individuals through passageways and narrow gates. We could generate a list of mappings like that given above for the *water-flow* model, based on the following foundational mappings: CURRENT corresponds to number of entities moving past a point per unit of time. VOLTAGE corresponds to the force with which the entities push their way along. RESISTORS correspond to narrow gates which slow the movement of the entities.

In the Gentner and Gentner experiments people were asked to solve basic problems concerning serial and parallel combinations of batteries and resistors. They were shown four wiring diagrams: batteries in serial order, batteries in parallel, resistors ordered serially, resistors in parallel. They were asked questions about whether such combinations would give *more, less,* or *the same* current. Let us consider the correct answers. For serial combinations we get a simple pattern: more batteries give more current and more resistors lead to less current. For parallel combinations the results are more tricky: parallel batteries generate the same current as a single battery, while parallel resistors lead to *more* current than a single resistor.

Given these facts, Gentner and Gentner predicted the following differences for the inference patterns, depending on the model employed:

1. *Fluid-flow model.* People using this model should perform best on the battery questions, since the battery combinations would be analogous to serial and parallel reservoirs. On the resistor problems, however, they would be expected to have more trouble, because people with the hydraulic model tend to view resistors as impediments, which, they think, will slow the flow of current. So they would be likely to think that two resistors slow the flow more than one (which is incorrect).

2. *Moving-crowd model.* Subjects with this model were expected to do less well on the battery problems, due to the absence of good analogs for batteries wired serially or in parallel. On the other hand, this model would seem to work quite well on the resistor problems, since resistors can be viewed as narrow gates. One would conclude, correctly, that parallel resistors increase current (adding more gates lets more entities through), while serial ordering reduces the current.

Were these predictions confirmed? In general, yes, but with certain qualifications. There were two experiments, one in which subjects were asked to solve the problems and then to report on how they did so, and the second in which subjects were taught one of the two models (including two versions of the *fluid-flow* model) and asked to apply them to the problems. In the first experiment the results were clear and unambiguous. Subjects with the *fluid-flow* model did best on the battery problems, while those with the *moving-crowd* model did better on the resistor problems. In the second experiment subjects with the *moving-crowd* model handled the resistor problems better than those who were taught either of the *fluid* models. However, there was no significant difference for any of the models in solving the battery problems. The anticipated superiority of the *fluid* models was not confirmed. The reason for this seems quite clear: most people do not adequately understand fluid dynamics in the first place, so they cannot make the appropriate metaphorical projections to draw the proper conclusions. Unless you know how the height of fluid in reservoirs affects flow and pressure, you cannot calculate the results of serial versus parallel combinations.

For our purposes, however, the results of these experiments are relatively unproblematic. What they show is that people draw definite inferences based on their underlying metaphorical conceptions of the domain they are investigating. And the first experiment shows that people do use image-schematic models and operations to understand various domains of experience and to solve problems. When we understand the behavior of electrical circuits by projecting structural relations from the domain of hydraulic systems, we are led to specific inferences about the target-domain. Thus, metaphorical structures of understanding *do* constrain some of our reasoning processes, both when we are consciously reflecting on our models (experiment 2) and when we are employing them in a less reflective fashion.

Someone who presupposes a strict theory/practice separation might argue that these experiments show only an obvious fact—that humans use different models to apply their knowledge. But these are not just cases of "application" of independently existing knowledge. I am suggesting the stronger thesis that such models *constitute* an individual's understanding of a phenomenon and thereby influence their acts of inference. The metaphors, or analogies, are not merely convenient economies for expressing our knowledge; rather, they *are* our knowledge and understanding of the particular phenomena in question.

How Image Schemata Constrain Metaphorical Projections

Throughout this book I have analyzed cases in which metaphorical structures in our understanding are the basis for meaning relations and for inferential patterns in our reasoning. For this to be the case, there must be sufficient internal structure to these metaphorical systems to permit specific inferences. We must answer the charge that metaphors are too ambiguous, too lacking in internal structure, to constrain our reasoning. To respond to this criticism, I want to consider more fully the internal structure of certain basic source-domains that determine the nature of metaphorical projections.

It is well beyond the scope of this book to survey the full range of possible source-domains, to explore their structure, and to show how they can be mapped onto various target-domains. I have done this in a partial way for a few instances, such as metaphors based on image schemata for CONTAINMENT, FORCE, and BALANCE. In this section I want to examine, in addition, the schemata for PATHS, CYCLES, SCALES, LINKS, and CENTER-PERIPHERY to identify the internal structure of each image schema as it maps onto the target-domain in various related metaphors. The central problem in each case is always to identify the structure of the source-domain that constrains the metaphorical mapping onto a target-domain. In this way one is able to show that metaphorical projections are not arbitrary (i.e., that not just anything can be mapped onto anything else), and that they do influence our reasoning.

Basically, what we are interested in is why certain metaphorical mappings exist, that is, why certain source-domains get mapped onto certain target-domains. And we also want to know what constraints govern the nature of the metaphorical mapping.[8] In general, to explain how specific metaphorical projections constrain meaning relations and patterns of inference, we need to explore the structure of the image schemata upon which they are based, and we need to determine why the particular mappings of source-domains onto target-domains occur the way they do. In the remainder of this section, then, I want to consider a few additional image schemata that play prominent roles in recurring metaphorical projections. I will begin with a relatively detailed treatment of the PATH schema as it constrains one pervasive metaphorical projection in our understanding, and I will describe much more briefly the structure of a few other experientially basic image schemata.

Paths

Our lives are filled with paths that connect up our spatial world. There is the path from your bed to the bathroom, from the stove to the kitchen table, from your house to the grocery store, from San Francisco to Los Angeles, and from the Earth to the Moon. Some of these paths involve an actual physical surface that you traverse, such as the path from your house to the store. Others involve a projected path, such as the path of a bullet shot into the air. And certain paths exist, at present, only in your imagination, such as the path from Earth to the nearest star outside our solar system.

In all of these cases there is a single, recurring image-schematic pattern with a definite internal structure. In every case of PATHS there are always the same parts: (1) a source, or starting point; (2) a goal, or endpoint; and (3) a sequence of contiguous locations connecting the source with the goal. Paths are thus routes for moving from one point to another.

PATH

As a consequence of these parts and their relations, our image schema for PATH has certain typical characteristics. (a) Because the beginning and end points of a path are connected by a series of contiguous locations, it follows that, if you start at point A and move along a path to a further point B, then you have passed through all the intermediate points in between. (b) We can impose directionality on a path. Paths are not inherently directional—a path connecting point A with point B does not necessarily go in one direction. But human beings have purposes in traversing paths, so they tend to experience them as directional. That is, we move along a path *from* point A *toward* point B. (c) Paths can have temporal dimensions mapped onto them. I start at point A (the source) at time T_1, and move to point B (the goal) at time T_2. In this way, there is a time line mapped onto the path. It follows that, if point B is further down the path than point A, and I have reached point B is moving along the path, then I am at a later time than when I began. Such a linear spatialization of time gives rise to one important way we understand temporality.

This definite internal structure for our PATH schema provides the basis for a large number of metaphorical mappings from concrete, spatial domains onto more abstract domains. Let us examine the way the PATH schema grounds the metaphor PURPOSES ARE PHYSICAL GOALS. Here *goals* are understood as end points toward which my various physical actions can be directed. In the metaphor we are thus understanding very abstract *purposes* (such as writing a book, getting a Ph.D., finding happiness) in terms of the performance of various physical acts in reaching a spatial goal.

What possible experiential grounding could give rise to this particular metaphorical structure? The PURPOSES ARE PHYSICAL GOALS metaphor is based on the PATH schema and the metaphor STATES ARE LOCATIONS, according to the following mapping:

Starting location onto initial state.
Goal (final location) onto final state.
Motion along path onto intermediate actions.

Based upon this mapping of structures of concrete physical achievement of a goal onto the abstract domain of achieving a purpose in general, we can have a large range of linguistic expressions:

PURPOSES ARE PHYSICAL GOALS

Tom has *gone a long way* toward changing his personality. You have *reached the midpoint* of your flight training. I've got *quite a way to go* before I get my Ph.D. She's just *starting out* to make her fortune. Jane was *sidetracked* in her search for self-understanding. Follow me—this is *the path* to genuine happiness. You'll never achieve salvation unless you *change your course*.

In these cases of abstract purposes, we understand our progress in terms of the metaphorical interpretation of the PATH schema by mapping *states* onto *physical locations*. Once again, we can ask why this mapping occurs in the way that it does. The answer seems to be that there is a basic correlation in our experience, which gives rise to the metaphor.

Consider the common goal of getting to a particular location. From the time we can first crawl, we regularly have as an intention getting to some particular place, whether for its own sake, or as a subgoal that makes possible some other activity at that place. There may well be no intention satisfied more often than physical motion to a particular desired location. In such cases, we have a *purpose*—being in that location—that is satisfied by moving our bodies from a starting point A, through an intermediate sequence of spatial locations, to the end point B.

Here there is an identity between the domain of intention (or purpose) and the physical domain. In the domain of intention there is an initial state, where the intention is not satisfied, a sequence of actions, and a final state where the intention is satisfied. Thus, there is a correlation in our experience, in which structure in the intentional domain is paired with structure in the physical domain.

> Initial state = location A.
> Final (desired) state = location B.
> Action sequence = movement from A to B.

This special case of a pairing of purposes with physical functioning is not itself metaphorical but sets constraints on the structure and entailments of the PURPOSES ARE PHYSICAL GOALS metaphor. This, of course, is an extremely important special case, since the metaphor it establishes is used constantly over and over, every day, and is absolutely vital to our successful functioning.

Let us compare this recurrent experiential pairing of purpose and physical motion, on the one hand, with the metaphor used to understand purposes in general, on the other. There is an isomorphism between the pairing and the metaphor. Each equality statement in the pairing corresponds to a mapping statement in the metaphor.

The experiential pairing constrains the metaphor in two ways. First, it constrains the choice of source- and target-domains. MOTION ALONG A PATH is the source-domain. ACHIEVEMENT OF PURPOSE is the target-domain. Second, the experiential pairing constrains which elements of the source-domain get mapped onto which elements of the target-domain. That is, the metaphorical mapping is isomorphic with the experiential pairing.

This is what is meant by saying that a correspondence in experience serves as the basis for a metaphor. What we have here is a case where an abstract domain, the domain of purpose in general, is understood via metaphor. But the metaphor is anything but arbitrary and unstructured. Its structure is based on the structure of the source-domain, which involves the PATH schema. The details of the mapping are constrained by a pairing that recurs so often in our experience that we hardly notice that it exists. It is the isomorphism between the structure of that pairing and the structure of the metaphor that allows us to understand abstract purpose in terms of motion along a path. Once again, this understanding is so natural, so pervasive, and so immediate that we hardly notice it.

This example shows the kind of account that is required to explain the nature of, and constraints on, metaphorical understanding. Recall that we had to answer three questions:

(1) What determines the choice of a possible well-structured source-domain?

(2) What determines the pairing of the source-domain with the target-domain?

(3) What determines the details of the source-to-target mapping?

Let us sum up the answers to these questions that emerge from the details of our analysis of the PURPOSES ARE PHYSICAL GOALS metaphor:

(1) The PATH schema is one of the most common structures that emerges from our constant bodily functioning. This schema has all the qualifications a schema should have to serve as the source domain of a metaphor. It is (a) pervasive in experience, (b) well-understood because it is pervasive, (c) well-structured, (d) simply structured, and (e) emergent and well-demarcated by virtue of (a)–(d). In fact (a)–(d) provide some criteria for what it means for a structure to be emergent and salient as a gestalt structure in our experience.

2. There is an experiential correlation between the source-domain (motion along a path to a physical location) and the target-domain

(achievement of a purpose). This correlation made the mapping from the source to the target domain natural.

3. The details of the mapping are governed by the details of the experiential correlation. The cross–domain correlations in the experiential pairing (e.g., desired state with final location) determine the details of the metaphorical mapping. The result is an isomorphism in which the structure of the PATH schema determines the basic character of the metaphorical projection.

To give a comprehensive analysis of the PATH schema and its role in our understanding would require a book-length study. We have examined only part of the PURPOSES ARE PHYSICAL GOALS metaphor, which is but one of several important metaphors constrained by the PATH schema. In our culture, for example, we have a metaphorical understanding of the passage of time based on movement along a physical path. We understand mental activities or operations that result in some determinate outcome according to the PATH schema. And we understand the course of processes in general metaphorically as movement along a path toward some end point. Obviously, it would be impossible to do justice to the PATH schema in the present treatment; however, I have tried to exemplify the type of analysis that would be required to show how various image schemata provide structure that constrains metaphorical projections in our understanding and reasoning.

In the rest of this section, I shall not even attempt to elaborate various metaphorical extensions of the schemata under consideration; instead, I offer only a brief description of a few of the most pervasive image-schematic structures in our understanding. For each image schema I explore (a) its pervasiveness in our experience, (b) its internal structure, and (c) the range of metaphorical elaborations of it in our understanding of more abstract domains.

Links

Without links, we could neither be nor be human. We come into existence tethered to our biological mothers by umbilical cords that nourish and sustain us. But this merely physical linking is never the full story of our humanity, which requires a certain nonphysical linking to our parents, our siblings, and our society as a whole. The severing of the umbilical cord launches us into an ongoing process of linking, bonding, and connecting that gives us our identity.

The combination of our perceptual capacities and the circumstances of our perceptual environment gives rise to a massive, interwoven complex of concrete and abstract linkages. To begin with, we experi-

ence the *coupling of physical objects:* two pieces of wood are nailed together, the child holds the parent's hand, the snaps on the child's coat
are connected, the lamp is plugged into the wall socket. In these simple
physical cases there is a spatial contiguity and closeness of the linked
objects, and the connected objects are related via the link.

Linkages are not only physical and spatial. As the child develops it
learns to experience *temporal connections*. Event A is linked to event B
by a series of temporally interceding events. Instead of an actual physical bond, the events are linked because we *experience* them as temporally related, as somehow being part of the same temporal sequence.

Given such temporal relatedness, we can experience *causal connection*
between temporally linked events. Even where we do not experience
the causal linking, we understand our world as a connected and coherent expanse held together by networks of causal connection. A *network* (causal or otherwise) is nothing more than a set of links. Without
such causal conjunction we could never experience our world as a relatively comprehensible place.

Genetic connections are specifications of the causal network in which
one or more objects are related to (connected with) a source. In its biological manifestation the offspring is dependent for its existence upon
some other physical being. Two or more offspring get connected indirectly via their link to a common source.

Another instance of causal relatedness is the *functional linking* of
parts or entities. One object may be intrinsically unrelated to another,
yet they can become connected by virtue of their relation within a
functional unity. Linking is a fundamental way of forming unities, of
which functional assemblies are a prominent type.

Links in our spatial and temporal experience thus share a common
schematic structure of the sort shown in figure 21. In its simplest
manifestation the internal structure of the LINK schema consists of two
entities (A and B) connected by a bonding structure. Typically, those
entities are spatially contiguous within our perceptual field. Extended
cases might involve many related entities (rather than merely two) and
might include spatially and temporally discontinuous or noncontigu-
ous entities (as in "action-at-a-distance").

The simple LINK schema makes possible our perception of *similarity*.

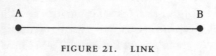

A   B

FIGURE 21.   LINK

Two or more objects are similar be⟨ ⟩use they share some feature or features. Those shared features are their cognitive links in our understanding. Here, obviously, we have a highly abstract notion of linkage, in which the "third thing" that binds or relates two objects is a perceptual or logical feature. The LINK schema must be metaphorically interpreted to apply to abstract objects or connections, since there is no actual physical bond of the required sort to relate the objects.

There are two basic sorts of metaphorical interpretations of the LINK schema. If the link is interpreted abstractly, we have an instance of similarity relations or functional unities. Two or more objects might be related, for instance, by sharing the abstract metaphorical link of "solubility" or "compressibility." If the entities are also interpreted abstractly, we have the notion of formal or abstract systems or networks. In logical systems, for example, "logical entities" (such as predicates or propositions) can be related via "logical connectives" ("and," "but," "or," "if-then") in acts of intellectual linking. In this fashion, the metaphorical elaboration of the LINK schema is one of the primary ways in which we are able to establish connectedness in our understanding.

Cycles

We come into existence as the culmination of a reproductive cycle. Our bodily maintenance depends upon the regular recurrence of complex interacting cycles: heartbeat, breathing, digestion, menstruation, waking and sleeping, circulation, emotional build-up followed by release, etc. We experience our world and everything in it as embedded within cyclic processes: day and night, the seasons, the course of life (birth through death), the stages of development in plants and animals, the revolutions of the heavenly bodies.

Most fundamentally, a cycle is a temporal circle. The cycle begins with some initial state, proceeds through a sequence of connected events, and ends where it began, to start anew the recurring cyclic pattern. The simplest CYCLE schema is thus represented by a circular motion (fig. 22). The circle represents the return to the original state. The cycle moves in one direction from start to finish in a forward-moving sequence of temporally related events. Backtracking is not permitted, so that once a certain stage in a cycle is passed through it is not repeated in that cycle.

This circular representation of the CYCLE is inadequate insofar as it fails to include a salient dimension in our experience of cycles, namely, their climactic structure. For us, life patterns do not simply repeat; they exhibit a character of build-up and release. In some natural cases

FIGURE 22.   CYCLE

this pattern is in the cycle itself, such as the build-up of sexual or emotional tension followed by a release, or the course of an illness that gradually drains our energy before we recover and return to our former "healthy" state. This climactic structure of the cycle is perhaps best represented by the sine wave with its periodic "rise" and "fall" (see fig. 23). It is important to see that this climactic pattern is typically *imposed* by us. The yearly cycle has no intrinsic high point, but we tend to experience it as having a nadir (winter) which builds to the heights of summer (or spring?). Likewise, we experience the life cycle as moving from birth to the fullness of maturation followed by a decline toward death.

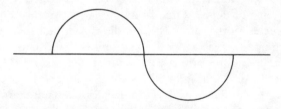

FIGURE 23.   CYCLIC CLIMAX

In addition to our natural cycles, our reality is structured by a mass of overlapping, interwoven, and sometimes conflicting *conventional* cycles. Zerubavel has explored the nature of these conventional cycles in great detail.[9] They include our weekly cycle and others our society and culture impose upon time in the name of business, politics, religion, social welfare, and so forth. Connelly and Clandinin[10] have followed Zerubavel's lead in a study of the cycles in schooling (e.g., annual, holiday, monthly, weekly, six-day, duty, daily, report, and within-class). The following set of recurring features of conventional cycles emerges from these studies:

i) Cycles constitute temporal boundaries for our activities, and these tend to be extremely rigid in most cases. Although these boundaries may be "invisible," their reality and rigidity is evident whenever we trespass or bump against those hidden boundaries, such as occurs in attempts to lengthen the school day cycle or to shorten the week to five days (an experiment that failed miserably in the Soviet Union).

ii) Cycles are multiple, overlapping, and sequential. Our temporal existence is defined by the distinctive set of cyclical patterns in which we find ourselves embedded. Such cycles may be differentiated temporally (hour, day, week, month, etc.) or functionally (e.g., cycles for nurses vs. doctors vs. orderlies in a hospital). In addition, any set of cycles will involve partial overlapping (e.g., hospital duty cycles) and will exhibit both harmonious and conflicting relations.

iii) Cycles can be quantitatively measured according to various mathematics of time, but they will also have a certain qualitative differentiation. Zerubavel shows that the "night" and "day" cycles are experienced in qualitatively different ways by their participants, and that "weekend" cycles have a different character than "weekday" cycles. Thus, to be fair, hospitals must work out complex schedules to balance these qualitative differences.

iv) Finally, there is a difference between "natural" and "conventional" cycles. Zerubavel argues that conventional cycles seldom have any natural basis; however, they can become so pervasive that they come to define the character of our experience.

The upshot of this for our purposes is that, whether in the simple *circular* form, or in the sine-wave representation with its imposed climactic character, the CYCLE schema manifests a definite recurring internal structure. This structure constitutes one of our most basic patterns for experiencing and understanding temporality. It provides us a way of understanding an enormous range of event sequences and, metaphorically interpreted, even nontemporal sequences such as numbers.

Scales

Consider the metaphor MORE IS UP which organizes a large number of our linguistic expressions that concern *amount*.

MORE IS UP

The crime rate keeps *rising*. The number of books published *goes up and up* each year. That stock has *fallen* again. You'll get a *higher* interest rate with them. Our sales *dropped* last year. Our financial reserves couldn't be any *lower*.

Why is AMOUNT based on *verticality* rather than on containment, balance, force, or some other important schema? And why is MORE mapped onto UP rather than onto DOWN? Why do *these* specific mappings occur, when there are so many other possibilities?

As I suggested in the Preface, the answer is that there are certain basic correlations of structures in our experience that give rise to metaphorical projections of this sort. When we add *more* of a substance to a pile or container, the level *rises*. This particular metaphor is not based on similarity, since there are no relevant similarities between MORE and UP. Instead, it is based on a correlation in our experience, of the sort just mentioned. The fact of this experiential correlation is not trivial, since it makes possible an important structuring of our concept of AMOUNT.

The MORE IS UP metaphor is based on, or is an instance of, what I shall call the SCALE schema. The SCALE schema is basic to both the quantitative and qualitative aspects of our experience. With respect to the *quantitative* aspects, we experience our world as populated with discrete objects that we can group in various ways and substances whose amount we can increase and decrease. We can add objects to a group or pile, and we can take objects away. We can add more of a substance to a pile or container, and we can take it away. With respect to the *qualitative* aspects, we experience objects and events as having certain degrees of intensity. One light is brighter than another, one potato is hotter than another, one blue is deeper than another, and one pain is more intense than another.

To sum up, from one perspective, we can view our world as a massive expanse of quantitative amount and qualitative degree or intensity. Our world is experienced partly in terms of *more, less,* and *the same.* We can have more, less, or the same *number* of objects, *amount* of substance, *degree* of force, or *intensity* of sensation. This "more" or "less" aspect of human experience is the basis of the SCALE schema.

The SCALE schema can be represented rather inadequately by means of a modified PATH schema, as in figure 24. The SCALE schema can be roughly differentiated from the PATH schema on several points:

i) the SCALE schema has a more or less fixed directionality. I have already explained why it seems natural to correlate MORE with UP. Normally, the further along the scale one moves, the greater the amount or intensity. Paths, by contrast, are not inherently directional, though we tend to impose directionality upon them, depending upon our point of view or location.

ii) Scales have a cumulative character of a special sort. If you are collecting money and have accumulated $15, then you also have $10. But this does not usually hold for progress along a path; if you pass

FIGURE 24.   SCALE

through point A and arrive at point B, then you are no longer at point A (point A is not carried along into the present position).

iii) SCALES are typically given a normative character; PATHS are not. Having more or less of something may be either good or bad, desirable or undesirable. Having more heat in the winter can be desirable, while having more heat in the summer might be awful. In either case, however, norms are mapped on to the scale.

iv) A final feature is shared by both the SCALE and PATH schemata: they can be either closed or open. The path or scale may continue indefinitely in one direction, or it may terminate at a definite point. In the case of SCALES this point establishes the upper limit of quantity, intensity, or degree (e.g., 10 on the Richter scale, 100% on a grading scale, etc.).

One other aspect of SCALES that is extremely important in our culture is the possibility of imposing numerical gradients on a scale. We can calibrate scales in terms of regular, discrete fixed units of measurement. This simple fact has made possible activities of measurement, quantification, and prediction that have come to define part of the distinctive character of Western civilization. As an extreme manifestation of this tendency, the Pythagoreans of ancient Greece were enticed by the apparent susceptibility of every aspect of physical experience to numerical description into drawing the radical conclusion that *the Real is Number.*

At any rate, SCALARITY does seem to permeate the whole of human experience, even where no precise quantitative measurement is possible. Consequently, this experientially basic, value-laden structure of our grasp of both concrete and abstract entities is one of the most pervasive image-schematic structures in our understanding. The image schema which emerges in our experience of concrete, physical entities is figuratively extended to cover abstract entities of every sort (numbers, properties, relations, geometric structures, entities in economic models, etc.). On the basis of these metaphorical extensions we are able to comprehend virtually every aspect of our experience in terms of SCALARITY.

Center-Periphery

The fact of our physical embodiment gives a very definite character to our perceptual experience. Our world radiates out from *our bodies* as perceptual centers from which we see, hear, touch, taste, and smell our world. Our perceptual space defines a domain of macroscopic objects that reside at varying distances from us. From our central vantage point we can focus our attention on one object or perceptual field after another as we scan our world. What is "figure" or "foreground" at one moment may become "background" at another, as we move perceptually through our world. At a certain distance from this perceptual center our world "fades off" into a perceptual horizon which no longer presents us with discrete objects. We may move in one direction toward the horizon, thus opening up new perceptual territory, but this only establishes new horizons presently beyond our grasp.

What I have just described is the contour of the CENTER-PERIPHERY schema, which can be represented by figure 25. The center-point represents my perceptual and experiential center which defines my experiential space and fades off into my horizon (wavy line).

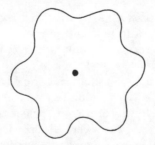

FIGURE 25.   CENTER-PERIPHERY

So far we have spoken of the CENTER-PERIPHERY schema as though it were totally a matter of perceptual space. But, obviously, the schema is a recurrent structure in my *experiential space.* In my "world" some things, events, and persons are more important than others—they loom larger in my experience and are more central to my interactions. Others are relatively peripheral at a given point in time. One's spouse, lover, or friend are more central forces in my interactional world. Understood in this way, we have already moved metaphorically to a more abstract interpretation of the CENTER-PERIPHERY schema. It shows itself not only in the structure of my perceptual field but equally important as a structure of my social, economic, political, religious, and philosophical world. Those "objects" that stand forth as significant in my experiential field are both concrete *and* abstract entities toward which my interest is directed. Even more abstractly, we can say that all of our understanding exhibits a horizonal contour.[11] For our purposes, the key point is that the nature of our bodies, the constraints on our perception, and the structure of our consciousness give prominence to the CENTER-PERIPHERY organization of our experienced reality.

The CENTER-PERIPHERY schema is almost never experienced in an isolated or self-contained fashion; instead, a number of other schemata are superimposed upon it to define my orientation toward my world. To name just a few: (i) Given a center and a periphery we will experience the NEAR-FAR schema as stretching out along our perceptual or conceptual perspective. What is considered near will depend upon the context, but, once that is established, a SCALE is defined for determining relative nearness to the center. (ii) We almost always superimpose a CONTAINER schema on our CENTER-PERIPHERY orientation. Where we draw the bounding container will depend upon our purposes, interests, perceptual capacities, conceptual system, and values. But we tend to define both our physical and mental identities by virtue of their containment (within "bodies" and "minds"). (iii) When such a CONTAINER schema is superimposed we experience the center as *inner* and define the *outer* relative to it. Likewise, we perceive this same INNER-OUTER orientation for objects existing in our perceptual field, and, by extension, to certain abstract objects (e.g., models, theories, geometrical figures). (iv) The INNER-OUTER pattern also supports the imposition of a SUBJECT-OBJECT orientation, in which our subjectivity is defined in terms of that which is inmost or central to our conscious being. (v) This "inmost" dimension gives rise, in turn, to a SELF-OTHER distinction, which can have the MINE-THINE valuation imposed upon it.

In this way, by superimposition of schematic structures, which can be metaphorically understood at a number of different levels, we develop a host of complex meaning structures central to our experience and understanding.

Other Basic Schemata

By virtue of such superimpositions our world begins to take shape as a highly structured, value-laden, and personalized realm in which we feel the pull of our desires, pursue our ends, cope with our frustra-

tions, and celebrate our joys. Much of the structure, value, and purposiveness we take for granted as built into our world consists chiefly
of interwoven and superimposed schemata of the sort just described.
*My chief point has been to show that these image schemata are pervasive,
well-defined, and full of sufficient internal structure to constrain our understanding and reasoning.* To give some idea of the extent of the image-
schematic structuring of our understanding (as our mode of being-in-
the-world or our way of having-a-world), consider the following partial list of schemata, which includes those previously discussed:

CONTAINER	BALANCE	COMPULSION
BLOCKAGE	COUNTERFORCE	RESTRAINT REMOVAL
ENABLEMENT	ATTRACTION	MASS–COUNT
PATH	LINK	CENTER–PERIPHERY
CYCLE	NEAR–FAR	SCALE
PART–WHOLE	MERGING	SPLITTING
FULL–EMPTY	MATCHING	SUPERIMPOSITION
ITERATION	CONTACT	PROCESS
SURFACE	OBJECT	COLLECTION

This brief list is highly selective, but it includes what I take to be
most of the more important image schemata. If one understands
"schema" more loosely than I do, it might be possible to extend this
list at length. The architect Christopher Alexander, for example, has
developed an account of some 253 recurring "patterns" that influence
our experience.[12] The central notion is that of a "unitary pattern of activity and space, which repeats itself over and over again, in any given
place, always appearing each time in a slightly different manifestation."[13] Alexander's patterns cover an enormous range of experiential
structures, from the grand scale (AGRICULTURAL VALLEYS, INDEPENDENT
REGIONS) to a smaller scale (POSITIVE OUTDOOR SPACE, SUNNY PLACE,
NATURAL DOORS AND WINDOWS) down to small areas (POOLS OF LIGHT,
WARM COLORS, TREE PLACES). Most of Alexander's patterns are not image schematic, in my sense, and would require a somewhat different
kind of analysis than the ones given above.

There is clearly nothing sacred about 253 patterns versus 53 or any
other number of patterns, but it is certain that we experience our world
by means of various image-schematic structures whose relations make
up the fabric of our experience, that is, of our understanding. I have
surveyed *some* of the internal structure of a few prominent image schemata to show that they are sufficiently structured to constrain our
understanding and reasoning.

Image-schematic and Metaphorical Constraints on Reasoning[14]

Throughout this chapter I have been trying to show that image schemata and metaphorical structures based on them are not internally "mushy"; on the contrary, they are one of the chief means by which our understanding is structured to give us a more or less comprehensible, patterned world that we can partially make sense of and function within. My examples so far have been isolated image schemata and metaphors taken out of their rich contexts (and thereby distorted in important ways). I now want to consider a much more extended, realistic (and, consequently, messy) case of understanding and inferences based on metaphorical systems. The case involves Hans Selye's lifelong research into the nature of stress reactions, which led him to infer a new model of disease and new strategies for the treatment of disease. My analysis is meant to show that metaphorical systems of understanding are sufficiently rich in internal structure to generate definite inferential patterns. Reasoning based on metaphors, I shall argue, is neither arbitrary nor unstructured.

Hans Selye is the founder of modern stress research. He was the first to define stress as a biological syndrome, as a general reaction to some shock to an organism's system:

Experiments on rats show that if the organism is severely damaged by acute non-specific nocuous agents such as exposure to cold, surgical injury, production of spinal shock . . . a typical syndrome appears, the symptoms of which are independent of the nature of the damaging agent . . . and represent rather a response to damage as such.[15]

This syndrome is the manifestation of a state Selye labeled "stress," which includes all the specific changes induced within the biological system of an organism. The agent of this state of stress is labeled the "stressor." Selye's main thesis is that stress is a general reaction that occurs in response to a variety of different stimuli, and which is characterized by a general increase in the production of certain hormones from the pituitary and adrenal glands that strengthen bodily defenses against stressors.

Selye saw the stress reaction as an adaptive syndrome (the General Adaptation Syndrome) of the organism in response to external stressors. The GAS consists of three phases. Confronted with some stressor, the organism enters the first phase, the *alarm reaction,* in which overall resistance to the stressor initially decreases, although bodily defenses, such as inflammation, are mobilized. This leads to the second stage, *resistance,* in which the organism adapts to the presence of the stressor and maintains itself. In short, it goes to war against the stressor. However, each organism has only a limited capacity to adapt and to fight, since its resources are eventually depleted, leading to the third stage, *exhaustion,* where the organism breaks down or dies. This view of stress response as developed by Selye is, with a variety of refinements, still widely accepted.

Given this general background, let us return to the beginning of Selye's research to examine the underlying metaphorical systems out of which it developed. In this way we can identify various inferential patterns grounded in metaphorical structures of understanding for a given domain of experience.

The first important event reported by Selye in his discovery of stress occurred during his first course in internal medicine at the University of Prague in 1925.[16] In several encounters with patients suffering the early stages of various infectious diseases, Selye was impressed by a collection of symptoms ignored by his professor. As one patient after another was brought into the lecture room, they all seemed to Selye to share a large number of symptoms: coated tongue, aches and pains in the joints, intestinal distress, loss of appetite, and in many cases fever, enlarged spleen or liver, inflamed tonsils, and skin rash, etc. Since these symptoms were common to many different diseases, they were of no interest to Selye's professor, because they did not fit the accepted models of disease and bodily function (which looked for *specific* causes for *specific* or *unique* symptoms). Furthermore, these *general* or *pervasive* symptoms could not be used to establish a definite, specific, unique diagnosis. Still, Selye was intrigued by the fact that so many symptoms were common to so many diseases. Although this realization made a strong impression upon him, the pressures of the medical curriculum forced Selye to direct his attention to more orthodox matters.

It was not until several years later, when he ran into trouble with his sex hormone research, that Selye recalled his earlier classroom puzzlement with the cluster of nonspecific symptoms. Now a young researcher, Selye believed that he was close to discovering a new sex hormone. When he injected rats with various ovarian and placental extracts to check for organ changes, he consistently found enlargement of the adrenal cortex, shrinking of the thymus, spleen, lymph nodes, and all other lymphatic structures, plus stomach and intestinal ulcers. Selye's hypothesis was that this cluster of symptoms was caused by an as-yet-undiscovered ovarian hormone.

In testing his hypothesis further, he found to his dismay that injections of pituitary, kidney, and spleen extracts produced the *same* cluster of symptoms. This result was devastating to his hypothesis, because these organs were thought not to produce sex hormones. It occurred to Selye that the observed symptoms might be due not to any hormonal activity but to the impurity of his extracts. In order to test this conjecture he injected a (toxic) formalin solution into his laboratory animals. As he feared, the same cluster of symptoms was produced.

It was at this point that the dejected Selye began to glimpse a new way to understand these phenomena:

As I repetitiously continued to go over my ill-fated experiments and their possible interpretation, it suddenly struck me that one could look at them from a different angle. If there was such a thing as a single nonspecific reaction of the body to damage of any kind, this might be worth study for its own sake. Indeed, working out the mechanism of this kind of stereotyped "syndrome of response to injury as such" might be much more important to medicine than the discovery of yet another sex hormone.

As I repeated to myself, "a syndrome of response to injury as such," gradually, my early classroom impressions of the clinical "syndrome of just being sick" began to reappear dimly out of my subconsciousness, where they had been buried for over a decade. Could it be that this syndrome in man (the feeling of being ill, the diffuse pains in the joints and muscles, the intestinal disturbances with loss of appetite, the loss of weight) were in some manner clinical equivalents of the experimental syndrome, the triad (adrenocortical stimulation, thymicolymphatic atrophy, intestinal ulcers) that I had produced with such a variety of toxic substances in the rat?[17]

What Selye began to see was the possibility of a general, *nonspecific, nonunique* reaction pattern to any number of stressors of various sorts.

What we are witnessing here is a change in the basic metaphorical structuring of Selye's understanding. He moved, I suggest, from one dominant metaphorical grasp of the situation, namely, BODY AS MACHINE (and thus not organic or homeostatic), to a novel understanding, that of BODY AS HOMEOSTATIC ORGANISM. When Selye began his research project he operated under the influence of the BODY AS MACHINE metaphors that he had acquired in medical school.[18] There he had assimilated a model of the human organism (i.e., as MACHINE) that came to control every aspect of his practice, such as his range of possible diagnoses, what he looked for in examining patients, what his treatment options were, and what his research focused on.

Under the head metaphor (BODY AS MACHINE) there are, of course, several interlocking subsidiary metaphors that contributed to the structuring of Selye's medical experience, metaphors such as those of isolated parts, functional assemblies, and repair and replacement of malfunctioning units. For example, the prevalent attitude at that time conceived the goals of surgery as repair of injuries and exturpation of diseased areas. Later in the twentieth century, when Cannon's theory of homeostasis became generally accepted (i.e., that various body functions exist to preserve certain functional equilibria), there would be a correlative change of attitude toward the goals of surgery, which came then to be seen as a way to restore the body's functional balances (homeostasis) by surgical intervention.

The key point in all of this is that the BODY AS MACHINE metaphor was not merely an isolated belief; rather, it was a massive experiential structuring that involved values, interests, goals, practices, and theorizing. What we see is that such metaphorical structurings of experience have very definite systematically related entailments. For instance, consider a small selection of the extensive range of such values, discriminations, expectations, and practices that are potentially tied up with the metaphor:

THE BODY IS A MACHINE
The body consists of distinct, though interconnected parts.
It is a functional unity or assembly serving various purposes.
It requires an energy source or force to get it operating.
Breakdown consists in the malfunctioning of parts.
Breakdowns occur at specific points or junctures in the mechanism.
Diagnosis requires that we locate these malfunctioning units.
Treatment directs itself to specific faulty units or connections.
Repair (treatment) may involve replacement, mending, alteration of parts, and so forth.
Since parts causally interact, we must be alert for failures in causal connections.
The parts of the functioning unity are not themselves self-adapting.

For someone whose understanding (i.e., whose experience) is structured by the BODY AS MACHINE metaphor, it is entailments like these that influence his or her perception, diagnosis, treatment, theorizing, and other practices. Such entailments *constitute* one's grasp of the medical situation at hand. Even though they are here represented propositionally, they actually involve patterns of discernment (both visual and epistemic), certain skills (nonpropositional), and various activities and operations. For example, it is an entailment of the MACHINE metaphor that when the physician examines a patient the physician will see certain things and miss others. One "learns to look" for certain clues and marks and thereby comes to filter out other factors as irrelevant. Thus, when Selye was in medical school and when he first started his research, any injuries or diseases were thought to be accompanied by a *specific* or *unique* set of essential characteristics or symptoms, since under the BODY AS MACHINE metaphor disease was understood and experienced as the breakdown of a specific part or as an invasion by a foreign object or substance. The idea that there might be a general *nonspecific* reaction to disease (or stress) did not have any place in the models, frameworks, and metaphors that defined medical science, experience, and practice at that time. As a result, Selye's professor had not been interested in the nonspecific symptoms shared by all the patients with infectious diseases. The recurrent grouping of symptoms simply was not (could not be) seen, at that time, as a significant cluster. In short, the MACHINE metaphor was systematically structuring medical experience *in a very definite manner.*

The employment of the HOMEOSTASIS metaphor made it possible to understand the biological purpose of the cluster of symptoms previously discovered. Selye drew on Walter B. Cannon's notion of homeostasis: the maintenance of the ability to regulate and control steady, healthy states.[19] At last, the nonspecific reactions made sense as the body's attempt to maintain a steady state in the face of stress. My reenactment of the pattern of thought involved during this stage of Selye's discoveries is as follows. The first step was his recognition that he was dealing with a syndrome of response, rather than a mere aggregate of symptoms. In searching for an explanation of the frustrating results of his sex hormone research, Selye began explorations we see as depending upon the power of the HOMEOSTASIS metaphor. Under the BODY AS HOMEOSTATIC ORGANISM one would tend to see every bodily response as serving some function.[20] Thus, Selye began to understand this syndrome of response as having a general function. Selye had observed that the introduction of a toxin into laboratory animals caused this syndrome in every case, and moreover, the dosage of the toxin correlated with the strength of the reaction. *Now* a new explanation was possible for these facts under the HOMEOSTASIS metaphor—the syndrome could now be seen as the body's general adaptive response to toxicity.

At this point we can begin to trace out a series of *entailments* of the

HOMEOSTASIS metaphorical structure. In what follows I shall not be
focusing on any strict deductive logical connections; however, there is
a definite inferential pattern—the following out of a pattern of entailments suggested by the change to the new metaphorical understanding. I use the term "entailment" here in an extended and enriched
sense to include the perceptions, discriminations, interests, values, beliefs, practices, and commitments tied up with the metaphorical understanding. We are not concerned here merely with what one *believes*
(though that is part of the story), but also with what the metaphorical
understanding means for the nature of one's world. Among the chief
entailments are the following:

   1. Based upon the prior entailment mentioned above, namely, that
the syndrome might be a response to a toxin, Selye drew the further
conclusion that the syndrome was a *general adaptive response to any*
stressor (toxins, cold, injury, fatigue, fear, etc.).

If this were so, the general medical implications of the syndrome would be
enormous! Some degree of nonspecific damage is undoubtedly superimposed
upon the specific characteristics of any disease, upon the specific effects of any
drug.[21]

In following out this insight the mechanistic (BODY AS MACHINE) metaphor was not dismissed completely, but it became background and was
superceded by the HOMEOSTASIS metaphorical structuring. The new
structuring emerged gradually as various previously unrelated parts of
Selye's experience began to take on a new unified organization.

   It is important to see that the MACHINE metaphor would not permit
this inference. As we have seen, the MACHINE metaphor entails the view
that significant bodily responses must be tied to *specific* injuries, breakdowns, or damages to *specific* regions of the organism's body. There is
no place, on this perspective, for a *general* adaptive response to a stressor: machines cannot repair or protect themselves on the basis of some
perceived "threat."[22] But under the HOMEOSTASIS metaphor, such a
general response makes perfectly good sense, as a self-generated way
of maintaining balance within the organism.

   2. This tentative synthesis (organizing experience under the HO-
MEOSTASIS metaphor) bore fruit—it led to further entailments. In par-
ticular, questions that seemed inappropriate given the BODY AS MA-
CHINE metaphor now seemed dictated by the BODY AS HOMEOSTATIC
ORGANISM understanding. That is, the emergence of the new meta-
phorical structuring opened up new questions, made possible new dis-

criminations, and suggested new connections. Selye recognized that this new understanding meant

that my first classroom impressions about the onesidedness of medical thinking were quite justified and by no means sterile questions without practical answers. If the "damage syndrome" is superimposed upon the specific effects of all diseases and remedies, a systematic inquiry into the mechanism of this syndrome might well furnish us with a solid scientific basis for the treatment of damage as such.[23]

Given that the goal of the body was homeostasis, Selye was led to ask such questions as: To what extent is this syndrome really nonspecific? What other manifestations are part of this syndrome? How does it develop in time? To what extent are the manifestations of the nonspecific syndrome influenced by the specific actions of the agent that elicit it? What is the mechanism of this reaction? In short, these and many other questions were sanctioned by Selye's new metaphorical understanding.

Once again, these questions would not have been generated by the MACHINE understanding—since it entails no notion of a nonspecific response, none of these questions would make sense. Without the HOMEOSTASIS metaphor, there would be no motivation for this line of inquiry.

Experimental work done to answer these questions led, among other things, to the development of the theory of the General Adaptation Syndrome, described above as consisting of three basic stages (alarm reaction, resistance, exhaustion).

3. A third major entailment of the BODY AS HOMEOSTATIC ORGANISM was a new view of disease. Early on, Selye recognized that the existence of the General Adaptation Syndrome suggested a new way of looking at illness:

If this were so (if there were a general adaptive response to stress), everything we had learned about the characteristic manifestations of disease, about the specific actions of drugs, would be in need of revision. All the actually observed biological effects of any agent must represent the sum of its specific actions and of this nonspecific response to damage that is superimposed upon it.[24]

Selye saw clearly that previous theories of disease (under what I have been calling the BODY AS MACHINE metaphor) could in no way account for the role of nonspecific response to stress.

What we have seen up to now however, gives us no reason to believe that *nonspecific* stress plays any role in this [disease]. As far as we can see at this point, each damaging agent—every germ or poison—may be opposed by a special highly specific defense mechanism.[25]

In contrast to this, under the HOMEOSTASIS metaphor, disease must be understood as "not just suffering, but a fight to maintain the homeostatic balance of our tissues, despite damage."[26]

This changing view of disease led to the dislocation of the notion of DISEASE AS LESION (i.e., as *specific* localized injury or damage) and its subordination to an ORGANIC model of disease. The previous understanding of DISEASE AS LESION entailed a view of medicine whose task was to attack and destroy the cause of the malady. This involved excision, patching, poisoning, bombarding with X-rays, etc., as counterattacks against the invader. Under the ORGANIC model, by contrast, treatment is not just directed at a specific invader but also takes into account the organism's overall balance, both internal and in relation to its environment.

Stress therapy is not offensive; it is not specifically directed against any one disease-producer (as are specific serums, antibiotics, and other chemotherapeutic agents).

Stress therapy is not symptomatic, nor strictly *substitutional*; it does not act by merely eliminating any one specific symptom (as does aspirin in a headache), or by patching up a defect (as when a loss of skin is repaired with a graft, or a lack of vitamin with a curative amount of it).

Stress therapy is instead *tactically defensive* in that it adjusts active defense (for instance, barricading off a disease-producer with inflammation) and passive submission (as permitting local death of limited cell-groups, or the spread of inoffensive disease-producers) in a manner favorable to the organism as a whole.[27]

For example, on the LESION model, obesity has been treated surgically by removing portions of the stomach or the intestine so that only small amounts of food could be eaten or digested. On the ORGANIC model one would consider not only the mechanism of digestion but also general environmental factors (exercise habits, self-image, personal relationships, work pressures, etc.). This is not to say that LESION model treatments are eliminated altogether but rather that they must now be seen in relation to the wider, dominant ORGANIC model.

4. A further important entailment of this ORGANIC model of disease based on the HOMEOSTASIS metaphorical structuring of experience is the rejection of the dichotomy between sickness and health, and its replacement by the notion of disease as a matter of degree. According to the LESION metaphor of disease based on the BODY AS MACHINE metaphor, stress at any point is taken as a sign of disease. But under the ORGANIC model of disease, stress is only a sign of disease when it is so

intense that the body cannot maintain its adaptive response. Therefore, disease is a matter of degree.

Textbooks usually define health as the absence of disease, and vice versa. The two conditions are alleged to be opposites of each other. Is this really so? Are they not rather different only in degree and in the position of vital phenomena within time-space.[28]

For example, a loss of weight is typically an indicator of disease (as in cancer); however, this same phenomenon might occur as a normal response to the stress of an important vocational change. In the latter case, we do not want to say that the person is sick, yet he or she does not seem completely healthy either. This indicates that disease is a matter of degree of imbalance, and what counts as sufficient imbalance to constitute disease is context dependent. That is, reference to the complete situation is essential to a medical evaluation of the symptoms.

5. Still another entailment grew from the developing exploration of the HOMEOSTASIS metaphor and its associated implications—the entailment that every response of the body must have some function. Selye's work, and that of his colleagues, was revealing more and more of the specific mechanisms by which the body identifies and responds to various threats. But also, they were learning the ways the body has to turn off responses to threats when some other threat or injury is more important. For example, when confronted by a major burn over a large portion of the body, the system will stop paying attention to a small infection in a finger and throw all its resources into dealing with the burn. In other words, researchers learned more and more about the *anti*-inflammatory responses in the body and the purposes they serve for overall well-being.

Once this much was understood, it was realized that whenever a stress response is unimportant for the long-range welfare of the animal, anti-inflammatory agents could be employed to relieve the animal's distress. Thus, for example, reactions to hay pollen—"hay fever"—can be turned off safely, because the pollen is not otherwise dangerous to the body. These sorts of subordinate entailments and their clinical applications have in time helped to develop the large body of techniques for control of immune responses, allergies, etc., through "telling" the body *not* to carry out its usual efforts to preserve homeostasis.

All of the examples we have explored so far have been cases of the following-out of entailments from the general metaphorical understanding of BODY AS HOMEOSTATIC ORGANISM. In each case, the experi-

mental questions posed, and the discoveries they gave rise to, were
made possible by the understanding that I have called the HOMEOSTASIS
metaphor. It does not seem plausible that these questions would even
have been formulated, let alone answered, had the researchers been
operating under the point of view established by the BODY AS MACHINE
metaphor.

But the HOMEOSTASIS metaphor and all its potential entailments,
many of which doubtless remain to be explored, are themselves subordinate to an even more far-reaching metaphorical structure: BODY AS
PURPOSEFUL ORGANISM (which requires teleological explanation). Selye
says that "it is evident that our whole unified concept is based upon
teleologic thought: the principle of purposeful causality."[29] In all these
cases where we have reenacted the patterns of inference basic to Selye's
discoveries, the notion of bodies as goal-directed (acting to achieve or
maintain a dynamic, healthy situation) was vital to the framing of
questions, the interpretation of results, and the building of a unified
theory. As Selye says: ". . . all my factual observations were made possible by experiments planned on the assumption that stress responses
are purposeful, homeostatic, reactions."[30]

The MACHINE metaphor has no place for this *teleological* understanding of bodily functioning—machines are not purposive. Organisms,
on the other hand, can be purposive, to the extent that they are not
mechanistically determined. It thus seems fair to say that the entire research program would not have been possible without the change in,
and working out the entailments of, dominant metaphorical structures
of experience.

To sum up: my analysis of Selye's project highlights the way in
which underlying metaphorical structures have entailments that generate definite patterns of inference, perception, and action. What is possible under one metaphorical understanding is not always possible
under another. The cluster of symptoms Selye came to regard as crucially important were not significant under a different metaphorical
understanding (namely, BODY AS MACHINE). Taking certain groupings
of symptoms led, in turn, to the asking of specific kinds of questions
and engaging in certain kinds of activities. This entailed looking for
answers to *those* questions (and ignoring others), and it suggested
where to look for those answers. This, in turn, entailed certain diagnostic techniques and sanctioned selected interpretations of available
data (e.g., how to interpret the symptoms). Finally, a huge system of
therapeutic practices rested on these other discriminations, questions,
experiences, and diagnostic devices. The foregoing analysis of Selye's

case suggests that vast domains of our experience, understanding, reasoning, and practice are metaphorically structured (and irreducibly so).

Constraints: A Summary

In this chapter I have been arguing that image schemata and the metaphorical systems they help to constitute are rich enough in internal structure to constrain our understanding and to generate definite patterns of inference. I continued my exploration of the nature and operation of some of the more prominent image schemata (LINKS, PATHS, SCALES, CYCLES, CENTER-PERIPHERY) to show just how much structure they have and how pervasive they are in human meaning and understanding. I then analyzed a small part of an actual case of extended scientific research to give some idea of what it means to say that underlying metaphorical systems give rise to and constrain inferences by virtue of metaphorical entailments. We saw also that such systems include perceptual discernment, skills and capacities, and patterned activities—none of which consists merely of grasping or manipulating finitary propositional representations.

To say that image schemata "constrain" our meaning and understanding and that metaphorical systems "constrain" our reasoning is to say that they establish a range of possible patterns of understanding and reasoning. They are like channels in which something can move with a certain limited, relative freedom. Some movements (inferences) are not possible at all. They are ruled out by the image schemata and metaphors. But within these limits, there is a measure of freedom or variability that is heavily context-dependent. Which inferences are sanctioned will depend, as we have seen, on the metaphorically organized background against which phenomena appear, questions are posed, investigations are performed, and hypotheses are formulated.

Crucial to this notion of constraints is the enriched view of understanding elaborated at the beginning of the chapter. I urged the view that understanding is never merely a matter of holding beliefs, either consciously or unconsciously. More basically, one's understanding is one's way of being in, or having, a world. This is very much a matter of one's embodiment, that is, of perceptual mechanisms, patterns of discrimination, motor programs, and various bodily skills. And it is equally a matter of our embeddedness within culture, language, institutions, and historical traditions.

It will not do, therefore, to pretend that one's understanding consists only of one's beliefs—these beliefs are merely the surface of our embodied understanding which we peel off as abstract structures. It might be more satisfactory to say that our understanding is our bodily, cultural, linguistic, historical situatedness in, and toward, our world. And my main point in the present chapter has been that image schemata, their abstract extensions, and their metaphorical elaborations constitute a great part of the constraining structure of this understanding.

6

Toward a Theory of Imagination

Up to this point, I have presented evidence for the existence of image-schematic structures that can be metaphorically extended to structure our network of meanings and, thereby, to direct and constrain our reasoning. My evidence has been chiefly linguistic, but has also included descriptions of structures of our bodily experience that help to explain how anything (an event, object, person, word, sentence, story) can be meaningful for us. I now want to support the sweeping claim that *all* of these structures and patterns are matters of *imagination*.

Until now, I have been careful to downplay the notion of imagination, for two basic reasons:

1. For most people the term "imagination" connotes artistic creativity, fantasy, scientific discovery, invention, and novelty. This is chiefly a result of nineteenth-century Romantic views of art and imagination that have strongly influenced our common understanding, especially of our concept of art. I shall argue that creativity and fantasy are only one aspect of imagination and that it has other facets that are equally important. Thus, I have had to avoid using the term in my previous analyses, in order to forestall the mistaken view that image schemata and their metaphorical elaborations play a role only in discovery and creativity and have no serious role in our understanding and reasoning.

2. The second reason for waiting until now to introduce the term "imagination" is that some philosophers and psychologists regard imagination as an artifact of an outdated faculty psychology. The idea that cognition depends on distinct "faculties" or capacities for per-

forming specific mental operations dates back to early Greek philosophy. These faculties typically included at least sensation, imagination,
and intellection (or semantic variants of these). In the seventeenth
through the nineteenth centuries, when "psychology" was first splitting off from philosophy and becoming a distinct discipline, philosophers still used faculty talk in their accounts of knowledge. With the
rise of sophisticated neurophysiological accounts of human cognition,
many have come to regard faculty talk as an inadequate substitute for
"genuine" scientific understanding of cognition.

   With both of these objections in mind, I shall push ahead with the
important task of developing a theory of imagination. I will respond
to the first objection by recovering earlier notions of imagination to
complete and complement our Romantic view of it as the capacity for
novelty. Imagination is our capacity to organize mental representations
(especially percepts, images, and image schemata) into meaningful,
coherent unities. It thus includes our ability to generate novel order. In
response to the second objection, I have already given an account of
image-schematic structures and metaphorical projections independent
of a theory of imagination. So the elaboration of such a theory is not a
substitute for empirical evidence.

   Moreover, I argue that it is important to revive and enrich our notion of imagination if we are to overcome certain undesirable effects of
a deeply rooted set of dichotomies that have dominated Western philosophy (e.g., mind/body, reason/imagination, science/art, cognition/
emotion, fact/value, and on and on) and that have come to influence
our common understanding. We need to explore the role of imagination (in my suitably enriched sense) in meaning, understanding, reasoning, and communication. Only in this way can we begin to understand how it is possible for us to "have a world" that we can make sense
of and reason about.

   Because the present chapter is lengthy, it may help to give a brief
synopsis of it in advance to explain what I hope to show, and how I
hope to show it. I begin with a short history of our concept of imagination that reveals a deep prejudice against it in Western thinking. This
history shows that imagination is located relative to a problematic set
of dichotomies that have led us to separate reason from imagination.
The next few sections attempt to show why such a separation is problematic. I do this with a fairly detailed treatment of Immanuel Kant's
account of imagination, because I believe that he offers us the most
promising foundation for an adequate theory, even though his view

has serious limitations. I then suggest how we might go beyond Kant's position toward a more satisfactory theory, and I draw out some of the implications of such a theory for our view of meaning, understanding, and reasoning. Finally, I end with a description of what an adequate theory of imagination would consist.

I regard my treatment of imagination from a Kantian perspective as crucial to my project, insofar as I am urging an enriched view of rationality that includes structures of imagination. My entire undertaking focuses on elaborating a more adequate theory of embodied imagination. The four middle sections on Kant's view are fairly technical and detailed. This is somewhat unavoidable, given the nature of Kant's work, but I have tried to explore his account of imagination as straightforwardly as possible. However, those who find my analysis too technical may wish to skip to the last three sections, where I summarize my conclusions and explore their implications.

A Short History of "Imagination": The Platonic and Aristotelian Themes

A survey of some of the most influential discussions of imagination in the Western tradition reveals two quite different approaches to the subject—one that associates it with art, fantasy, and creativity, and another that treats it as a faculty that connects perception with reason. I shall argue that an adequate theory must incorporate both themes, and that Kant was the first to undertake such a project with any thoroughness. Let us consider these two dominant themes in more detail.

Until the Enlightenment we find nothing that could be called a fully worked out theory of imagination.[1] Before that period we must piece together brief passages and even random remarks where the concept comes into play. As Harold Osborne has noted, there was no classical theory of what we today call "imagination," that is, of the capacity to mold experience, to bring something new out of the old, or to sympathetically project oneself into the position of another.[2] In spite of this absence of any unified theory explicitly elaborated, we can identify two traditions of thought about imagination that influenced Enlightenment views and that are still influential today.

The Platonic Tradition

The first tradition is what we may call a *Platonic suspicion of imagination*. I use the term "Platonic" to denote a historical tradition that developed

MODES OF COGNITION		OBJECT OF COGNITION
INTELLIGIBLE REALM (Realm of Knowledge)		
Knowing—WHY (first Principles)	{ Intellection (noesis)	Form or Idea (eidos or idea)
Knowing—WHAT (hypothetical method)	{ Discursive Thinking (dianoia)	Mathematical Objects (mathemata)
VISIBLE REALM (Realm of Opinion)		
Knowing—HOW Useful correct opinions without reasons	{ Belief (pistis)	Living Things (zoa/pheteuton/skeuaston)
Conjecture/Guess	{ Imagining (eikasia)	Images, Shadows, Reflections (eikones)

DIAGRAM I

from interpretations of Plato's writings, even though some scholars argue convincingly that Plato never held such views.³ In this Platonic tradition imagination is regarded with considerable suspicion, on the grounds that it is not a genuine mode of knowledge. This prejudice rests on a very specific interpretation of the famous Metaphor of the Divided Line in Book VI of the *Republic* (509c). Plato employs the DI-VIDED LINE metaphor to show the various modes of cognition by which we can grasp objects in our attempt to gain knowledge of them. As the Line in diagram I indicates, imagination, as a power of forming images, is taken to the *lowest* form of cognition, offering us no real knowledge of any object.⁴

According to what I am calling the "Platonic" reading of this diagram, imagination is our way of grasping objects through their images, shadows, and reflections. But, as we all know from our experience, such images can be fleeting, changeable, and illusory. Knowledge, in this tradition, would involve grasping the unchangeable essence of a thing, and it would seem that images don't supply such essential knowledge. In fact, on this account, *nothing* in the physical world gives us real knowledge, since all perceptible objects are constantly changing, while their essences are fixed. To grasp such essences, therefore, it is necessary to jump to the "intelligible" realm beyond the senses—to transcend all sensuous and imaginative cognition. Only in this way are we able to find out the "essence" of an object, that is, to find out what properties all objects *of that same kind* have. In the Platonic tradition, then, the Divided Line is interpreted as a scale of ascending levels of cognition, from the lowest, imagining, to the highest, intellection.

Given this (distorted and inaccurate) interpretation of Plato's view of knowledge, it is easy to see why imagination fell under suspicion, as an inadequate mode of cognition. This view was reinforced by the traditional interpretation of Plato's criticism of imitative poetry in Book X of the *Republic*. The connection is straightforward—the imitative poet must be banned from the Republic for two related reasons:

i) The poet makes inferior imitations (using images) that are far removed from the Ideas or Forms, which alone could reveal the real essences of things. Socrates concludes,

Then must we not infer that all the poets, beginning with Homer, are only imitators; they copy images of virtue and the like, but the truth they never reach? The poet is like a painter who, as has already been observed, will make a likeness of a cobbler though he understands nothing of cobbling . . . [*Republic* 600b] . . . Thus far then we are pretty well agreed that the imitator has no knowledge worth mentioning. Imitation is only a kind of play or sport, and the tragic and epic poets are imitators in the highest degree? [*Republic* 601]

ii) Through imagination the poets "feed and water the passions," using powerful images to stir up the emotions that override our rational faculty. This ability to form vivid images that ignite our passions is the distinctive strength of the poet. But imagination of this sort is *not a rational faculty;* rather, it is the result of a kind of demonic possession in which the poet loses rational control. Possessed by the *daimon* (the muse), the poet is given the images to inflame the emotions of the audience:

For the poet is an airy thing, a winged and a holy thing; and he cannot make poetry until he becomes inspired and goes out of his senses and no mind is left in him; so long as he keeps possession of this, no man is able to make poetry and chant oracles. Not by art, then, they make their poetry with all those fine things about all sorts of matters—like your speeches about Homer—not by art, but by divine dispensation. [*Ion* 534c]

In short, the prejudice of the "Platonic" tradition against imagination is based on the claim that no true knowledge can rest on either sense experience or, even worse, upon images of things. This "epistemological" argument is then coupled with the "psychological" argu-

Basis for what model?
Unjustified model?

ment that poetic imagination is not a rational process but only an act of possession by the *daimon*. Moreover, to the extent that succeeding generations saw imagination as an activity of "aesthetic" or "artistic" making, they tended to regard it as nonrational and unsuitable for serious cognitive undertakings.

The Aristotelian Tradition

The second major tradition derives from Aristotle's brief remarks on imagination, which he regards as the faculty that mediates between sensation and thought. It is dependent on the former and makes possible the latter.

> For imagination is different from either perceiving or discursive thinking, though it is not found without sensation, or judgment without it. That this activity is not the same kind of thinking as judgment is obvious. For imagining lies within our power whenever we wish (e.g., we can call up a picture, as in the practice of mnemonics by the use of mental images), but in forming opinions we are not free: we cannot escape the alternative of falsehood or truth. [*De Anima,* bk. 3, chap. 3, 427b]

Imagination thus seems to be a power to form images from present or prior sense perceptions, though it is not identical with mere sense perception, since it can form images in the absence of sensation (e.g., as in dreams). Discursive thought leading to knowledge, moreover, requires the prior operation of imagination to supply the empirical content. John Herman Randall explains this crucial role of imagination for all knowledge as follows:

> For Aristotle there can be no knowledge of the what or the why of things without sensing them, without at least having sensed them, without images, *phantasmata,* persisting in the *phantasia* (imagination): that is, there can be no knowledge without sense observation. This phantasia or imagination is a kind of motion generated by actual sensing: it is a physical occurrence. And sense images, phantasmata, are corporeal, not "mental."[5]

What I am calling the *Aristotelian* tradition, then, sees imagination as an indispensable and pervasive operation by which sense perceptions are recalled as images and are made available to discursive thought as the contents of our knowledge of the physical world. This tradition, in contrast with the Platonic, does not see imagination as an unruly faculty needing control, since it downplays what we today would see as imagination's creative and spontaneous mode.

From Hobbes to Kant

What I have distinguished as the "Platonic" and "Aristotelian" traditions might be construed as two dominant themes that have more or less defined the issues discussed in standard treatments of imagination to the present day. The Platonic theme gets associated with treatments of art and beauty, in which imagination is seen chiefly as a creative and wild artistic faculty unsuited for scientific or theoretical cognition. Thus, in the period leading up to the Enlightenment, imagination (or "Fancy") makes its appearance as a regular topic in treatments of artistic creativity, literature, and rhetoric. Imagination is typically regarded with a cautious suspicion of the sort expressed by Samuel Johnson:

Imagination, a licentious and vagrant faculty, unsusceptible of limitations, and impatient of restraint, has always endeavored to baffle the logician, to perplex the confines of distinction, and burst the enclosures of regularity.[6]

In this same context, however, we see also the emergence of a more positive assessment of the creative powers of imagination, as necessary for beauty. In his essays on "The Pleasures of the Imagination," Addison praises the faculty for its capacity to "fancy to itself things more great, strange or beautiful than the eye ever saw."[7]

The Aristotelian theme, in which imagination is a faculty between sensation and understanding, is stressed in medieval and modern philosophical accounts of the processes of human cognition leading to knowledge. In contrast to its definition as a creative faculty for producing beautiful art, imagination is regarded as an indispensable, yet not particularly creative, process necessary for connected experience of any sort. When this Aristotelian view is emphasized, imagination is considered more a mechanical operation tied to the sensing faculties than a creative process constitutive of genius. In short, empiricism came to treat imagination as a mechanical means for obtaining unified images and recalling past sense contents in memory. In becoming philosophically respectable, imagination also became somewhat tame and unremarkable.

It is during the seventeenth century, with its growing concern for a science of human cognition, that the Platonic and Aristotelian themes are woven together in a serious way. In search of a unified theory of cognition, philosophers sought the connections between the mundane operations of imagination in memory and image formation and those more spontaneous operations of artistic genius. An excellent example

of these developments is Thomas Hobbes, who tried to lay out universal and comprehensive principles governing cognition. He begins with
his famous principle that all knowledge and all the contents of cognition stem from experience: ". . . there is no conception in a man's
mind, which hath not at first, totally, or by parts, been begotten upon
the organs of sense."[8]

Knowledge begins when objects impinge upon our external senses,
leaving sense impressions or images that are stored in memory and can
later be recalled and recombined. All of this work is the operation of
imagination, which is "nothing but *decaying sense*" or "memory," the
term we use "when we would express the decay, and signify that the
sense is fading, old, and past."[9] This elegant model is extended to explain all knowledge and artistic making as resulting from the workings
of imagination. We have a process in which initial, forceful impressions
on the senses grow weaker and weaker as the force is passed through
one stage of cognition after another. Hobbes summarizes this process:

Time and Education begets experience; Experience begets memory; Memory
begets Judgment and Fancy; Judgment begets the strength and structure, and
Fancy begets the Ornaments of a Poem. The Ancients therefore fabled not ab-
surdly in making memory the Mother of the Muses. For memory is the World
(though not really yet so as in a looking glass) in which the Judgment, the
severer Sister, busieth herself in a grave and rigid examination of all the parts
of Nature, and in registring by Letters their order, causes, uses, difference, and
resemblances; Whereby the Fancy, when any work of Art is to be performed
findes her materials at hand and prepared for use.[10]

Finally, based upon this account of the workings of imagination,
Hobbes introduces elements of the Platonic theme when he warns
that, although Fancy can produce "very marvellous effects to the benefit of mankind" (*Answer to D'Avenant*), yet it must be kept under the
control of rational judgment:

Without steadiness, and direction to some end, a great fancy is one kind of
madness; such as they have, that entering any discourse, are snatched from
their purpose, by everything that comes in their thoughts.[11]

Hobbes is representative of Empiricist treatments of imagination in
the period leading up to Kant. Imagination is understood as a very
broad-ranging faculty that gives unified images and allows us to recall
them in memory (the "decaying sense"). But all of this processing
gives rise to "fancy," which is the specific form of imaginative activity
that generates novel ideas, vividness, and ornamentation in art and

literature. The chief problem Kant inherited was not so much that of explaining imagination as a capacity to form images, recall them in memory, and associate them in regular patterns; rather, he inherited the problem of explaining how structures of imagination can be constitutive of our (objective) experience and how imagination can be creative.

Kant's Account of Imagination

Kant's impressive attempt to elaborate a unified theory of imagination must be situated within his principal philosophical project from about 1770 until his death in 1804. That project, known as the Critical Philosophy, sought to investigate the nature and limits of human reason. The results of these inquiries are presented in Kant's three famous *Critiques* (of *Pure Reason, Practical Reason,* and *Judgment*). Each Critique selects one or more kinds of mental activity, characterizes the judgments (as products) each generates, and then examines the mental processes that must be involved to produce such judgments. Thus, each of the Critiques focuses upon certain types of judgments (e.g., propositions within science, moral precepts, judgments of natural and artistic beauty, judgments of teleology in nature).

The obvious connecting thread that ties together the successive stages of the Critical Philosophy is the notion of *judgment*. According to Kant, "All judgments are functions of unity among our representations" (A69, B93), where a function is "the unity of the act of bringing various representations under one common representation" (A68, B93).[12] So, one way to construe Kant's project is to see it as an exploration of the ways in which meaningful unity and order are achieved in our experience and cognition. I shall argue that imagination (*Einbildungskraft*) is the chief means by which this order is accomplished. There are four major stages in the development of Kant's view of imagination: (a) reproductive imagination, (b) productive imagination, (c) the schematism, and (d) the creative operation of imagination in reflective judgment. Let us consider each stage in turn, in search of a unfied theory of imagination.

The Reproductive Dimension of Imagination

When Kant set forth the epistemological foundations of his Critical Philosophy in the *Critique of Pure Reason* (1781, 1787), he focused chiefly on one type of judgment, *determinate* judgment, resulting in empirical knowledge. Kant asks what mental operations must occur to produce the universal objective judgments about experience that underlie mature science. His answer is that all knowledge of objective (shared, universally communicable) experience must involve two components: (1) some perceptual content given to our senses, and (2) mental structures to organize and make sense of that content. Kant thought of the perceptual contents as *material* elements that must be structured by *formal* elements (which include [a] concepts, and [b] the structures of spatial and temporal organization for all our experience). In our experience of physical objects, the material component is given to our senses from outside us, while the formal component is given by the structure of our understanding and of our capacity for having sensations. The form is something that we impose on our experience.

On this account, knowledge is the result of judgments in which the contents of our sense perception are organized by concepts. A *concept* is a rule by which a series of perceptual representations can be structured in a definite way. The concept "dog," for example, is a rule specifying the properties any object must have if it is to be a "dog." When you experience something as a dog, you are making a sort of automatic judgment that the perceptual object before you has the appropriate properties to fall under the concept "dog." Objective knowledge is thus built up by combining concepts (in acts of judgments) that are tied to sense perceptions at some point in our experience. For instance, when we make the judgment "All whales are mammals," we are asserting a specific relation between the concept "whale" and the concept "mammal" (we combine them in judgment), and both of these concepts, in turn, are general representations of sets of properties common to many physical objects.

To sum up, all knowledge involves judgments in which mental representations (sense percepts, images, or even concepts) are unified and ordered under more general representations. For Kant, imagination is *the* faculty for achieving this synthesis, defined as "the act of putting different representations together, and of grasping what is manifold in them in one act of knowledge" (A77, B103). To understand imagination is to understand the nature of its synthesizing or unifying activity.

Kant accepted the Empiricist assumption that whatever is given to our senses in perception cannot have its own principle of organization within itself. That is, he assumed that each of our mental representations, in itself, occurs singly and atomistically, so that any unity we experience in sense perception must be the result of the synthesizing work of the imagination. This experiential unity is described as being the result of a simultaneous "three-fold synthesis":

1. *Synthesis of apprehension in intuition.* In order to cognize a series of separate representations as one object, we must first grasp them as one unified image at a single point in time. I can't experience a dog unless I can get a unified image of a dog as distinct from other possible unities in my perceptual field.

2. *Synthesis of reproduction in imagination.* It is not enough, however, merely to have one unified image; we apprehend objects as persisting through time, so to experience unified objects we must keep before our awareness representations (i.e., previous images) that were given to us at a prior time (i.e., the moment before the present one, the moment before that, and so on). It is imagination, as a power of representing what is no longer present, that performs this synthesis.

3. *Synthesis of recognition in a concept.* It is still not enough merely to apprehend unified images over time, if we are to grasp objects in perception. In addition, we must recognize what it is we are experiencing. Kant says that this involves a more or less automatic recognition of the rule (concept) that tells us that *this present object* is an object *of a certain kind* (say, a dog). In other words, we must be able to distinguish one unity from another, which we do by recognizing the different organizing properties and relations that make them different kinds of objects.

Now, since every appearance contains a manifold, and since different perceptions therefore occur in the mind separately and singly, a combination of them, such as they cannot have in sense itself, is demanded. There must therefore exist in us an active faculty for the synthesis of the manifold. To this faculty I give the title, imagination. Its action, when immediately directed upon perception, I entitle apprehension. Since imagination has to bring the manifold of intuition into the form of an image, it must previously have taken the impressions up into its activity, that is, have apprehended them. But it is clear that even this apprehension of the manifold would not by itself produce an image and a connection of impressions, were it not that there exists a subjective ground which leads the mind to reinstate a preceding perception alongside the subsequent perception to which it has passed, and so to form whole series of perceptions. This is the *reproductive* faculty of imagination. [A120]

There is nothing particularly novel about this account of reproductive imaginative activity. Kant is only presenting the standard empiricist view of *imagination as a power to form unified images, and to recall in memory past images, so as to constitute a unified and coherent experience.* As Hobbes, Locke, Berkeley, and especially Hume had already noted, reproductive acts of imagination can be explained as involving merely empirical rules of *association*. Hume had argued that the unity of our experience and cognition were the joint result both of general psychological principles that exert a "gentle force" to unify representations and of principles of association developed by habitual practice.[13]

Kant granted the existence of such empirical rules for the association of representations, but he argued that no merely empirical principles could account for the possibility of *objective* experience, that is, of our experience of public objects subject to universal natural laws. If the order in our representations is the result of subjective psychological principles of association, then there could be no guarantee of a shared objective world. With only reproductive imagination we might each have our own privately structured realities. Thus, Kant argued that because a science of nature which finds universal laws is possible, there must be a synthesizing function of imagination that is not merely reproductive (and subjective) but is transcendental and *productive*.

The Productive Function of Imagination

Let us restate the problem Kant is addressing. It might be the case, if there is only reproductive imagination, that each of us organizes our experiences of objects differently. You might associate and unify them in one way, and I in another. In such a case, we would each have our own little isolated, solipsistic reality. But it is a fact that we do share a common world of physical objects; we are not locked up inside our subjective experiences. So the question is, How is this possible? What is there beyond reproductive imagination that could give this shared, objective structure to our world?

Kant poses this same problem in still another way. He points out that, if we organize our mental contents only by means of reproductive imagination, then our experience might consist only of one mental state (state of consciousness) after another with no objective principle tying them all together. Experience would then be only a *series of successive states of consciousness*. But, of course, our experience is not this way. We are not just one conscious state after another. Instead, there is something that unifies my successive states of consciousness, a structure that makes them *my* conscious states. In short, what we experience is not a series of successive states of consciousness but rather *our consciousness of these successive states as belonging to us (as "ours")*. In Kant's words, "Only in so far, therefore, as I can unite a manifold of given representations in *one consciousness,* is it possible for me to represent to myself the *identity of the consciousness in (i.e., throughout) these representations"* (B133).

What Kant is claiming is that it is the unity of our consciousness, to which our experience is always subject, that is the ground of objectivity in our experience. We can have objective, public, shared experiences because there is an objective structure to our consciousness. Kant calls this objective structure a "transcendental" unity of consciousness, which constitutes the ultimate conditions for objective experience. It is "transcendental" because it is given by the structure of consciousness and is not derived from our empirical experience.

For our purposes, the important point is that Kant describes this ultimate unifying structure of consciousness as an operation of imagination, because it is a synthesizing activity that gives the general structure of objective experience as such. He also calls this transcendental synthesizing activity "productive" and "figurative," because it generates or produces the figure or structure that any set of representations must fit if they are to be experienced by us as objects in our shared world.

The section on productive imagination is one of the most difficult and obscure passages in all of Kant's writing. This is not surprising, since he is probing the very emergence of structure in the depths of our experience. I would sum up his chief conclusions as follows: the *productive* function of imagination is what makes it possible for us to experience public objects that we all share in our common world. This productive imagination is none other than the *unifying structures of our consciousness* that constitute the ultimate conditions for our being able to experience any object whatever. There can be no objective experience that is not subject to these structures, which are the categorical patterns imposed by the transcendental structure of human consciousness.

We are thus brought to a momentous conclusion about the importance of human imagination, namely, *there can be no meaningful experience without imagination,* either in its productive or reproductive functions. As productive, imagination gives us the very structure of objectivity. As reproductive, it supplies all of the connections by means of which we achieve coherent, unified, and meaningful experience and understanding. We are talking here about operations of the imagination so pervasive, automatic, and indispensable that we are ordinarily not aware of them. Nevertheless, our ordered world, and the possibility of understanding any part of it, depends on the existence of this synthesizing activity.

Imagination as Schematizing Function

So far, we have talked about imagination in a rather abstract manner, as a basic synthesizing activity for ordering our mental representations. But how does imagination really work? The closest Kant comes to answering this question is in the section on the schematism of the understanding in the *Critique of Pure Reason*. It is here that the Aristotelian theme is most evident, for we see imagination as an activity mediating between sensation and understanding or thought.

The section on the schematism is Kant's answer to a problem in his philosophy about how categories (as pure concepts) can apply to sensible intuitions (as empirical). For our purposes, it is not necessary to explore Kant's view about categorization, nor must we accept his view in all its details. Briefly, the categories are the most basic concepts to which any representation that lays claim to objectivity must be subject. The categories are "pure" concepts, that is, they are nonempirical rules that give the structure for objects as such. A good example of a Kantian category is *causality,* for there can be no objective experience that does not fall within some causal network. Causality is thus one of the basic structures of all experience of objects. As "pure" concepts, the categories are distinguished from mere empirical concepts, such as "dog," which are derived from experience. The categories are the structures of consciousness that we "bring to experience" and to which all our experience of objects is subject.

The problem of the schematism section is this: How can pure concepts relate a priori to empirical intuitions (i.e., to sense perceptions)? How can categories, which are pure forms, connect up with experience, which has empirical content? How can the formal (i.e., without empirical content) map onto or structure the material? Kant describes what is required to answer this question:

Obviously there must be some third thing, which is homogeneous on the one hand with the category, and on the other hand with the appearance, and which thus makes the application of the former to the latter possible. This mediating representation must be pure, that is, void of all empirical content, and yet at the same time, while it must in one respect be intellectual, it must in another be sensible. Such a representation is the *transcendental schema*. [A138, B177]

Even if we are not convinced by Kant's treatment of the categories, we have here a genuine problem that any account of experience must address. How is it that abstract mental structures can connect up with the contents of our sense perception? The "third thing" that connects the two is a *schema,* which is the *structure of a schematizing activity of imagination in time.* What Kant discovers is that imagination *always* involves a temporal ordering of representations, whether or not those representations are also spatial. Kant had argued earlier that time is an a priori form of inner sense and thus a form of *all* cognition (since all cognition, either of internal states or external objects, occurs in inner sense).

The key point here is that, regardless of whether or not we accept Kant's view of time, he is correct in claiming that all cognition occurs in time and thus is subject to the structure of temporality. Kant describes the characteristics of time structure that permit it to connect pure concepts with sense contents ("appearances" or "intuitions," as he calls them):

Now a transcendental determination of time is so far homogeneous with the category, which constitutes its unity, in that it is universal and rests upon an *a priori* rule. But, on the other hand, it is so far homogeneous with appearance, in that time is contained in every empirical representation of the manifold. Thus an application of the category to appearances becomes possible by means of the transcendental determination of time, which, as the schema of the concepts of understanding, mediates subsumption of the appearances under the category. [A138–139, B177–178]

Kant thought of time as a pure, formal structure of consciousness to which all of our representations are subject. Thus, since time is universal and pure, it can connect up with the pure concepts (the categories); and since it organizes all representations, it is connected to our perceptions. It can serve, therefore, as the mediating link between concepts and percepts.

Whatever problems there are with Kant's account of time,[14] there is still an important insight about imagination that is not dependent upon his particular theory of time. That insight is that *imagination is a schematizing activity for ordering representations in time.* The schematic operation of imagination can show itself either as a transcendental determination (as when it connects the categories to sensation in general) or as an empirical determination (when it connects empirical concepts, e.g., "dog," to specific sensible intuitions, e.g., this four-footed furry object impinging on my senses). The key point in all of this is the temporal character of imagination as the chief means for establishing order in our experience.

Kant clarifies the irreducible character of imaginative schematic activity by distinguishing the *schema* from the *concept* and also from the

	"dog"	"number 5"	"triangle"	category (pure concept of the understanding)
CONCEPT	"dog"	"number 5"	"triangle"	category (pure concept of the understanding)
SCHEMA	"Representation of a rule according to which imagination can delineate the figure of a four-footed animal in a general manner"	"Representation of a method for representing a multiplicity in conformity to a concept"	"Rule of synthesis of imagination, in respect of pure figures in space"	"Product of transcendental synthesis of imagination constructing an object of intuition in general" (i.e., the figure of any object of possible experience)
IMAGE	 in thought	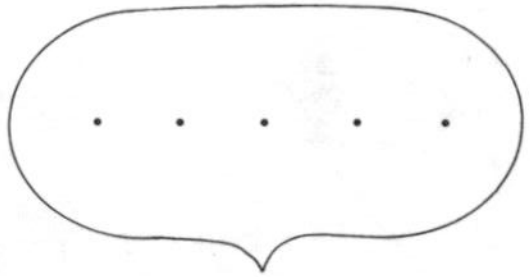 in thought	 in thought	No Image! (We have no image for the thought of an object in general, but only for particular objects)
OBJECT PERCEIVED	 (an actual dog)	(5 dots in space, 5 pigs, 5 trees, 5 of anything)	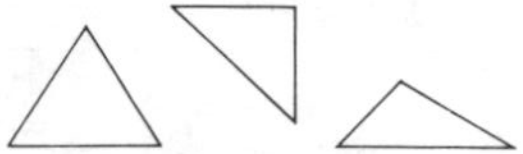 (drawn objects, triangular objects)	Any object as such (object in general)
		for empirical concepts		for pure concepts

DIAGRAM 2

specific *image*. The *image* is a mental picture that can be traced back to sense experience. This is what I have called the "rich image" in Chapter 2. The *concept* is an abstract rule specifying the characteristics a thing must have to "fall under that concept." The concept "dog," for instance, would be a "rule" (Kant's term) of the following sort: a dog is a four-footed, furry, domesticated, carnivorous mammal of the canine family. Whatever satisfies these properties is a dog. The *schema* is, for Kant, a procedure of imagination for producing images and ordering representations. It is thus partly abstract and intellectual, while also being a structure of sensation. So, it provides the needed bridge between concepts, on the one hand, and images and percepts, on the other. The schema for DOG would be a procedure for delineating the figure of a four-footed animal of a certain sort in a general manner. It would not be an image of a specific dog, nor a mere abstract concept "dog."

Diagram 2 is based on Kant's examples and shows the difference between the concept, schema, image, and physical object.

Let us examine Kant's treatment of the triangle, to illustrate the key distinctions. First, there is my concept "triangle": a triangle is a three-sided, closed plane figure. Then there are actual physical objects that are triangular, such as triangles drawn on paper, or triangular pieces of cardboard. Third, I can form images of specific triangles, even though no actual triangle is present to my senses. Finally, there is my schema of a triangle. This is not the same as my image; rather, it is a procedure for synthesizing pure triangular figures in space, whether in my mind (as images) or in actual physical reality. The schema of a triangle is what allows me to generate images of triangles, but it must be distinguished from the image. Kant makes this point in the passage I cited earlier in Chapter 2:

No image could ever be adequate to the concept of a triangle in general. It would never attain the universality of the concept which renders it valid of all triangles, whether right-angled, obtuse-angled, or acute-angled; it would always be limited to a part only of this sphere. The schema of a triangle can exist nowhere but in thought. [A141, B180]

The schematizing activity of the imagination, then, mediates between images or objects of sensation, on the one hand, and abstract concepts, on the other. It can accomplish this mediation because it can be a rule-following or rule-*like* activity for creating figure or structure in spatial and temporal representations. And, since all representations occur in time, we can say, with Kant, that schematic activity is a matter of time determination.

My notion of the *image schema* is directly influenced by, and is a slight variation on, Kant's concept of a "schema." The points where my view diverges from Kant's are identified below; but I would argue that Kant saw correctly that the ability of humans to have, and dwell in, a "world" is tied directly to such schematic structures of imagination as we have been describing.

It is not clear in Kant's account whether he wants to say that the schema is a "procedure," or whether he thinks that it is a "product" of a process. He speaks both ways. Sometimes he describes it as a product or structure resulting from imaginative activity in which concepts get connected to percepts (A142, B181). But he also describes it frequently as the procedure or rule at work in imaginative structuring (A140, B179). Perhaps we cannot resolve this ambiguity in Kant's treatment, but it is quite clear that he is insisting on the existence of structures of imagination that mediate between concepts and percepts.

What I have tried to show so far is the absolutely fundamental role Kant attributes to imagination (reproductive and productive) in our ability to have *any* meaningful and connected experience that we can comprehend and reason about. In exploring the workings of the imagination at this most basic level, we are probing the preconceptual level of our experience at which structure and form first emerge for us. Thus, it is not surprising that even Kant would acknowledge the limitations of his analysis. In one of the few places where he ever confesses a measure of bafflement, Kant both summarizes his view and recognizes its incompleteness:

This schematism of our understanding, in its application to appearances and their mere form, is an art concealed in the depths of the human soul, whose real modes of activity nature is hardly likely ever to allow us to discover, and to have open to our gaze. This much only we can assert: the *image* is a product of the empirical faculty of reproductive imagination; the *schema* of sensible concepts, such as figures in space, is a product and as it were, a monogram, of pure *a priori* imagination, through which, and in accordance with which, images themselves first become possible. These images can be connected with the concept only by means of the schema to which they belong. [A141–42, B180–181]

The metaphor of the MONOGRAM suggests that the schema is a figure or outline in imagination that can be "filled in" by particular images or percepts. This is the closest Kant comes to describing the schema in the sense I am employing it in this book (as elaborated in Chapter 2). I have given considerable attention to Kant's account, because he makes a point upon which the entire argument of my book rests, namely, *that all meaningful experience and all understanding involves the activity of imagination which orders our representations (the reproductive function) and constitutes the temporal unity of our consciousness (the productive function).* If imagination were not always at work, we could never have any coherent and unified experience or understanding. It is for this reason that I am trying to ground my account of human meaning and reasoning upon an elaboration of the operations of imagination (construed in this broad, Kantian sense).

The Creative Function of Imagination

Up to this point we have not even mentioned the definition of imagination that is generally taken for granted by most of us. Due to the influence of Romanticism, most of us understand imagination as the capacity for creativity and novelty in art, literature, and science. It is one of the strengths of Kant's account that he does treat imagination in this sense, and he tries to relate it to the other functions we have just described. Let us then ask how successful he is at explaining creative imagination as a function that makes use of the same synthesizing capacity we have just seen to be crucial for the structuring of our ordinary experience.

Kant does not describe either the reproductive or the productive operations as creative. He couldn't, within the constraints of his system, since that would loosen the rigor of their rule-determined activity. Both operations are treated within the context of his account of *determinate* judgment, whereby some more particular representation(s) is brought under (determined by) a more general representation (such as a concept). But by the time Kant wrote the third and last of his great Critiques, in which he tried to tie together his entire Critical project, he recognized the existence of another basic kind of judgment. This he called *reflective* judgment, which is the subject of the *Critique of Judgment* (1790). Kant saw that the mind does not go about only with a fixed stock of concepts under which it organizes what it receives through its senses. It also engages in the creative act of reflecting on representations in search of novel orderings of them, which thereby generates new meaning. Thus, in addition to determinate judgment, there is reflective judgment. Kant explains:

The judgment can be regarded either as a mere capacity for *reflecting* on a given representation according to a certain principle, to produce a possible concept, or as a capacity for *making determinate* a basic concept by means of a given empirical representation. In the first case it is the *reflective,* in the second the *determining* judgment. To reflect (or to deliberate) is to compare and combine given representations with other representations or with one's cognitive powers, with respect to a concept which is thereby made possible. The reflective judgment is called the critical faculty.[15]

Kant held that reflective judgments do not constitute acts of knowledge, since they do not involve the determinate structuring of a field of representations according to a definite concept. Reflection is an imaginative activity in which the mind "plays over" various representations (percepts, images, concepts) in search of possible ways that they might be organized, although this process is free from the control of the understanding (which is the faculty that supplies concepts). Reflective judgment is thus distinguished from determinate judgment in the following way: determinate judgments involve the recognition of some set of representations by means of a concept that is already available. Seeing a furry, four-footed thing as a *dog* would be a determinate judgment—you are simply applying a preexisting concept to your experience.

In reflective judgment, on the other hand, there is no pre-given concept that is automatically applied to experience. Instead, we must *reflect* imaginatively on a series of representations in an attempt to come up with a concept or other representation under which they can be organized. Consider, for example, my dog Zobie. There is nothing in my knowledge of the characteristics of the species to which Zobie belongs that *guarantees* that I can find a genus (or more general concept) to which Zobie's species belongs. However, I can imaginatively reflect on the nature of Zobie's species and other species and sometimes come up with a unifying genus for them all. This ability to generate new concepts and new organization in my experience is the result of reflective judgment. My reflection is not guided by any concept that guarantees my success, but it results in novel structurings that can make sense.

Kant explores imagination's role in reflective judgment by investigating its operation in judgments of natural and artistic beauty, and in teleological reasoning in science. His fullest account of creative imagination is situated chiefly within his treatment of the judging and making of beautiful objects. To see what, according to Kant, distinguishes judgments of beauty, let us consider some of the kinds of judgments I might make, for instance, about a rose. First, I might take a certain sensuous and immediate pleasure in its color or its smell. These "judgments of sense" are based upon the pleasure I experience because of my body chemistry. I don't claim any universal validity for such judgments, since others might find the odor too rich or the color too dark as a result of their particular perceptual makeup.

Second, I might judge the rose good for a certain purpose, such as the production of rosewater. Here I can expect others to agree with my judgment, because I base it upon a concept of the qualities that make a rose good for making rosewater. If you disagree, we can argue about the matter, either by debating the concept (of what makes a rose suitable for rosewater), or else by discussing whether *this* particular rose has all of the properties specified by the concept. In either case, it is by referring our judgment to some concept that we carry on our debate.

A third way to judge the rose is with an interest in its various parts and the way they serve some purpose in the rose's survival. Thus, I might make judgments about how certain parts of the rose are useful for reproduction. Here again, I bring concepts to bear as the basis for my judgment, and it is on the basis of these concepts that I can argue with those who disagree with my judgment. There is at least a ground for a possible universal agreement with my judgment, since it rests on concepts we can all share.

But now suppose I approach the rose in a fourth way, not caring what immediate sensual pleasure it gives, nor what purposes it serves, nor how its parts work for reproduction; instead, I simply engage in an intellectual reflection on its form (i.e., its shape, inner structure, and composition) and on various possible ways of relating its structures. Such a reflective judgment might give me pleasure as I sense a certain "rightness" in its formal features. Its form is not "right" (or beautiful) merely because it fits some concept (some purpose the object can serve) but rather because there is a certain harmony and grace in the relation of its formal features.

Kant calls this fourth sort of cognition of the object a "judgment of taste." He argues that such judgments are based on the pleasure we experience as we imaginatively reflect on the formal rightness of the object (think, for instance, of grasping the form of a musical composition). He also insists that we can rightly claim universal validity for judgments of taste, even though they are not grounded on any shared concept that could be the basis for possible agreement. The claim to universal validity is based, instead, on the judgment attending only to formal properties of the object, which, Kant argues, can be reflected upon by everyone in the same manner. To explore Kant's extended argument for the universality of judgments of taste would divert us from our project, which is to investigate the workings of creative imagination. I have dealt with the universality issue elsewhere.[16]

Setting aside, then, the issue of whether universality can be grounded on the perception of formal features, let us consider Kant's contention that judgments of taste are exemplary of the *freedom of imagination* in reflective judgment. In Kant's terms, judgments of taste consist of a free play of imagination as it reflects on possible structurings of the object being experienced. By "free play" is meant that this imaginative reflection is not guided or determined by any definite concept (any rule) that structures its operations. In other words, being beautiful is not a matter of possessing a fixed set of properties specified by some concept "beauty." Strictly speaking, there is no *concept* of beauty, even though we speak as if beauty consisted of properties in an object. Yet the object on which we reflect does give rise to a free play of imagination that, rather than being nonsense, really does make good sense to us. So imagination is acting *freely* (without the guidance of concepts) as it would *if* the understanding really were controlling the judgment with conceptual rules.

Kant describes this non–rule-governed conformity of imaginative activity to structures of understanding as a special kind of "purposiveness" (*Zweckmassigkeit*) that the object has for my cognitive faculties. More precisely, there is a "purposiveness without any definite purpose," since there is no definite concept (of a purpose the object serves) guiding the reflection, and yet it is somehow fitting (purposive) for mental activity that makes sense to me. Objects judged to be purposive or fitting in this way are called "beautiful," and we say that they put our imagination in a playful harmony with our intellect or understanding (i.e., our conceptual faculty). Thus, we judge objects to be beautiful by a free (non–rule-governed) preconceptual imaginative activity that has a rational character and can lay claim to the agreement of other judges, since it focuses only on the formal features of the object, which imagination allows us all to experience in the same way.

In sum, Kant is articulating some of the major implications of the commonplace that there can be no fixed canon for judging beauty, that is, no set of rules (concepts) to follow in deciding whether or not something is beautiful or is a compelling work of art. There is no concept "beauty" that specifies a set of properties shared by all beautiful things. There are no rules to follow in judging the beauty of something. What you must do is experience the object by imaginatively reflecting on its formal features to see whether they give rise to a certain sort of cognitive harmony, which one feels as pleasure. Yet, even though there is no underlying concept, no set of rules for the judgment, it is not merely subjective or arbitrary. We can defend such judgments of taste by directing the attention of others to aspects of the object, so that they, too, can experience its formal rightness, its beauty.

Let us take stock of Kant's somewhat convoluted and strained argument. Kant is struggling to express a deep insight which the confines of his system seem to exclude, namely, he sees that *there is a kind of shared meaning that is not reducible to conceptual and propositional content alone.* He sees that there is a *preconceptual activity of imagination that is not merely subjective,* even though it is not objective in the strict sense of being conformable to public rules. That is, he sees that there is a *rationality without rules, that is subject to criticism, and so is not arbitrary.* He sees that there are *structures of imagination that can be shared by communities of people.*

In short, I am suggesting that Kant is grappling with the recognition that imagination plays a far more central role in meaning and rationality than his own restrictive framework will allow. Since he has defined rationality in terms of rules, concepts, and judgments (propositions), he cannot find a place for a rationality for which there is no algorithm. I shall take up this criticism in a later section, where I suggest that the Third Critique (which explores a non–rule-governed level of meaning and rationality) ought to be seen as fundamental for the project of the First Critique.

At present, I want to explore my contention that the schematic and metaphoric structures I described earlier are part of imagination in this Kantian sense. So far we have considered only the free play of imagination in the *judging* of beauty. Kant's hypothesis is that the same kind of free imaginative activity required to *judge* a beautiful object must also go into the *creation* of beautiful objects by artists. Just as there are no useful rules or objective principles for judging or criticizing beautiful art, so in making art there must be a parallel non–rule-governed activity. This is not to say, of course, that there are *no* rules involved in making art; on the contrary, there will always be technical rules to be observed. Thus, Kant defines "art" in a broad, somewhat Aristotelian fashion, as production by a will acting from some rational principle.[17] So, all art must conform to some rules, since the artist has, at the very minimum, some concept of the kind of object to be produced. Yet *beautiful art* is not the result of specifiable rules, because there is no definite concept at its ground. Beautiful art is the result of *genius,* which Kant defines appropriately as "the exemplary originality of the natural gifts of a subject in the *free* employment of his cognitive faculties" (*CJ*, §49). We might say that genius is the capacity to initiate a free harmonious play of imagination that issues in a new ordering of representations that makes sense to us without the use of concepts.

Genius, for Kant, does not fit the Greek notion of possession by the *diamon* or spirit that speaks through the poet who is without reason (i.e., out of their senses). Rather, Kant offers a more psychological and proto-Romantic view of genius as a free psychological process by which novel order is generated, which yet makes sense:

(T)he imagination (as a productive faculty of cognition) is very powerful in creating another nature, as it were, out of the material that actual nature gives it. We entertain ourselves with it when experience becomes too commonplace, and by it we remold experience, always indeed in accordance with analogical laws, but yet also in accordance with principles which occupy a higher place in reason . . . Thus we feel our freedom from the law of association (which attaches to the empirical employment of imagination), so that the material supplied to us by nature in accordance with this law can be worked up into something different which surpasses nature. [*CJ*, §49]

The important question for us is whether we can say anything more revealing about the way in which genius allegedly surpasses the merely associative laws of empirical imagination. Kant offers a partial answer by describing genius as a faculty for producing an *aesthetical idea,* defined as "that representation of the imagination which occasions much thought, without however any definite thought, i.e., any *concept,* being capable of being adequate to it; it consequently cannot be completely compassed and made intelligible by language" (*CJ*, §49).

Aesthetical ideas are not conceptual in Kant's sense, but they can "connect up with" our network of concepts. They involve more play of imaginative structuring, more meaning, than can be represented in a concept. They thus create new meaning, new significance, by going beyond the confines of our established conceptual system. Kant explains:

If now we place under a concept a representation of the imagination belonging to its presentation, but which occasions in itself more thought than can ever be comprehended in a definite concept and which consequently aesthetically enlarges the concept itself in an unbounded fashion, the imagination is here creative, and it brings the faculty of intellectual ideas (the reason) into movement; i.e., by a representation more thought (which indeed belongs to the concept of the object) is occasioned than can in it be grasped or made clear. [*CJ*, § 49]

To speak less technically, Kant is saying that there is a preconceptual activity in which imagination freely grasps something of the meaning and significance of an object or experience, even though there is no conceptual way to express this insight. What imagination shows us is not arbitrary or merely subjective—it really is part of the meaning of the object or experience. Thus, Kant says that the imagination *enlarges* the concept, opening up *new* significance in a creative generation of new structure and order.

To bring this rather esoteric discussion down to earth, let us consider Kant's examples of aesthetical ideas. First, there is the image of "Jupiter's eagle with the lightning in its claws" as a symbol for "the mighty king of heaven." The image of the eagle does not

represent what lies in our concepts of the sublimity and majesty of creation, but something different, which gives occasion to the imagination to spread itself over a number of kindred representations that arouse more thought than can be expressed in a concept determined by words. [*CJ*, §49]

This is a symbolic presentation, in which a certain image sets into motion an imaginative reflection that results in new insight about the object symbolized. The symbol points beyond itself to the thing symbolized.

This is not, however, the only type of aesthetical idea, for Kant also describes a process very similar to what I have been calling "metaphorical projection." He discusses the imaginative activity required to comprehend a passage from a poem by Frederick the Great, in which images of the serene end of a beautiful summer day are used to suggest the proper disposition one would desire at the end of his or her life. In this case, imagination works through a projective process in which structures from one domain (e.g., summer evening) are projected to order our understanding of another domain (the end of life). This is a metaphorical structuring.

Kant is describing here what he later calls (in §59) "hypotyposis" (literally, bringing under a type), or "presentation." There are two ways in which this can be accomplished, either "directly" or "indirectly." *Direct* (or schematical) presentation of a concept is simply the act of supplying a sensible object corresponding to the concept. If asked, for example, to present the concept "dog," I would simply call my dog, Zobie, into the room, thereby providing the physical instantiation of the concept. *Indirect* (or symbolic) presentation is necessary when we want to illustrate a concept for which no sense perception is adequate. Then we use some physical appearance to point indirectly to the idea we want to express. To speak of immortality, for instance, which has no instantiation in nature, I must use metaphorical and symbolic language and images to point indirectly to it.

It is important to see that Kant is actually talking about metaphorical and analogical thought processes as basic to creative imaginative activity. He summarizes his view and describes the relevant "double function" of the projective mechanism as follows:

All intuitions which we supply to concepts *a priori* are therefore either *schemata* or *symbols,* of which the former contain direct, the latter indirect, presentations of the concept. The former do this demonstratively; the latter by means of an analogy (for which we avail ourselves even of empirical intuitions) in which the judgment exercises a double function, first applying the concept to the object of a sensible intuition, and then applying the mere rule of the reflection made upon that intuition to a quite different object of which the first is only the symbol. [*CJ*, §59]

This is the closest Kant comes to explaining the operation of imagination that I have called *metaphorical projection*. In fact, his examples of this "symbolic hypotyposis" are *all* metaphors, such as when he suggests that a despotic state might be presented metaphorically as a handmill. We project structure and significance from our understanding of the nature of a handmill onto our understanding of the nature of a despotic state.

And, then, in a very remarkable passage, Kant goes on to mention the following examples of symbolic hypotyposis, which are metaphors in the sense I have been discussing (in previous chapters):

. . . *ground* (support, basis), *to depend* (to be held up from above), *to flow* from something, and *substance* (as Locke expresses it, the support of accidents) . . . [*CJ*, §59]

In the context of the argument I am developing in this book (i.e., my account of image schemata and metaphorical extensions of them), this passage is especially important for two reasons. (i) Words such as these are typically regarded as *literal,* and yet Kant is claiming that they involve complex metaphorical and symbolic projections that are tied up with their meaning. In other words, he seems to recognize that even our grasp of the meaning of what we take to be literal or conventional language depends upon underlying metaphorical systems of understanding. This is exactly the situation I have been describing in my treatment of image schemata and their metaphorical elaboration to give structure to our network of meaning and to our reasoning.

(ii) Kant also recognizes that our understanding, reasoning, and communication are inextricably bound up with imaginative structures that are nonpropositional in nature. We cannot make sense of our experience as a whole without both metaphorical projections and symbolic presentations, neither of which is propositional in any Objectivist senses.

A Summary of Kant's View of Imagination

Kant's treatment of imagination is complex, full of technical jargon, and subject to certain limitations that I shall indicate below. In light of the difficult nature of the previous four sections, a brief summary of the main points, and of the chief problems, may prove useful at this point. Above all, Kant showed *why* and *how* it is that there could be *no* meaningful experience without the operation of imagination in its many functions. Kant understood imagination as a capacity for organizing mental representations (especially images and percepts) into meaningful unities that we can comprehend. *Imagination generates much of the connecting structure by which we have coherent, significant experience, cognition, and language.*

There were four related functions of imagination. As *reproductive*, it gives us unified representations (such as mental images and percepts) in time, and unified, coherent experiences over time, so that our experience is not random and chaotic. It allows us to grasp a series of perceptual inputs as connected, so that we experience objects that persist through time. As *productive* it constitutes the unity of our consciousness through time. My consciousness has a structure that it imposes on all experiences that I can be aware (conscious) of. For something to be an object of my experience, it must satisfy certain conditions established by the nature of my consciousness. These conditions of organization are structures of imagination. As a *schematizing* function, imagination mediates between abstract concepts and the contents of sensation, making it possible for us to conceptualize what we receive through sense perception. Imagination can make this connection because it is both formal and embodied (i.e., tied to sensation). It is a more abstract organizing structure than rich images (it generates their structure), yet it is not an abstract concept or a proposition. Finally, as *creative,* imagination is a free, non–rule-governed activity by which we achieve new structure in our experience and can remold existing patterns to generate novel meaning. This creative structuring occurs as symbolic presentation and as metaphorical projection. It operates throughout our entire system of meaning, understanding, and language. Moreover, creative imagination is nonalgorithmic and non-propositional, insofar as it is not a process determined by concepts or rules.

I am not able to find a completely unified theory of imagination in Kant's writings. There seems to be a gap between the creative function, on the one hand, and the reproductive, productive, and schematizing functions, on the other. What connects them is that they all involve the structured ordering of mental representations into meaningful unities within our experience. But the freedom of creative imagination (the production of novelty) is not explicable solely in terms of the automatic and orderly reproductive and productive functions. Kant does not bridge this gap—it seems that it cannot be bridged within his system. He *describes* the operation of creative imagination but does not *explain* it.

It was Kant's genius to grasp the scope, pervasiveness, and importance of imagination for human experience. Unfortunately, the very theoretical framework that generated this insight also made it impossible for Kant to provide a satisfactory account of the workings of imagination. I shall now identify the chief limitations of Kant's system that blocked (unnecessarily) his success in achieving a unified theory comprehensive enough to encompass the various operations of imagination we have been exploring. Such a criticism suggests how we might advance a more satisfactory theory of imagination.

Beyond Kant to a Richer View of Imagination as Constitutive and Creative

There are two obvious problem areas in Kant's view. The first is his placement of imagination midway between conceptualization and sensation. Somehow imagination is supposed to have a foot in both worlds (in the "formal" and the "material"), and yet it is not clear how it can have this dual nature. The second problem is closely related to the first, because it, too, concerns the gap between the intellectual and the sensuous. The problem is how to explain a faculty that sometimes seems controlled by rules, while at other times it appears to be free of such constraint. As free and non–rule-governed, this faculty is regarded by Kant as nonrational, and yet it seems to play a role in what is meaningful for us and in how we reason about our world.

Both of these problems have the *same* roots in the structure of Kant's philosophical system. Both problems arise because Kant assumes a certain kind of metaphysical split—he sees reality as divided into two radically different and irreducible realms. On the one side, there is the physical or material realm governed by strict deterministic natural laws. This is the realm of our bodily being, of sensations, of emotions, and of physical objects in space. On the other side, there is a realm beyond the physical, wherein freedom is possible. This is the realm of understanding, reason, and our capacity for spontaneous action.

As Gadamer has shown, the rigid separation of understanding from sensation and imagination relegates the latter to second-class status as falling outside the realm of knowledge.[18] As a result, judgments of taste can never, for Kant, be determinative or constitutive of experience. Neither can they be "cognitive," for he regards the cognitive as the conceptual, and there is no concept or rule guiding reflective judgment. There are vague intimations here of the Platonic view of imagination, insofar as reflective judgments are accorded the status of a diminished rationality. Furthermore, Kant was forced by this metaphysical split to consider the imaginative activity of symbolic (indirect) presentation to be a hindrance to theoretical cognition.[19] He claimed that we turn to symbolic presentation (such as metaphorical projection) only when we have a "poverty of concepts" available for understanding some aspect of experience. So the nonconceptual imaginative activity of indirect presentation cannot measure up to conceptual judgment.

Now, what would happen if we deny the alleged gap between understanding, imagination, and sensation? What if, following the consensus of contemporary analytic philosophy, we deny the strict separation of the analytic from the synthetic, the a priori from the a posteriori, and the formal from the material?[20] If we regard these as poles on a continuum, then there is no need to exclude imagination from some supposed pristine realm of "cognitive content" or "objective structure." Such a view supports the somewhat unorthodox reading of Kant's contribution that I gave earlier, according to which he is seen as recognizing a vast realm of shared meaning structure (in imagination) that lies beyond concepts (in his overly narrow sense of that term). We saw that he couldn't quite bring himself to grant this dimension objective status, since it wasn't properly rule-governed in an algorithmic fashion. But he also couldn't quite deny that its operations could support claims to universal agreement (i.e., it was not merely subjective and private).

Here we are reminded of Frege's more-or-less Kantian objections to imagination in his account of meaning. Recall that Frege wanted to ex-

clude imagination from "objective sense," on the grounds that products of imagination are valid only for the mind that entertains them.
Frege argues:

People speak, e.g., of such-and-such a mental image, as if it could be in public
view, detached from the imagining mind. And yet a man never has somebody
else's mental image, but only his own; and nobody even knows how far his
image (say) of red agrees with somebody else's; . . . [21]

For the sake of argument, let us assume that Frege was exactly right
about mental images—they are private and tied to the mind that experiences them. But even if we grant this highly questionable assumption, it does not apply to image schemata of the sort we are exploring,
for they are structures of imaginative activities that can be *shared* by a
community. While they are not propositional in any Objectivist sense,
they provide relations in a shared basis of meaning that makes concepts
and propositions possible. They are thus "propositional" only in the
non–Kantian, non–Objectivist sense of "possessing sufficient internal
structure to constrain reasoning."

So, I am suggesting that the objectivity of meaning relations and
rational inference structures is not tied solely to Objectivist propositional contents and to algorithmic operations. I would even suggest
that, though Kant could never admit it, his remarkable account of
imagination actually undermines the rigid dichotomies that define his
system. It shows very powerfully that they are not absolute metaphysical and epistemological separations. I would defend this interpretation in the following way. Imagination is a pervasive structuring
activity by means of which we achieve coherent, patterned, unified
representations. It is indispensable for our ability to make sense of our
experience, to find it meaningful. The conclusion ought to be, therefore, that imagination is absolutely central to human rationality, that
is, to our rational capacity to find significant connections, to draw inferences, and to solve problems. Kant, of course, pulls back from this
conclusion, because it would undermine the dichotomies that underlie
his system.

Thus, the answer to the first problem—how imagination can be
both formal *and* material, rational *and* bodily—is that there is no unbridgeable gap between these two realms in the first place. Once we no
longer demand a disembodied (or nonphysical) rationality, then there
is no particular reason to exclude embodied imagination from the
bounds of reason.

This brings us to the second problem. How can imagination, which is not algorithmic, be part of rationality, which is rule-governed? This is a problem for a Kantian view in which understanding and reason are faculties of rules and principles, respectively. This ceases to be a problem, however, if we once again deny the assumption of an unbridgeable gulf between reason and imagination. If Kant's account of imagination shows us anything, it shows us that imaginative activity is absolutely crucial in determining what we will regard as meaningful and how we will reason about it. Instead of being nonrational, imaginative structures form the body of human rationality. Therefore, if imagination is not strictly algorithmic, then this cannot be essential for rationality, either. In other words, the Third Critique ought perhaps to be regarded as the "First" Critique in importance, insofar as it elaborates a notion of imaginative meaning and understanding that makes possible our more abstract conceptual and propositional structures.

One reason that creative imaginative activity has been considered "irrational" is that there does not appear to be a *logic of creativity,* that is, a definite pattern, algorithm, or inferential structure for creative reasoning. So it is a commonly held, and widely espoused, idea that there is nothing that can be said to explain the mystery of creativity. Yet in spite of its importance and indispensability, it is still regarded as a nonrational process. Furthermore, if you think of creativity as a process of generating new connections among *ideas,* then it does seem inexplicable, for we cannot figure out where the connections come from, if not from rule-governed relations among the concepts or ideas themselves.

The answer, I think, is that the novel connections come out of our experience. To see what this amounts to, of course, we need a full-blown theory of imagination, and that is what we do not yet have. However, we can at least say this much: creativity is possible, in part, because imagination gives us image-schematic structures and metaphoric and metonymic patterns by which we can extend and elaborate those schemata. One image schema (such as the PATH schema) can structure many different physical movements and perceptual interactions, including ones never experienced before. And, when it is metaphorically elaborated, it can structure many nonphysical, abstract domains. Metaphorical projection is one fundamental means by which we project structure, make new connections, and remold our experience.

Now this is surely only a small part of the complete story of creativity. But it at least takes a first step beyond the standard view that creativity is a miracle, or that new ideas just pop inexplicably out of thin air. Creativity occurs at all levels of our experiential organization and not just in those rare moments when we discover novel ideas. We are imaginatively creative every time we recognize a schema in a new situation we have never experienced before and every time we make metaphorical connections among various preconceptual and conceptual structures. For example, we are creative even when we come to see a dinner conversation as a process moving from a beginning point toward some indeterminate completion, for example, a new understanding of the participants in the conversation. This creativity is modest and unnoticed, but it is the basis for our more remarkable acts of innovation, too.

Obviously, this account leaves creativity a wonderful mystery, but it dispels the notion that creativity is irrational (or nonrational) and unstructured. Our new ideas and connections *do* come from somewhere. They come from the imaginative structures that make up our present understanding, from the schemata that organize our experience and serve as the basis for imaginative projections in our network of meanings. The kinds of connections and projections we can make are determined, in part, by the kinds of schemata there are and by the possible relations they can stand in to one another.

The move I am making beyond Kant can be summed up in the following way: I am suggesting that Kant's greatest contribution to our understanding of meaning and rationality was his work on imagination, which, ironically, his system forces him to separate sharply from reason and understanding. I am thus led to deny that the metaphysical and epistemological dichotomies presupposed by his system are rigid and absolute. I regard them, rather, as poles on a continuum of cognitive structure. By taking imagination as central, I see its structures as a massive, embodied complex of meaning upon which conceptualization and propositional judgment depend. Meaning is broader and deeper than the mere surface of this entire experiential complex—a surface that we peel off (cognitively) as concepts and propositional contents. We also see that meaning is not always, or even usually, univocal as Kant seems to think when he defines concepts as rules specifying lists of features. At least where human conceptualization is metaphorical, there is not a core underlying set of literal propositions into which the metaphor can be translated. Finally, rationality resides in *all* of these structures taken together, *each* with *their* own special constraints.

The Nature of a Complete Theory of Imagination

My analysis of Kant's deep insights coupled with the explorations of the previous chapters suggests that an adequate account of meaning and rationality (as well as of understanding and communication) awaits a comprehensive theory of imagination. Such a theory would complement and influence our present theories of conceptualization, propositional content, and speech acts. In its broadest sense, it would give an account of structure in human experience and cognition. In this book, I have addressed, in a preliminary fashion, some of the more important dimensions of imaginative structures of understanding. As I see it, a fully adequate theory of imagination would include *at least* the following components:

1. *Categorization*. I speak here not of classical, set-theoretical views of categorization (which never probe the workings of imagination) but of a view that does justice to the way human beings really do break up their experience into comprehensible *kinds*. I have in mind here a theory of prototypical categorization and not one that seeks sets of necessary and sufficient conditions.[22]

2. *Schemata*. We need a comprehensive theory of schemata, both in the sense I am using that term (image schemata) and as it is used in much of cognitive science, that is, as general knowledge or event structures. We need to survey the basic kinds of schemata, to see how they can be developed metaphorically, to investigate their complex interrelations, and to explore their connections with propositional structures.

3. *Metaphorical projections*. Metaphor is perhaps the central means by which we project structure across categories to establish new connections and organizations of meaning and to extend and develop image schemata. We need to know more about what kinds of source-domains there are, about what kinds of projections are possible, and about constraints on them (which keep them from being arbitrary).

4. *Metonymy*. Another basic form of projection crucial to the development of meaning is the general category that includes both synecdoche (part-for-whole) and metonymy proper (salient or related attribute-for-whole). The same kinds of questions raised by metaphor will be relevant here, too.

5. *Narrative structure*. When it comes to explaining how it is that humans experience their world in ways that they can make sense of, there must be a central place for the notion of "narrative unity." Not only

are we born into complex communal narratives, we also experience, understand, and order our lives as stories that we are living out. Whatever human rationality consists in, it is certainly tied up with narrative structure and the quest for narrative unity.[23]

As I noted in detail in the footnotes to the Preface, there is a large and rapidly growing body of research on all of these areas. We are beginning to construct the required basis for a more comprehensive theory of imagination that is sensitive to the workings of human understanding. To be a "comprehensive" theory, it would need to investigate the relations among all five of the above components, plus others that are bound to emerge as relevant. The central focus of the present study has been on image schemata and metaphorical projections, but each of the five areas is being explored in depth by researchers working in philosophy, psychology, linguistics, mathematics, and computer science. Obviously, many people working on these topics would not regard themselves as investigating imagination; but that *is* what they are doing, if we understand imagination as it has been described here.

Imagination is central to human meaning and rationality for the simple reason that what we can experience and cognize as meaningful, and how we can reason about it, are both dependent upon structures of imagination that make our experience what it is. On this view, meaning is not situated solely in propositions; instead, it permeates our embodied, spatial, temporal, culturally formed, and value-laden understanding. The structures of imagination are part of what is shared when we understand one another and are able to communicate within a community. It is to the nature of meaning so described that I now turn my attention.

7

On the Nature of Meaning

A Non-Objectivist Account of Meaning

An Objectivist theory treats meaning as a relation between sentences and objective (mind-independent) reality. In the past few decades, the most popular way of specifying this relation has been to say that sentences have truth conditions which *are* their meaning. Thus Carnap claimed, "To know the meaning of a sentence is to know in which of the possible cases it would be true and in which not."[1] We have seen, in the Introduction, that this "truth-conditional" approach has become *the* dominant view today, since truth conditions seem to be universal and objective in just the sense required for an Objectivist semantics.

In this book I have been outlining a non-Objectivist, *semantics of understanding*[2] to take the place of Objectivist semantics, which has shown itself to be incapable of explaining the full range of semantic phenomena we have been investigating here. In this non-Objectivist (or "cognitive semantics")[3] approach there are three key notions that are regarded as central: *understanding, imagination, embodiment*.

As we saw in the Introduction, Objectivist theories mistakenly assume that embodied, imaginative understanding does not have the universal, public character necessary to yield objective meaning. As a consequence of this false assumption, Objectivism underestimates the value of these three basic notions, denying them a central place in semantics. Let us recall the alleged reasons for this devaluation.

First, Objectivist theories try to avoid any mention of "understanding," because this term calls up the mediating role of human subjectivity, and this is regarded as a serious threat to the "objectivity" of meaning. Once again, Frege is representative on this point in his insistence on the public, objective character of "senses" (or meanings) as existing in a special ontological realm of thought independent of any individual consciousness. Only in this way, he thought, could one insure the objectivity of senses, untainted by anything subjective or particular to individual minds, or to their understanding.

Second, there is no room for imagination in Objectivist theories, at least in specifying the nature of meaning. The reasoning behind this view is simple. Meaning is a relation between abstract symbols and states of affairs in the world, between signs and their references. The meaning of a sign is simply its sense, which is the "mode of presentation" of the reference. Grasping a sense is an act of thought and not an act of imagination of an individual mind.

Third, the embodiment of imagination and understanding is treated as wholly inappropriate to a theory of meaning. Meanings, conceptual connections, inference patterns, and all other aspects of rationality are distinguished, according to Objectivism, by their universality and independence from the particularities of human embodiment. They are supposed to be that which is shared by all of us, that which transcends our various embodiments and allows us to partake of a common objective realm of meaning.

The chief difference, then, between the Objectivist view of meaning and the non–Objectivist "semantics of understanding" being proposed here can be summed up as follows: For the non–Objectivist, *meaning is always a matter of human understanding, which constitutes our experience of a common world that we can make some sense of. A theory of meaning is a theory of understanding. And understanding involves image schemata and their metaphorical projections, as well as propositions. These embodied and imaginative structures of meaning have been shown to be shared, public, and "objective," in an appropriate sense of objectivity.*

The central issue is the nature, role, and importance of understanding for meaning and rationality. Objectivism, of course, grants that we must grasp the sense of a term, but it tends to treat understanding as though it were more or less transparent, as though the relation of sentences to truth conditions was mediated in a relatively unproblematic way. According to Objectivist semantics, a sentence specifies its objective truth conditions or other conditions of satisfaction, which constitute its meaning. There is no mention here of the way human beings might happen to understand the senses or meanings they have "grasped."

In sharp contrast, I have argued that, between symbols and the world, there falls understanding. I have tried to indicate the importance for our understanding of structures of our embodied imagination, which are a chief means by which we "have a world" that we can partially comprehend and reason about. These imaginative (in the sense elaborated in Chapter 6) embodied structures often *seem* to us to be quite transparent, just because they operate nonproblematically much of the time in our ordinary experience. But the fact is that they are able to function nonproblematically precisely insofar as they constitute our understanding, our way of being in the world.

This particular formulation of the relevant notion of understanding, as a way of "being in" or "having" a world, highlights the dynamic, interactive character of understanding (and meaning). Grasping a meaning is an *event* of understanding. Meaning is not merely a fixed relation between sentences and objective reality, as Objectivism would have it. What we typically regard as fixed meanings are merely sedimented or stabilized structures that emerge as recurring patterns in our understanding. The idea that understanding is an event in which one has a world, or, more properly, a series of ongoing related meaning events in which one's world stands forth, has long been recognized on the Continent, especially in the work of Heidegger and Gadamer. But Anglo-American analytic philosophy has steadfastly resisted this orientation in favor of meaning as a fixed relation between words and the world. It has been mistakenly assumed that only a viewpoint that transcends human embodiment, cultural embeddedness, imaginative understanding, and location within historically evolving traditions can guarantee the possibility of objectivity.

Against this erroneous claim, I have argued that, at the very least, image-schematic structures and their metaphorical projections have a shared, public character which gives them a central role in the objectivity of meaning. By "objectivity," of course, I mean that there are meaning gestalts connected to structures of bodily experience that we all can share. I take up this issue more thoroughly in the next chapter, where I argue that we need not be frightened by the threat of a rampant "anything goes" relativism, just because we acknowledge the historical embeddedness of events of meaning and understanding, and thereby renounce the quest for an unattainable ahistorical standpoint.

To sum up: a non-Objectivist theory of meaning is a semantics of understanding. Understanding is treated as a historically and culturally embedded, humanly embodied, imaginatively structured event. We cannot understand the nature of meaning, therefore, without a theory of understanding that explains how we can experience a shared, public world.

Meaningfulness and Linguistic Meaning

My remarks in the previous section apply to "meaning" in the broadest possible sense of the term. Meaning is a matter of human understanding, regardless of whether we are talking about the meaning of someone's life, the meaning of a historical happening, or the meaning of a word or sentence. A theory of meaning is a theory of how we understand things, whatever those things might be. Objectivist semantics denies this, claiming that the concept of "meaningfulness in life" has little or nothing to do with linguistic meaning. Thus, it is a standard ploy in introductions to books on semantics to list various uses of the term "means" (e.g., "Smoke means fire," "Life means nothing," "She means to leave," "The Revolutionary War means a lot to Americans," and "The word 'triangle' means a three-sided closed plane figure") and then to argue that only the last sense needs to be dealt with in semantics.[4]

In contrast to this approach, I have been working up to the view that "linguistic meaning" is only an instance or specification of meaning(fulness) in general. Linguistic meaning is distinguished by its distinctive use of syntactic categories (e.g., noun phrase, verb phrase, particle, etc.), by its semantic categories (e.g., object, event, agent, etc.), and by its elaborate employment of speech-act conventions. However, we have seen that even some of these speech-act structures, such as illocutionary force operators, may have bodily correlates (as in Chapter 3).

I have not developed the extensive argument that would be needed to show *in detail* how linguistic meaning is a specification of meaningfulness in its broadest sense. In general, one would first need to give an analysis of what it is that makes an event, a narrative, or a life meaningful. And it would then be necessary to show that these same structures and elements are crucial to what we call "linguistic meaning" (the meaning of words, phrases, sentences).

The hypothesis of the unity of the notion of meaning is not an insistence on a single unified literal concept "meaning"; rather, it is a commitment to the existence of a series of connections among the various senses of "means." It is a commitment to the conviction that we are unified human beings and not a cluster of autonomous modules. It is a commitment to the "cognitive semantics" view that humans have general cognitive mechanisms which can be specified to particular functions. So, linguistic meaning turns out to be a special instance (perhaps the most central) of our capacity to have meaningful experience.

In the absence of a full explication of the notion of linguistic meaning in relation to a general concept of meaningfulness, I would like to suggest two possible correlations that would seem to be central for a complete account of the matter:

1. Whether it be for human events or for words and sentences, meaning is always meaning *for some person or* community. Words do not have meaning in themselves; they have meaning only for people who *use* them to mean something. We say, of course, that a certain word or phrase or sentence has a certain meaning, and there is nothing wrong with this way of talking. But this can only be a shorthand for the statement that a word or phrase or sentence is used by a linguistic community to mean something. To say that the word "cup," for instance, means "a small open bowl-shaped vessel for holding liquids" is to say that because the English-speaking linguistic community has used the word "cup" *to mean* "a small open bowl-shaped vessel for holding liquids," that term has become conventionally associated with that meaning. In short, linguistic meaning consists of the *use* of words by a person or community *to mean something for that community.*

2. The meaning of the symbol stems from the imposition upon it of a certain intentionality, which is *always a matter of human understanding. Intentionality* is the capacity of a mental state or of a representation of some kind (concept, image, word, sentence) to be about, or directed at, some dimension or aspect of one's experience. Meaning, I am claiming, is irreducibly intentional in this sense: the capacity for a mental event or a symbol to be meaningful (to "have meaning") always presupposes some being or beings for whom the event or symbol is meaningful, by virtue of its relation to something beyond itself. How that mental event or symbol gets its relatedness will depend upon the understanding in which it is embedded.

Meaning is thus always a matter of relatedness (as a form of intentionality). An event becomes meaningful by pointing beyond itself to prior event structures in experience or toward possible future structures. The event is meaningful insofar as it stands against, and is related to, a background stretching from the past into the future. A word or sentence is meaningful because it calls to mind a set of related structures of understanding that are directed either to some set of structures in experience (either actual or potential), or else to other symbols.

On the view I have been developing in this book, the relevant structures called up will be image schemata, basic categorical structures, metaphorical and metonymic projections, propositions, and a host of specific gestalts that make up the fabric of our understanding and experience. The key point for the theory of meaning I am advancing is that meaning always involves human understanding and intentionality. It is never merely an objective relation between symbolic representations and the world, just because there can be no such relation without human understanding to establish and mediate it.

Furthermore, a non–Objectivist cognitive semantics insists that understanding is not a transparent medium through which words map onto the world. The apparent transparency of understanding is really only the pervasiveness of shared understanding in ordinary experiences within stable contexts. It can seem plausible to ignore understanding (as embodied and imaginative) if, as Objectivist semantics does, one focuses on a set of simple examples in which understanding is shared unproblematically by members of a culture or community. But one can see the "thickness," ubiquity, and indispensability of imaginative understanding in all of those cases, such as novel metaphor, in which conventionalized meaning proves inadequate, or is subjected to change. *Then* we see just how rich, value-laden, historically situated, and imaginative our understanding really is. And we see that grasping the meaning of something is an imaginative event we call understanding.

Searle's Theory: Meaning as Derived Intentionality

The theory of meaning that emerges from the previous chapters is intentionalistic—it locates meaning in the intentional directedness of human understanding. It shares some features with the theory elaborated by John Searle, most recently in his book *Intentionality*. However, it differs from Searle's view at certain crucial points where, I shall argue, Searle remains Objectivist. So, it is illuminating to play my view off against Searle's, first, to show how we both differ from mainstream truth-conditional semantics, and, second, to show where a genuinely non-Objectivist theory must go beyond Searle to develop a semantics of understanding. In order to work up to the crucial differences, and to explain the nature of the necessary addition made by a theory of image schemata, I shall begin with a brief outline of the basic tenets of Searle's account of meaning.

Searle's earliest definition of linguistic meaning is given within the context of his "speech-act" theory of language. "Speaking a language is engaging in a (highly complex) rule-governed form of behavior."[5] A comprehensive theory of language, therefore, would have to supply all of the phonetic, syntactic, semantic, and pragmatic rules governing this form of behavior. Since Searle's primary concern is with meaning, his central project is to identify and explain the rules by which speakers can utter sounds in order to mean something. Those rules will be both conventional and constitutive, that is, they will create or define certain forms of linguistic behavior.

Searle assumes that, generally, speech acts can be represented by the following formula:

$$F(p).$$

"F," the illocutionary force indicating device, specifies the kind of illocutionary act being performed, such as asserting, questioning, commanding, expressing; "p" specifies the propositional content, which consists of a referring expression and a predicating expression. In the utterance "Is John home now?" therefore, the F would be "questioning," and the p would be "John is home now." An adequate semantic theory would need to supply the rules governing the successful performance of all of the possible illocutionary acts, plus the rules governing successful referring and predicating for all literal utterances.[6] However, since there is a relatively limited range of common illocutionary acts (falling into five basic types), listing the relevant rules for each appears to be a manageable task.

Searle's earliest account of the nature of meaning was set within the framework of this general theory of speech acts.[7] Roughly, Searle improved upon Grice's well-known definition[8] by arguing that uttering a sentence and meaning it involves getting the hearer to grasp certain of your intentions by virtue of the hearer's knowledge of the conventional rules governing the sentence uttered. Searle goes beyond Grice by emphasizing the *conventional* aspects of meaning as well as the *intentional* aspects.

The chief congruence between the non-Objectivist theory of meaning I am advancing and that of Searle (and Grice) is our agreement, over against truth-conditional semantics, that all meaning is a matter of intentionality. The chief point of divergence concerns our respective interpretations of the nature and extent of this intentionality. I take up this disagreement later.

For our purposes, we can forego any careful analysis of Searle's early definition of meaning in favor of his more relevant and adequate recent remarks. In *Intentionality*[9] he places the theory of meaning (as part of the philosophy of language) within the purview of a theory of mind and action, since he regards meaning as primarily a matter of intentionality, and intentionality is a property of mental states.

The problem for a theory of meaning is to explain how a set of meaningless marks or sounds can come to have meaning. Searle's general answer is that sounds or intrinsically meaningless symbols can have meaning imposed upon them by human beings. More specifically, the "words" become meaningful when a certain kind of intentionality is imposed upon them. Intentionality is "that property of many mental states and events by which they are directed at or about or of objects and states of affairs in the world."[10] A given mental state (e.g., belief, desire, hope, fear) is intentional because it has conditions of satisfaction that specify some object or state of affairs toward which the mental state is "directed." Thus, my belief "that it is raining" has as its conditions of satisfaction (i.e., what would make it true) *that it is raining outside*. My desire "for a cold drink" has as its conditions satisfaction *my obtaining a cold drink*. Mental states, then, have intentionality, or directedness toward the world.

Now, for Searle, linguistic meaning is possible just because human beings can impose this intentionality of their mental states onto sounds or marks that become words and sentences. In this way, the words and sentences acquire conditions of satisfaction via the intentionality of speakers. Searle identifies a "double level of Intentionality" in the performance of an illocutionary act:

1. *Sincerity condition.* There is a psychological state (e.g., belief, desire, hope, etc.) expressed in performing the appropriate illocutionary act. For instance, when I *assert* that it is raining, I express my *belief* that it is raining, and this belief has conditions of satisfaction (namely, that it is raining).

2. *Meaning intention.* This is the intention with which the act is performed. When I assert that it is raining, I have the intention to perform an illocutionary act of asserting.

Based upon this double level of Intentionality, Searle explains how it is possible for there to be linguistic meaning:

The fact that the conditions of satisfaction of the expressed Intentional state and the conditions of satisfaction of the speech act are identical suggests that the key to the problem of meaning is to see that in the performance of the speech act the mind intentionally imposes the same conditions of satisfaction on the physical expression of the expressed mental state, as the mental state has itself. The mind imposes Intentionality on the production of sounds, marks, etc., by imposing the conditions of satisfaction of the mental state on the production of the physical phenomena.[11]

In other words, a speaker utters certain sounds with a certain intention to confer on those sounds conditions of satisfaction (this is the meaning intention). But these conditions of satisfaction become those of the psychological state expressed in the utterance (this is the sincerity condition). In this way the sentence gets a derived intentionality from the intentionality of the speaker who uses that sentence. It follows that *anything can have meaning that can have intentionality (conditions of satisfaction) imposed upon it.*

We are now in a position to identify the chief points of congruence between Searle's intentionalist theory and the kind of non-Objectivist theory I am urging. There are two fundamental points of agreement:

1. *Meaning always involves human intentionality.* Intentionality is primarily a property of human mental states, and only derivatively a property of sentences, upon which we impose our intentionality. If this is correct, then no theory of meaning has a chance of being adequate if it is not based on a theory of intentionality that makes reference to the understanding of human beings. It follows that any Objectivist theory which pretends that there *just is* an objective relation between sentences and states of affairs in the world independent of intentionality cannot account for meaning as we know it.

2. *All meaning is context-dependent.* Searle notes that the vast majority of intentional states (and, derivatively, meaningful utterances) have contents that specify conditions of satisfaction.[12] He then argues the crucial point that the conditions of satisfaction are determined *only relative to a contextual Network of other intentional states and a Background of preintentional practices, capacities, and stances.* Let us consider the two basic kinds of context involved:

i) *Network.* The "Network" is a holistic web of intentional states presupposed by a given intentional state. A certain belief, desire, or hope will specify conditions of satisfaction that presuppose other intentional states, such as other beliefs, desires, fears, etc. For example, my belief that my wife and I are married has conditions of satisfaction (namely, that we are married) that depend upon other intentional states (e.g., the belief in the existence of the institution of marriage, the belief that uttering certain words in a certain context with a legal representative of the state present constitutes marrying someone, and so forth).

ii) *Background.* The Network is not the whole story, for it consists only of more and more representational, intentional mental states, each with their own conditions of satisfaction. Searle claims that this interwoven Network of intentional structures does not extend forever in one massive, unending system of distinctions (differences), because human beings have a certain bodily engagement with their world that grounds the Network. The Network fades off into a *preintentional, non-representational* background of shared capacities, practices, and stances toward objects in the world. The Background consists chiefly of certain kinds of "know-how," knowing *how to do things,* and knowing *how things are,* in contrast with "knowing-that" something is the case. Consider, for example, my intention to get milk at the store. The conditions of satisfaction for this mental state presuppose, of course, a huge number of tacit mental states, such as believing that there is a store, believing that there will be milk at the store, desiring to have some milk, believing that the store will take money for that milk, believing that I have that money, and on and on. But there are other prerequisites for having the intention to go to the store for milk. To name a few: I must be able to drive a car (which involves a mass of preintentional capacities), open doors, pick out milk on shelves, manipulate shopping carts, count money, find my car in the parking lot, maneuver into my driveway, and so forth. And I "presuppose" a world of stable objects with which I perceptually interact in predictable ways. This involves my bodily orientation toward objects and is not just a matter of entertaining or implicitly supposing certain beliefs. All of this, and much more, lies behind my simple(!) intention to get milk for my son.

Beyond Searle's Account of the Background

The upshot of the previous discussion for a theory of linguistic meaning is quite obvious. If linguistic meaning is a form of derived intentionality, then what holds for Intentionality generally will hold for linguistic meaning, namely, that it presupposes a Network that is permeated by and fades into a Background. Consequently, we are not going to develop an adequate theory of meaning until we understand more about the structure of the Background.

Unfortunately, it is precisely the Background, with all of its embodied structures and imaginative patterns, that is excluded from Objectivist semantics. It is Objectivism's refusal to consider these dimensions of understanding that explains the shortcomings of its view of meaning and rationality.

The preceding chapters represent an exploration of some of the chief image-schematic and metaphorical structures that make up both the Background and the Network. Image schemata, as structures emerging in our perceptual interactions and bodily movements, fall clearly into Searle's notion of Background. But even though they have a continuous, connected character in our bodily experience, they are sometimes conceptualized and drawn up within a representational Network, too. This happens, for example, when a PATH schema is figuratively elaborated and becomes the PURPOSES ARE PHYSICAL GOALS metaphor that is both experientially real and can also be consciously entertained in a propositional form. As structuring our experience, it is not properly representational, but we can grasp it abstractly in a propositional form that is both representational and intentional.

It would be fair to describe my constructive project as an inquiry into the structures that populate and order the Background, with special emphasis on their possible transformations and on the constraints that make them criticizable and nonarbitrary.

It is not surprising, therefore, that when Searle gives evidence of the existence and necessity of the Background, his examples involve exactly the kinds of phenomena we have considered in previous chapters. I want to consider very briefly the *nature* of his evidence in order to suggest that our earlier treatment of image schemata and their metaphorical projections gives us a way of exploring the operation of the Background (in its constraint of meaning and inference patterns), rather than merely pointing to its existence (as Searle does).

Searle gives three kinds of evidence for the Background:

A. *Literal meaning*. Searle argues quite correctly that even the most ordinary assertions literally interpreted are inextricably tied to a Background. In his essay, "Literal Meaning,"[13] he shows convincingly the ineliminable Background assumptions for simple assertions ("The cat is on the mat") and imperatives ("Bring me a hamburger," and "Shut the door"). In *Intentionality* he considers a far more interesting and problematic set of sentences using the word "open" to show that "the same literal meaning will determine different truth conditions given different Backgrounds, and, given some Backgrounds, sentences which are semantically impeccable from the classical point of view are simply incomprehensible, they determine no clear set of truth conditions."[14] Briefly, Searle's examples and conclusions are as follows: Consider these uses of "open":

(1) Tom opened the door.
(2) Sally opened her eyes.

(3) The carpenters opened the wall.
(4) Sam opened his book to page 37.
(5) The surgeon opened the wound.

All of these five sentences, according to Searle, have the same literal sense of "open," the same semantic content. However, the different Background called up for each of the five allows us to understand the same semantic content differently, that is, to understand each sentence as having different truth conditions. These five are then contrasted with three further cases, which are alleged to have *three different literal senses:*

(6) The chairman opened the meeting.
(7) The artillery opened fire.
(8) Bill opened a restaurant.

So, in the first set of five, we are supposed to have a single shared semantic content that is different from each of the three different semantic contents for "open" in sentences (6)–(8). But the truth conditions for the first five are different, because of their different Backgrounds. Furthermore, the indispensability of the Background is made clear in sentences such as (9)–(11), which are grammatically correct but do not make sense because they call up no relevant Background that would give them conditions of satisfaction.

(9) Bill opened the mountain.
(10) Sally opened the grass. (The mowed, not the smoked, type.)
(11) Sam opened the sun.

While I reject Searle's analysis of the semantics of these eleven sentences, I do share his view that they all point to the existence of what he calls the "Background." I would analyze his cases of "open" as parallel in kind to other cases of image-schematic structures tied to spatial orientation and manipulation of objects (i.e., cases such as that of *in-out* orientation discussed earlier). I would analyze his examples (1)–(8) as instances of an OPEN schema that is extended and metaphorically elaborated to constitute a web of related senses of "open."

The important point is that a non-Objectivist view of meaning and understanding begins to explain precisely how it is that image schemata determine the various related meanings of "open." Searle can only point to the Background and assert that there are different conditions of satisfaction called up depending on the appropriate background for each sentence. The arguments of the previous chapters give us a way of being far more specific about how the Background plays a crucial role in each of these cases.

B. *Metaphor.* In his essay, "Metaphor,"[15] Searle tries to list general principles for identifying an utterance as metaphorical and for determining its meaning. I have already noted (Chapter 4) that his fourth principle amounts to an admission that, for a certain class of metaphors, we really don't have any idea how they work or where they come from. We are left with the unhelpful claim that some metaphors are grounded on connections in the Background.[16] Searle is much more explicit about this grounding in *Intentionality,* where he treats metaphor as inextricably tied to the Background. He still holds that there are general rules for figuring out that when a speaker says metaphorically "X is Y" he means "X is like Y with respect to certain features F." But he insists that "there is no algorithm for discovering when an utterance is intended metaphorically, and no algorithm for calculating the values of F, . . ."[17] Moreover, there are certain kinds of metaphors whose interpretation does not rest on the perception of any literal similarity between the X and Y terms. Taste metaphors (e.g., "sweet person," "sour disposition," "bitter argument") and temperature metaphors (e.g., "warm welcome," "heated debate," "cold stare"), for example, do not seem to rest on any literal similarities between the extensions of the two terms in the metaphor. Bitter things and arguments do not share any relevant similarities that would explain the meaning of "bitter argument." Searle concludes:

It just seems to be a fact about our mental capacities that we are able to interpret certain sorts of metaphor without the application of any underlying "rules" or "principles" other than the sheer ability to make certain associations. I don't know any better way to describe these abilities than to say that they are nonrepresentational mental capacities.[18]

I do not have an adequate analysis of the taste and temperature metaphors listed by Searle. However, our non-Objectivist account of meaning suggests that there is more to be said than Searle offers us, namely, we can extend our inquiry into the Background where these metaphorical connections arise. As a starting place, we need to survey the range of gestalt structures of meaning, and we need to explore the nature of metaphorical projections of image schemata along the lines set out in Chapter 4. This, of course, does not guarantee that answers to Searle's problem will be forthcoming, but it gives us a domain of image-schematic structure in which to look for answers. Lakoff and

Kovecses[19] have taken initial steps toward understanding the role of temperature in ANGER metaphors. Their work suggests how some temperature connections are established in experience, even though they make no claims about the grounding of temperature metaphors generally. Progress on such issues will depend, in part, on further inquiries into the image-schematic grounding of metaphorical projections.

C. *Physical skills*. Searle's final body of evidence for the Background consists in the claim that learning physical skills (such as skiing) does not consist in internalizing a set of "rules" by which one may have been introduced to the skill. Skiing isn't an activity of guiding one's movements by a very rapid series of calculations based on unconscious rules and intentional contents; instead, we develop certain physical capacities and skills that make the rules irrelevant.

As with the case of metaphor, I would argue that there is much more to be said about physical skills and their role in meaning than Searle would lead us to believe. Specifically, they are not just physical skills, consisting of neural connections, about which we can say no more; rather, they involve structured motor programs. Those programs involve image schemata and gestalt structures that recur over and over again in various related skillful performances. These structured movements, in turn, depend on schemata for perceptual interactions. If there were not such regular, recurring schemata, we could never recognize the structure of situations such that we could skillfully interact with them. When I walk, for example, I must recognize patterns in my environment to which I respond on the basis of the structures I perceive. It is true that *my body* does this responding, and I am not performing a rapid set of rule-governed calculations; yet, I must at least perceive certain structures which direct, shape, and help me to monitor my skillful responses, with varying degrees of adequacy.

Furthermore, as we have seen in Chapters 2–6, the image-schematic structures of our skillful actions do not exist only as preintentional gestalts. They can be cognitively extended and elaborated so that they come to play a role in our understanding of abstract, nonphysical, or nonspatial situations. Our ability to make such semantic connections depends on our ability to grasp structure in our skillful activities. In other words, physical skills are not merely foundational, inscrutable, "physical" givens. Their structure lends itself to cognitive extension, transformation, and projection as a means for achieving understanding of more abstract domains of experience.

Why the Background Is Part of Meaning

I have been stalking Searle's treatment of the Background for three reasons: (i) I wanted to argue that any adequate theory of meaning must explore its operation. (ii) I wanted to suggest that inquiries of the type advanced in the previous chapters are an important way of probing the role of Background understanding in meaning. The key point here is that *image schemata, with their metaphorical and metonymic extensions, have been the overlooked dimension of a satisfactory theory of meaning.* In ignoring the Background, Objectivist semantics ignores the basis in human understanding that first gives rise to meaning. (iii) I wanted to indicate the respect in which Searle's treatment of the Background still rests on Objectivist longings for ultimate foundations, a desire that must be overcome if we are to understand meaning. It is to this last important point that I now turn my attention.

According to Searle, the Background is not part of meaning. His argument is straightforward: The Background plays a crucial role in our understanding, but since it is nonrepresentational and preintentional, it is not part of meaning. "Meaning," says Searle, "exists only where there is a distinction between Intentional content and the form of its externalization, and to ask for the meaning is to ask for the Intentional content that goes with the form of externalization."[20] Searle claims that the "Background" cannot be part of meaning for it has no Intentional content and thus no conditions of satisfaction.

So far, I have been using Searle as a criticism of certain Objectivist assumptions of truth-conditional semantics. I have described a gradual move from the more Objectivist leanings of *Speech Acts* (with its rules and foundational literal propositions) toward a more subtle, richer, and less Objectivist orientation in *Intentionality*. But it is in his treatment of the Background that Searle's clearly Objectivist orientation persists. I suspect that Searle's chief reason for drawing the line (between Background and meaning Network) where and as he does is to save the possibility of foundations for meaning and knowledge. The alleged preintentional character of the Background provides Searle with a way of stepping outside the potentially infinite series of connected intentional states that might be relevant to the meaning of any given utterance. The Background terminates the quest for further explanation by serving as a "given" of physical skills and stances that claims to need no further analysis, since it is not intentional (i.e., directed beyond itself).

In short, Searle regards the Background as the ultimate, rock-bottom foundation for objective meaning. Were this foundationalist view to prove adequate, it would supply a preintentional bedrock of skills, practices, capacities, and stances against which Intentional states achieve definite conditions of satisfaction. It would "ground" meaning in bodily functioning and orientation, as that beyond which we cannot go in our semantic analyses.

Unfortunately, matters are not so simple and clear-cut. We have seen that there is no clear and distinct demarcation between intentional mental states and preintentional mental and bodily capacities. Image schemata (which are preintentional in Searle's sense) can be conceptually elaborated to establish connections in our network of meanings. We seem to have a continuum rather than a dichotomous gap. On one end of the continuum are Objectivist propositions and other abstract representations, and on the other end are image schemata. Searle seems, at times, aware of this fact. He calls capacities in the Background "*preintentional*" rather than "*non*intentional," for these capacities must have a character (structure?) that can somehow connect up with *intentional* contents.

In an important summary passage, he presents the image of the Background *permeating* the intentional Network and *shading into* it, which suggests a kinship of structures much closer than the preintentional/intentional split would indicate:

The Network shades off into a Background of capacities (including various skills, abilities, preintentional assumptions and presuppositions, stances, and nonrepresentational attitudes). The Background is not on the *periphery* of Intentionality but *permeates* the entire Network of Intentional states; since without the Background the states could not function, they could not determine conditions of satisfaction.[21]

As I see it, if the Background really does *permeate* and *shade off into* the Network, then it must have a character, a structure, somewhat akin to structure in the Network. That is not to say, of course, that it will be wholly propositional (for it will exist in our experience in a continuous, analog fashion), but only that image schemata must tie up with a host of intentional structures, including propositions. Where we draw the line as we move along the continuum of structures will depend upon our purposes, values, and other assumptions. But no line of demarcation will exist "in the nature of things."

In my view, the Background must be seen as part of meaning for the simple reason that certain semantic connections and relations are constituted by image-schematic structures that emerge from our skilled bodily performances. This is made clear in the earlier analyses of the role of image schemata and their metaphorical elaborations in the development of our system of meaning. Image schemata have a continuous, analog character, yet they provide a basis for, and can connect up with, propositional structures, by virtue of their internal structure (which is propositional in my non-Objectivist sense). Image schemata really do *permeate* our networks or webs of meaning. Without them, we cannot explain the connections and relations that obtain in our semantic networks.

I am claiming that the so-called Background is merely that part of meaning that is not focused on in a given intentional act. It is that which is presupposed and is unquestioned as part of the context in which we grasp and express what we mean. It is background, relative to the foreground on which we are now focusing; but it is still part of the web of connections that constitute meaning.

Our preliminary exploration of structures in the Background also suggests a reply to Searle's chief argument for excluding the Background from meaning. He argues that, because the Background is not intentional and does not itself have conditions of satisfaction, it cannot be part of meaning. In response, we can point out that the Background is full of structure that is crucial to meaning. Take, for instance, a skill like skiing. Our ability to ski is tied up with all sorts of perceptual and motor-program schemata that have plenty of internal structure. The term "skiing" calls up (potentially) all of these structures as part of its *meaning* when it is used in an utterance. Such structures are not just a background against which the meaning of the term stands out; rather, they are part of that meaning.

Furthermore, even though image schemata do not have "truth conditions" in the way that propositions do, they do support a notion of *fit* that is a close relative of truth conditions. In place of truth conditions for the Background, we have the grasping of a situation as instantiating certain schemata, or else failing to do so. It is *part of* our experience of meaningfulness that we grasp recurring patterns or structures in a situation. So the meaning of a word or sentence will also involve these patterns or gestalt structures.

In general, the principal basis for my disagreement with Searle is an important difference in our respective notions of intentionality. On Searle's account, mental states have intentionality insofar as they are directed toward "states of affairs" in the world. On my account, the mental states are directed at our *experience* of states of affairs in the world. But experience is always a matter of understanding, and so "states of affairs" never really stand over against our web of intentionality. Searle's view of the Background is ultimately his way of trying to get "outside" language, intentionality, and understanding to "plug into" the objective world. I shall argue in the next chapter that we cannot step outside our understanding, but that, fortunately, we need not do so to find perfectly satisfactory notions of objectivity and realism.

In the final analysis, the crucial issue here is not really that of whether or not we win the privilege of including the so-called Background within meaning. That is only a minor squabble. The crucial issue in all of this is whether or not we recognize that any adequate semantic theory must include an account of structures within the Background. What matters is the way we describe those structures and their role in meaning. I am claiming that *an adequate theory of meaning is a theory of understanding, which, in turn, requires a treatment of image schemata and their metaphorical extensions out of the Background.* Meaning and rationality are embodied to the extent that they are connected to such structures.

What a Theory of Meaning Ought to Include

We are finally in a position to describe the kind of theory of meaning needed to account for semantic phenomena of the sort dealt with in this book. The key to an adequate "cognitive semantics" will be the nature of the theory of understanding upon which it relies. To ask about the meaning of something (whether it be an experience, a word, a sentence, a story, or a theory) is to ask about our understanding of it. In short, a theory of meaning is a theory of how we understand things (of whatever sort). And we have seen that this is not merely a matter of how some *individual* might happen to understand something but rather about how an *individual as embedded in a (linguistic) community, a culture, and a historical context* understands. In other words, we are concerned here with *public, shared meaning*.

It is quite clear now how the view of meaning suggested here differs from that of Objectivism. Recall that Objectivism excludes from its account of meaning a theory of understanding of the sort I am urging. The only relevant "understanding" allowed is our grasp of the truth conditions of propositions or sentences. Thus, a recent representative account of Objectivist semantics gives the standard description of the project:

A truth-conditional theory of semantics is one which adheres to the following dictum: To know the meaning of a (declarative) sentence is to know what the world would have to be like for the sentence to be true. Put another way, to give the meaning of a sentence is to specify its truth conditions, i.e., to give necessary and sufficient conditions for the truth of that sentence.[22]

We can now see why such an Objectivist theory cannot be adequate for a semantics of natural languages. It assumes that propositions or sentences *just do* map onto objective reality via conditions of satisfaction, but it ignores the fact that there are conditions of satisfaction only by means of our understanding of the propositions or sentences. And this understanding itself involves, in addition to propositional structures in the Objectivist senses, a massive complex of image-schematic structures metaphorically and metonymically elaborated. The central thrust of the earlier chapters has been to explore some of the more important kinds of image-schematic structure that make such meaning possible.

As a complement to Objectivist specifications of truth conditions and recursive functions that preserve truth, we have to ask how it is possible for propositions to have the conditions of satisfaction they do, and this involves us in a theory of understanding. This latter theory, in turn, focuses our attention on nonpropositional phenomena, and thus reveals the limited and dependent character of Objectivist semantics, which is now recognized as telling only a (very important) part of the story of meaning. In short, we need to enrich the range of phenomena which semantics takes as its proper focus of attention.

When I speak of "enriching the range of phenomena" to be explained by a theory of meaning, I am referring, in part, to the kind of phenomena dealt with in this book. At the end of the previous chapter I listed several phenomena that are central to any theory of imagination. These are the kinds of structures that must be part of a theory of meaning, but which tend to be overlooked or ignored in Objectivist semantics, because they are thought to be too subjective, idiosyncratic, derivative, or irrelevant to meaning proper.

The following list suggests the kinds of phenomena that any acceptable theory would need to explain, in addition to standard problems (e.g., synonymy, referential opacity, indexicals, etc.):

1. *Categorization*. A theory of categorization is basic to any theory of cognitive structure, for it explores the way we organize our experience into *kinds*. Objectivist semantics has tended to favor the set-theoretical view of a category as specifying necessary and sufficient conditions for membership in a given kind. But, as I noted in the Pref-

ace, there is a growing body of empirical research that suggests a different view of categories as consisting of networks with prototypical members clustered in the center of the category with less prototypical members at various distances from the central members. A category thus forms a complex radial structure, and we would need an account of the nature of these structures, to the extent that they vary in kind.[23]

Furthermore, we need an analysis of the levels of categories, with special emphasis on those that are "basic level," the level of organization that is experientially predominant for a given organism. This level will be determined by the way people interact with parts of their environment, and thus will depend upon their gestalt perception, image formation, motor programs, functions, and purposes.

In short, categorization will be understood within a general theory of cognitive models and will be inseparable from each of the following phenomena in this list.

2. *Schemata.* We have explored the operation of a few representative image schemata as they play a crucial role in the formation of networks of meaning. A comprehensive theory would go beyond the brief survey of some of the more prominent kinds of image schemata to analyze the structure and possibilities for extension of all of the significant schemata. Then, image schemata, as I am using that term, must be related to the more general sense of schema as abstract knowledge or event structure. What is needed here is a theory of cognitive models. For both senses of schema we must explain how a given schema is called into play as relevant in a given situation (out of all the possible schemata available). And we must explain both how schemata can be transformed and can be adapted to novel situations different from those in which they first emerged.

3. *Metaphor.* I am speaking, of course, of the need for a more satisfactory theory that recognizes metaphor as one of the central projective operations by which we establish semantic connections. Traditional semantic theories treat metaphor only as a deviant or derivative function on literal meaning. On the contrary, we have seen that some kinds of metaphor must be regarded as irreducible, primary cognitive functions by which we create and extend structure in our experience and understanding.

4. *Metonymy.* I have not dealt with another basic principle of understanding of nearly equal importance with metaphor, namely, that of *part-whole* relations. But metonymy, regarded as a general cognitive structure, rather than an isolated figure of speech (as in traditional accounts), turns out to be central to categorization.[24]

5. *Polysemy*. The key to understanding polysemy is to see that we are not dealing merely with multiple meanings for a single word but rather with multiple *related* meanings. On the hypothesis of image-schematic structures that can be metaphorically and metonymically extended, we can explain these relations in a manner not available to standard views. We are not left with the inexplicable fact of multiple meanings, as Objectivism alleges; instead, we have a basis for explaining the connections among the related senses.

6. *Semantic change*. A theory of meaning should be able to explain semantic change over time. Once again, traditional views can trace connections and historical sequences, but there is no general account of why the changes should occur as they do. On the view proposed here, the same structures that made it possible to explain polysemy (namely, schemata with metaphoric and metonymic extensions) can begin to account for the direction and nature of such change.

To sum up: I am suggesting that an adequate theory of meaning must consider all of the above-mentioned phenomena, in addition to the standard focus on sentential conditions of satisfaction. The move is to extend the scope of semantic theory by broadening and enriching the range of phenomena to be considered. When this is done, it becomes immediately evident that meaning is inextricably tied up with understanding—understanding as involving at least the kinds of *imaginative* phenomena just discussed. Objectivism will grant that, of course, we must "understand" the sentences to grasp their truth conditions, but it regards the relevant understanding as not requiring all of the imaginative structures listed above. It tries to get by with such an impoverished notion of understanding that it can, in effect, disregard anything beyond some allegedly transparent notion of grasping truth conditions. But, *we have seen that this cannot be done—we cannot ignore the imaginitive structures of understanding by which meaning is made possible.* We cannot ignore image schemata, metaphorical projections, metonymy, and so forth, if we want to explain meaning for natural languages.

My central theme thus has been that a theory of meaning rests on a theory of understanding, which is a theory of cognitive models—of their structure, extensions, transformations, and relations. A theory of rationality thus would depend upon such an enriched theory of meaning, for all our reasoning is done within such cognitive models and by means of patterns for manipulating and relating them.

8

"All This, and Realism, Too!"

A Problem About Rationality

We have seen that human rationality is imaginative through and through, insofar as it involves image-schematic structures that can be metaphorically projected from concrete to more abstract domains of understanding. Obviously, this is not imagination in the Romantic sense of unfettered creative fancy; rather, I have been urging an extended Kantian view of imagination as a capacity for ordering mental representations into unified, coherent, meaningful wholes that we can understand and reason about. Imagination, in this sense, mediates between sense perception and our more abstractive conceptualizing capacities; it makes it possible for us to conceptualize various structural aspects of our experience and to formulate propositional descriptions of them.

On an Objectivist account, however, the idea that there exist irreducible structures of imagination that are indispensable to meaning, understanding, and reasoning is disastrous. As we saw in Chapter 6, Objectivists exclude imagination from rationality for two basic reasons. (i) Understood in the Platonic way, imagination is taken to be too tied to the body; it is held to be too particular, concrete, subjective, and idiosyncratic to achieve the status of objective rationality. Thus, Frege insisted that images exist only in the mind that entertains them, so no two people could ever be certain that they have the same, shared imaginative representation. (ii) Understood in the Romantic way, imagination is taken to be too unconstrained, arbitrary, and fanciful to achieve the status of objective, rule-governed, rationality. According to either interpretation, then, imagination is regarded as not sufficiently rule-governed, abstract, and objective to rise to the exalted status of "rational structure."

Now, it might seem that all of this argument about the embodied nature of imaginative structures of understanding (e.g., image schemata and their metaphorical extensions) is nothing more than a harmless debate about when it is permissible to apply the honorific term "rational" to some process. And if *that* is all that is at stake, then it makes this whole discussion rather esoteric and insubstantial.

On the contrary, the question of the status of image schemata and metaphors as structures of embodied understanding turns out to have considerable significance for a number of central philosophical issues. Most important, it bears directly on the question of what is to count as knowledge and objectivity. The key question here is this: Are embodied image schemata and metaphorical systems of understanding sufficiently shared to be considered relevant to knowledge, or are they too subjective, unstructured, and unconstrained?

The Objectivist complaint about such structures can be summarized as follows: the conflation of reason with imagination can only lead to relativism. There is alleged to be no way to demonstrate the universal (shared) character of any representation of imagination. But knowledge and objectivity require just this shared character that activities of imagination are accused of lacking. So, if reason is ineliminably contaminated with imagination, then relativism follows.

One Objectivist way to salvage objectivity under these conditions would be to demonstrate that there is an algorithm governing the operations of imagination. If this could be shown, then there could be standards for assessing the correctness of any product of imagination. There would be rules, for example, to generate *the* correct and unique interpretation of a given metaphor. But we have already seen, in the last four chapters, that metaphors are not algorithmic in this way— they cannot be reduced to sets of literal propositions that map directly onto reality. What most Objectivists conclude, therefore, is that structures of imagination cannot be an integral part of the logical structure of rationality; otherwise, we would be faced with an untenable relativism. Imagination is granted a role in the "context of discovery," wherein we imaginatively generate new ideas and connections; but it is excluded from the "context of justification," which is restricted solely to the tracing of logical connections.

In this chapter I shall argue that it *does not follow* at all that the recognition of the centrality of imagination in human meaning and rationality leads to a relativism in which "anything goes." Frege was too restrictive when he claimed that structures of imagination must always be relativized to the mind that entertains them. His polemic was directed against specifically "psychological" ideas, including what I have called "particular rich images." He seems not to have been aware of image schematic structures of the sort described in the previous chapters, so it is not surprising that he doesn't acknowledge the central role of imagination.

In response to criticisms of this kind, we have seen that image schemata *can have a public, objective* character (in a suitably defined sense of "objective"), because they are recurring structures of embodied human understanding. They are part of the structure of our network of interrelated meanings, and they give rise to inferential structures in abstract reasoning. They are thus quite public and communicable in the required sense—they play an indispensable role in our sharing of a common world that we can have knowledge of.

In short, we ought to reject the false dichotomy according to which there are two opposite and incompatible options: (a) Either there must be absolute, fixed value-neutral standards of rationality and knowledge, or else (b) we collapse into an "anything goes" relativism, in which there are no standards whatever, and there is no possibility for criticism.

Against this rigid dichotomy, I have argued that there exists a large middle ground between the two extremes of foundationalism and relativism. In this book we have explored some of the more prominent imaginative structures of this intermediate domain of embodied understanding and have traced, in a general way, their role in meaning and reason. We now need to ask the question: How is it that knowledge and objectivity are possible given the irreducibly imaginative and embodied character of human understanding and rationality?

The idea that there is a middle ground between Objectivism and Relativism has been made much of in the last decade by philosophers such as Thomas Kuhn, Hilary Putnam, Richard Rorty, Richard Bernstein, and Harold Brown.[1] These and many other philosophers have argued against the view that Bernstein describes as Objectivism:

By "objectivism," I mean the basic conviction that there is or must be some permanent, ahistorical matrix or framework to which we can ultimately appeal in determining the nature of rationality, knowledge, truth, reality, goodness, or rightness.[2]

Richard Rorty has shown that some form of Objectivism has defined mainstream Western philosophy for at least the last three-and-a-half centuries. He has traced its chief formulations from Descartes' search for a method of certain knowledge, through Kant's belief in the possibility of a rational critique of all forms of judgment, up to attempts in recent analytic philosophy to formulate "the logic" or "the grammar" of a given cognitive activity or mode of inquiry.[3] In the present century Objectivism has been preserved in analytic philosophy in its claim to offer "*the* analysis of X" in a value-neutral and final fashion. Rorty explains that

analytic philosophy is still committed to the construction of a permanent, neutral framework for inquiry, and thus for all of culture.

It is the notion that human activity (and inquiry, the search for knowledge, in particular) takes place within a framework which can be isolated prior to the conclusion of inquiry—a set of presuppositions discoverable a priori—which links contemporary philosophy to the Descartes-Locke-Kant tradition.[4]

The previously mentioned assault on this form of Objectivism denies the existence of a neutral, universal framework for evaluating products of human rationality. It thus raises the specter of relativism, which Bernstein describes as the view that all of the concepts that philosophers have regarded as fundamental—those of rationality, truth, reality, knowledge, goodness, rightness—"must be understood as relative to a specific conceptual scheme, theoretical framework, paradigm, form of life, society, or culture."[5]

For most people, relativism of this sort evokes a gut-level revulsion. We cannot live with the idea that we are merely expressing "our opinion" when we condemn the wanton butchering of innocent children as morally impermissible and repugnant. We reject the implication that the moral laws that seem to bind humankind together are merely cultural prejudices erected into supreme principles. Nor can we comfortably entertain the idea that science (thought to be our most objective form of rational inquiry) is not really progressing toward *the* correct description of reality. There is something about the progress of science (or what we take to be its "progress") that leads us to think that our science really has employed human rationality in the proper way, or that we are at least moving in the right direction.

It is not surprising, therefore, that debates concerning Objectivism versus Relativism are typically carried on with great seriousness and vehemence. The reason for this earnestness seems to be tied to our deep desire for fixed standards against which to measure our actions and reasonings, and thereby to avoid a frightening indeterminacy in our experience. There lurks in most of us a gnawing fear that, should Objectivism prove untenable, the floodgates holding back the raging currents of relativism would be opened forever. We would all drown in the ensuing chaotic inundation.

In the face of the threat of relativism, therefore, there has been a tendency to return to ever more subtle and sophisticated forms of Objectivism by seeking out ever new ways to "ground" logic, science, philosophy, morality, politics, social theory, or whatever else seems threatened. And it is not surprising that philosophers have traditonally conceived their chief task as that of providing just such a "grounding." Again and again we see philosophy regarding itself as the highest rational discipline, in which all forms of rational judgment can be analyzed and critiqued—in short, as claiming to elaborate ultimate standards of rationality.

Throughout much of the twentieth century, the debate over the nature of rationality has been carried on principally, as we might expect, within the philosophy of science. Science (especially physics) is often treated as the paradigmatic model of cognitive virtue, so it seemed natural that a logical investigation into its structure and methods might reveal the core of rationality. This inquiry into the "logic of science" was carried out most notably in the movement known as Logical Empiricism.

The Failure of Logical Empiricism's Defense of Objectivism

Logical Empiricism undertook an investigation of the rationality of science on the assumption that science is our highest achievement in rational inquiry. What is supposed to distinguish science from other modes of inquiry is its logical rigor and its empirical grounding. It was held that science gives us genuine empirical knowledge because it is testable against objective data, whereas investigations in metaphysics and theology could never yield testable claims. So, it seemed that science had a *formal* part (the logical structure of theories) and an *empirical* part (its grounding in objective data). Logical Empiricism was thus faced with two tasks necessary for a defense of scientific objectivity. (i) It had to show that the rationality of science could be analyzed in terms of mathematical logic, since logic was regarded as the essence of rationality. (ii) It had to show that scientific theories were grounded in, and testable against, objective, theory-independent empirical data. In other words, Objectivist assumptions could be defended by showing that science was firmly rooted in the soil of empirical evidence and that its theories and laws were connected to that empirical ground via logically correct relations.

The failure of Logical Empiricism to accomplish either task is now well documented.[6] Early on it became quite clear that one cannot reduce the structure of scientific explanation to any form of logic available. Even the most impressive attempts along these lines typically include confessions of their own limitations.[7] This failure is especially evident in any history of attempts to formalize in logical terms the connections holding between laws and what they describe, or between scientific terms and observable states of affairs. As Hempel has shown, the Verificationist theory of meaning failed to tie empirical meaning to independent observable data, first, at the level of the single term, then, at the level of the statement, and even at the level of clusters of statements.[8] Quine is forced to conclude that only at the level of *science as a whole* is there any grounding in experience for our theories.[9]

Another aspect of the claim for empirical grounding also came under criticism. Logical Empiricism was committed to the testability of scientific theories against neutral observational data. There have now appeared a sequence of compelling arguments to the effect that there are no neutral data in the required sense.[10] Although there may be uninterpreted perceptual inputs, it is only such inputs comprehended in acts of propositional judgment that can serve to ground knowledge claims—and *these* are theory-laden by virtue of the very fact that they are taken up into propositional judgments.

The central point so far for our purposes is that all of these difficulties were the result of an inadequate Objectivist view of meaning and rationality. The Logical Empiricist view of meaning tried to tie terms or sentences down to independent, theory-neutral objective reality in a univocal fashion. In the "rational reconstruction of theories" no role was allowed for imaginative structures of understanding of the sort I have been examining. Furthermore, the attendant Objectivist view of rationality also excluded understanding of this sort, by seeking out a "pure" logical structure algorithmically governed. In sum, it was an unsatisfactory Objectivist theory of meaning, understanding, and rationality that undermined the entire project.

The failure of Logical Empiricism to give the desired Objectivist grounding of scientific knowledge seemed, once again, to open the way for a vicious relativism. But this fear of relativism is predicated upon a false assumption about the nature of objectivity—that either we have absolute foundations, or there are no foundations of any sort whatever.

In contrast to this Objectivist oversimplification, it is simply not the case that either we find some neutral, ahistorical matrix of rationality, or else we are thrown into relativistic anarchy. There are other ways to account for the objectivity of science and morals that do not rest on Objectivist assumptions. This point has been made more and more frequently by philosophers and historians of science in the last decade. Kuhn, Suppe, Feyerabend, Putnam, and Rorty have all emphasized what Brown summarizes as "the new image of science," in which most scientific research consists

of a continuing attempt to interpret nature in terms of a presupposed theoretical framework. This framework plays a fundamental role in determining what problems must be solved and what are to count as solutions to these problems; the most important events in the history of science are revolutions which change the framework. Rather than observations providing the independent data against which we test our theories, fundamental theories play a crucial role in determining what is observed, and the significance of observational data is changed when a scientific revolution takes place. Perhaps the most important theme of the new philosophy of science is its emphasis on continuing research, rather than accepted results, as the core of science.[11]

Philosophers of science are coming to recognize that scientific rationality is distinguished, not by manifesting a God's-Eye, value-neutral framework, but rather by the critical nature of its historically evolving, value-laden, and goal-directed investigations.

Objectivist Theories of Reference

This "new image of science," in which standards of evaluation evolve through history, still strikes many philosophers as far too relativistic to explain the *progress* of science. In light of the apparent failure of Logical Empiricism to ground scientific knowledge, a new Objectivist theory of meaning has arisen to take up the cause. The new program seeks a theory of reference that can explain how language (in particular, scientific language) can correctly map onto reality. The central notion is that our knowledge claims are the result of external objects causally determining our conceptual network. Logical Empiricists had earlier sought to ground knowledge in both its formal component (logical structure of theories) and in its material component (uninter-

preted perceptual data). But there turned out to be no "bare sensations" of the sort that could serve as useful foundations of knowledge.
The New Objectivism, therefore, replaces talk of "bare particulars"
and "sense data" with the general claim that it is possible to construct
an adequate theory of objective reference.

Such a theory of reference would not try to show how particular
terms are tied to sense data, or even how entire sentences map onto
states of affairs in the world. Instead, this new theory of reference
offers very abstract and subtle arguments that, since science does progress, we must be getting closer to telling the truth about the way the
world is; so there must be *some* mapping relation connecting our language to "the world." We must be "realists," that is, we must believe
that our language is tied to real objects and objectively existing categorical structures independent of us. Richard Rorty describes this new
"technical realism":

Whereas Frege, like Kant, thought of our concepts as carving up an undifferentiated manifold in accordance with our interests . . . Kripke sees the
world as already divided not only into particulars, but into natural kinds of
particulars and even into essential and accidental features of those particulars
and kinds. The question "Is 'X is Φ' true?" is thus to be answered by discovering what—as a matter of physical fact, not of anybody's intentions—"X" refers to, and then discovering whether that particular or kind is Φ. Only by
such a "physicalistic" theory of reference, technical realists say, can the notion
of "truth as correspondence to reality" be preserved.[12]

This new "technical" realism reasserts the Objectivist assumption
that issues of truth are not relative to human understanding, or human
intentionality. It wants to exclude intentions and structures of imagination by which we grasp our world as meaningful from having *any*
role in the determination of objective knowledge and truth. On this
view, the issue of truth is a question of the way in which words (or
sentences) map onto particulars ("things"). Whether they do or not,
on this Objectivist account, is not a matter of how humans come to
grasp and make sense of these particulars (and kinds of particulars).

Rorty's "pragmatist" reply to technical realism rests on the claim
that there can be no grasp of an object for the purpose of referring to it
that is not entwined within some particular semantic network, some
system of description. As Putnam phrases the crucial point: "[*W*]*hat
objects does the world consist of?* is a question that it only makes sense to
ask *within* a theory of description."[13] Putnam argues that there is no

useful or interesting sense in which words simply connect up with
things, independent of observers:

[S]igns do not intrinsically correspond to objects, independently of how those
signs are employed and by whom. But a sign that is actually employed in a
particular way by a particular community of users can correspond to particular
objects *within the conceptual scheme of those users*. "Objects" do not exist independently of conceptual schemes. *We* cut up the world into objects when we
introduce one or another scheme of description. Since the objects *and* signs are
alike *internal* to the scheme of description, it is possible to say what matches
what.[14]

Putnam is not an idealist, or an anti-realist, for whom there is nothing "outside us." To deny that there are things existing independent of
us (of perceivers) is a ridiculous view that we needn't take seriously.
Putnam (and even Rorty) grants, of course, that we live, move, and
have our being within an environment populated with physical things
that can stand off against us, resist us, and sometimes even destroy us.
So, the issue known as *realism* does not rest on whether or not there is
something in the physical world besides human beings, "minds,"
"conceptual schemes," or "language"—that is agreed upon by almost
everybody.[15] The issue actually concerns what it means for there to be
an "object" and what is required for us to be able to refer to "objects."

Putnam is correct about this issue—things are only meaningful
"objects" *for us* when we grasp them within some scheme, network, or
system of meaning structures. Words do not simply refer to objective
states of affairs independent of human beings. *People use words to refer to
objects,* and they must employ intentionalistic structures of meaning to
do this. How we carve up our world will depend both on what is "out
there" independent of us, and equally on the referential scheme we
bring to bear, given our purposes, interests, and goals. On Putnam's
view we *are* in touch with our world but always in a mediated fashion.
There is thus no single, God's-Eye way of carving up the world. But it
does not follow from this that we can carve it up any way we wish.[16]

Putnam summarizes these points nicely in a passage where he emphasizes that the inputs of sense perception do indeed *constrain* reference, and thus knowledge, but they do not uniquely determine them.
As Putnam formulates the crucial point, the nonobjectivist does not
deny

that there are experiential *inputs* to knowledge; knowledge is not a story with
no constraints except *internal* coherence; but it does deny that there are any
inputs *which are not themeselves to some extent shaped by our concepts,* by the vo-

cabulary we use to report and describe them, or any inputs *which admit of only one description, independent of all conceptual choices.*[17]

Rorty points out that the technical realist's standard response to this "internalist" or "pragmatist" relativizing of reference to a community of inquirers or agents is that it confuses the *test* of truth with the *nature* of truth. According to the technical realist, it may be that we always *determine or test* truth claims according to standards raised within a community for specific purposes; so, the internalist is correct on this point. But, it is argued, we cannot make sense of scientific progress or objective knowledge unless there is some theory-independent notion of truth as correspondence. The *nature* of truth is a correspondence or mapping between statements and states of affairs independent of human interference.

Rorty's response is simply to deny the alleged distinction—to say that there is no difference that makes any difference between the *test* of truth and its *nature*.[18] Seen in this light, we can still preserve the important claim *that we can make true statements that correspond to states of affairs in the world.* Given some specific scheme of description, which will carve up the world into particulars and kinds of particulars (i.e., categories), some statements will correspond to the world more accurately, for our purposes, than others—some of them will be obviously true, others will be clearly false, and many will be problematic borderline cases. But in every case, this "correspondence" will always be relative to our *understanding* of our world (or present situation) and of the words we use to describe it.

We can say, if we feel the need to, that we are getting better and better descriptions of reality, because we are now better able to predict the causal effects of certain events. Surely, such predictive capacity assures us that we are somehow "plugged into" the real world. But prediction is not the only value that constrains what we take as knowledge; and prediction presupposes a semantic network in terms of which the relevant relations of objects and events can be understood, for purposes of prediction. So, our ability to make correct predictions is not a proof that we have found *the* unique, God's-Eye account of reality; it only assures us that we are in touch with reality from one possible perspective.

This "being in touch with reality" is *all the realism we need.* Our realism consists in our sense that we are in touch with reality in our bodily actions in the world, and in our having an understanding of reality sufficient to allow us to function more or less successfully in that world.

Our understanding is our way of being situated in our world, and it is our embodied understanding that manifests our realist commitments.

In attempting to defuse the entire realism debate, Searle has been tempted into the extreme view that realism is not even a *theory* at all, so that it is not something worth arguing about. He suggests that treating realism as though it were a theory ordinary people hold about the world leads to unnecessary and misbegotten attempts to answer radical skeptical fears that there might be nothing in the world outside us. But, he claims, if we give up the idea that realism is a theory, all of these insoluble skeptical problems vanish.

My commitment to "realism" is exhibited by the fact that I live the way that I do, I drive my car, drink my beer, write my articles, give my lectures, and ski my mountains. Now in addition to all these activities, each a manifestation of my Intentionality, there isn't a further "hypothesis" that the real world exists.[19]

While I share Searle's view that realism is not the monumental issue it has been treated as in recent years, I think he is mistaken in denying a theoretical character to realism. The argument is simple. Minimally, ordinary people are committed to some description, or set of descriptions, of their world. *But every description presupposes some (usually implicit) theory.* So, our commitment to realism is, if only in the most general sense, a theoretical commitment.

But even if Searle is wrong in denying a theoretical status to realism, he is still right in pointing out that realism is not the kind of issue one needs to lose sleep over. We need not fear that we have lost our world when we acknowledge the theory-impregnated nature of our understanding. "Things" outside us talk back to us, and proclaim their presence, with a very loud voice most of the time. And it is our being situated in relation to them, and interacting with them, that assures us that we are realists.

The mistake that generates so much heated argument about the existence and character of the external world is the transformation of our sense of being situated in the world into the claim that we have access to a God's-Eye perspective. This "metaphysical realist" orientation requires us to show how such a perspective is possible, that is, how we can prove that there is one correct description of reality. This project, in turn, requires an ahistorical, neutral rationality and a theory of meaning and reference in which words can map directly (unmediated by understanding) onto objective reality. Finally, it is alleged that only an Objectivist metaphysical realism of this sort can withstand the attack of an "anything goes" relativism. Thus, the problems of meaning, reference, realism, rationality, and relativism cluster together within the Objectivist program.

Objectivist views generate a dual problem of reference and realism by creating a gap between concepts, propositions, meanings, and words, on the one hand, and physical objects, events, and causal interactions, on the other. The metaphysical problem of reference thus comes to be defined as a problem of how objects of one kind (ideas, concepts, meanings, words) can possibly map onto objects of a wholly different kind (physical objects or events) in an unmediated fashion. In effect, Objectivism drives a huge metaphysical wedge between these two allegedly distinct realms. And it comes to seem as though only "technical realism" and objective reference can ground a workable correspondence theory of truth.

A Non-Objectivist Defense of Realism and Knowledge

It is simply not the case that only an Objectivist perspective can justify our cherished notions of realism, objectivity, and truth. I want to suggest that the account of imaginative structures of understanding developed in this book gives the lie to the Objectivist picture of realism and reference, and it offers a more adequate and detailed way of explaining how we can have objective knowledge of our .vorld.

On the view developed here, the key notion is *embodied understanding*. We are never separated from our bodies and from forces and energies acting upon us to give rise to our understanding (as our "being-in-the-world"). The world is always with us, to a greater or lesser degree, to the extent that we have been able to function more or less successfully in our environment, and have found theories, schemes, and paradigms that make partial sense of our world. This is the sum of our realism. It is what Putnam calls an "internal" realism, since it recognizes that we only have "objects" relative to, or within, conceptual or descriptive schemes.

None of what I have said is meant to suggest that the problems of realism and reference will (or ought to) somehow magically disappear. But image schemata, as structures of our organizing activities in our embodied experience, give us a more satisfying way of talking about relations between symbols and perceptual inputs. They are structures that emerge as part of our meaningful interaction with things "outside" us. They are structures that relate us to energies and forces that we encounter in the ongoing interactive process that constitutes our understanding, our having of a world. In this manner, our realist commitment is evident, only it is not a God's-Eye ("metaphysical") realism. It is a realism based on our mediated understanding of our experience. And it would require a theory of reference based on a theory of understanding. The proper response to the threat of relativism (in its anti-realist form) is not the general overhaul of Objectivist projects (such as theories of reference and technical realism), but rather the further exploration of operations of imagination by which we have a meaningful world about which we can reason and make knowledge claims.

Let us consider briefly what is required for an adequate account of knowledge which supports the sort of realist orientation I have been defending. What is needed is an exploration of human understanding that includes image schematic structures and their imaginative metaphorical and metonymic projections, in a way that reveals our engagement in a physical environment and shows how it is possible to lay claim to objective knowledge. In general, an adequate view would have the following features:

1. First of all, it would be a view of *human* knowledge and not one of absolute, God's-Eye knowledge that could only be accessible from God's point of view. That project has been shown by Putnam and others to be hopeless in principle. All knowledge requires structure and categorization. Specifically human knowledge requires structures and categories of understanding that human beings can make sense of in terms of their own mediated experience and can use for their human purposes.

2. All knowledge is mediated by understanding. To know is to understand in a certain manner, a manner which can be shared by others who join with you to form a community of understanding.

3. Shared understanding is not merely a matter of shared concepts and propositions. It is also a matter of embodied structures of understanding, such as image schemata, which constitute a large part of what we mean by *form* itself in our experience. Such structures, as we have seen in detail, emerge in our bodily functioning; they are recurring patterns in our dynamic experience as we move about in our world. They include CONTAINERS, BALANCE, COMPULSION, BLOCKAGE, ATTRACTION, PATHS, LINKS, SCALES, CYCLES, CENTER-PERIPHERY, and a host of other patterns we did not explore. Without them our experience would be an undifferentiated mush; but because of their internal structure they constrain our understanding and reasoning. Image-schematic structures of this sort are not something imposed by our minds upon some infinitely malleable "stuff" outside us. Rather, they

are definite, recurring patterns in an interaction of an organism with its environment. Thus our experience and understanding partake of the reality of both our bodily organism and our environment, broadly conceived to include our history, culture, language, institutions, theories, and so forth.

4. It is a mistake, however, to think of an organism and its environment as two entirely independent and unrelated entities; the organism does not exist as an organism apart from its environment. The environment as a whole is as much a part of the identity of the organism as anything "internal" to the organism. As Levins and Lewontin have argued,

Natural selection is not a consequence of how well the organism solves a set of fixed problems posed by the environment; on the contrary, the environment and the organism actively codetermine each other. The internal and the external factors, genes and environment, act upon each other through the medium of the organism.[20]

It is for this reason that both Idealism and Objectivism are wrong. They both assume that the organism and its environment are two wholly separate things, and then ask *how* the two are related, and *which* one is responsible for the structure of the world. Contrary to idealism, *we* do not impose arbitrary concepts and structure upon an undifferentiated, indefinitely malleable reality—we do not simply construct reality according to our subjective desires and whims. Contrary to Objectivism, we are not merely mirrors of a nature that determines our concepts in one and only one way. Instead, our structured experience is an organism–environment interaction in which both poles are altered and transformed through an ongoing historical process.

In other words, the environment is structured in ways that limit the possibilities for our categorizations of it. But the structure of the environment by no means strictly determines the structure of our experience, which is to say, of our *understanding* of our world. When we speak of "experience," therefore, we do not mean merely a flow of mental representations. We mean to include bodily experience in all of its richness, and all that goes to make it up—the organism and its nature, the environment and its nature, and our understanding (our way of grasping) their ongoing interaction.

5. We are organisms that have adapted to and transformed our environments in the course of our evolution. We have evolved ways of functioning that are more or less successful given our purposes and needs, both for our survival and for enhancing the quality of our expe-

rience. It is not surprising, therefore, that psychologists have recently discovered a "basic level" of experience and a corresponding conceptual organization.[21] Such a level of organization permits us to function well most of the time. It is the level defined by gestalt perception of overall shape, by our capacities for motor movement in interaction with the object, and by our ability to form rich mental images of the object. It is thus the level of organization that permits us to characterize relatively accurately those discontinuities in nature that matter most for our everyday functioning. Tables and chairs, for example, are basic level objects for most of us—we function effectively in interaction with them, we can perceive their overall shapes easily, and we can readily form rich images of them. While most of us also happen to know that chairs and tables are clusters of atoms, atomic structure does not form an experientially basic level of organization for us. In fact, we needn't move all the way down to atoms to leave the basic level. If CHAIR is a basic-level category, then FURNITURE is a superordinate category, and ROCKING CHAIR is a subordinate category. All of these concepts map onto reality, but our basic level categories represent a level of organization that seems to serve our human purposes well and to favor our getting on in the world.

6. Thus, our conceptual system is "plugged into" our most relevant experiences very accurately at two levels. (a) The *basic level,* at which we distinguish elephants from giraffes and tigers, and at which we distinguish walking from running, and standing from sitting. This is the level of understanding that we have evolved to permit us to function passably well in our environment. It is not the only way to function, and we become aware of this when certain of our basic-level concepts change over time. (b) The *image-schematic* level, which gives general form to our understanding in terms of structures such as CONTAINER, PATH, CYCLE, LINK, BALANCE, etc. This is the level that defines form itself, and allows us to make sense of the relations among diverse experiences.

Both of these are real levels of structure in our understanding, each motivated by interactions with our environment. The concepts that result from these interactions must have been, and continue to be, tested constantly, instant by instant, by billions of people over our history as a species. They work pretty well, or we wouldn't be here to talk about them. Different kinds of organisms might well have developed different levels of organization to insure their survival and flourishing by giving them a hold on reality. But because we are the kinds of organisms we are, living in the kinds of environments that shape our being in countless ways, it is *our* basic-level and image-schematic structures that mesh with our experience.

One important consequence of this is that our knowledge is relative to just such mediating structures of embodied understanding as these. What counts as knowledge, therefore, is relative to our understanding that permits our more or less successful interaction with our environment. This is not to say, of course, that we live in the "best of all possible worlds," or that we have gotten everything right. On the contrary, there isn't any such thing as "getting everything right." What we have done, rather, is to exclude quite a few inaccurate and unuseful schemes and structures of understanding. There are, no doubt, many other as-yet-unexplored schemes that will prove even more useful in pursuing our purposes as they are currently shaped.

7. Finally, though basic-level and image-schematic structures are meaningful for us in the most immediate and automatic way, they by no means exhaust our understanding. We need a lot more than concepts at those levels to function successfully for our purposes. To make sense of our experience, we need categories that are superordinate and subordinate to basic-level categories. We also need ways to understand one domain of experience in terms of structures from a domain of a different kind, that is, we need metaphor. And we often need to understand one aspect of a single domain in terms of another aspect of that domain, that is, we need metonymy—as when we need to understand a whole in terms of a part of that whole, or in terms of some related attribute.

To summarize: we have conceptual systems that are grounded in two ways—in basic-level and image-schematic understanding—and are extended imaginatively by category formation and by metaphorical and metonymic projections. There is no aspect of our understanding that is independent of the nature of the human organism. And that is why this book is devoted to an exploration of the way meaning and rationality are grounded in recurring structures of embodied human understanding. *Understanding is an event*—it is not merely a body of beliefs (though it includes our beliefs). It is the means by which we have a *shared, relatively intelligible world*. The basic epistemological finding of this "experientialist" (cognitive semantics) approach is that knowledge must be understood in terms of structures of embodied human understanding, as an interaction of a human organism with its environment (which includes its language, cultural traditions, values, institutions, and the history of its social community). This finding is set within a realist conception of the world and our understanding as part of the world.

A Non-Objectivist Account of Truth and Objectivity

The outline of an account of shared knowledge given above has some rather obvious implications for a view of objectivity and truth. The central problem with Objectivism is that it does not take embodied understanding seriously enough. It assumes that words or sentences can map directly onto objective reality because it regards understanding as more or less transparent. But we have seen that understanding is actually quite thick, rich, and imaginative. Because Objectivism leaves imaginative human understanding out of the picture, it can only treat reference as a relation between abstract symbols and objective states of affairs. We saw that meaning and rationality do not work that way. Signs do not just map onto objective reality all by themselves—they can relate to "the world" just because *people* understand both the symbols and their world and can relate one to the other. Both cases of understanding involve image-schematic and basic-level structures that can be the basis for metaphoric and metonymic projections. Thus, it is not surprising that those symbols, understood in that fashion, can be seen to pick out objects, events, and persons in our experience *as we understand it*.

Truth-as-correspondence is still a workable notion only if it is not understood in the Objectivist fashion, as requiring a God's-Eye-View of an external relation between words and the world. Of course, we can say true things about our world, as we understand those words and that world. What is true will depend upon how our reality is carved up, that is, how our understanding is structured. And that, as we have observed, depends on many things: the nature of our organism, the nature and structure of our environment, our purposes, our conceptual system, our language, our metaphorical and metonymic projections, our values, and our standards of accuracy. When all of these interrelated factors are put together, we have the complex structure of our ongoing, ever-changing experience. But since our experience does have structure and differentiation, we can make statements that correspond, more or less adequately, to some part of that structure. Some of the things we say will not correspond very well and will be false. Many of our statements will, given our purposes and interests, neither fit precisely, nor fail to fit, our understood experience. These will be open to debate and further inquiry, in the course of which we may even change our interests, standards, or basic concepts. In short, given the nature of our bodies, our environment, our purposes, and our conceptual system, we will understand the world as carved up into objects and kinds of objects. And, based on our understanding of these, we can make claims that correspond more or less accurately to our experience.

The idea that standards of truth—that what counts as accurate correspondence of statement to fact—depend on our systems of description and our purposes for having descriptions is often very distressing to people. To some philosophers it seems as though there must either be absolute standards (specifying one correct view), or else no standards at all. But we have seen that this is not so, that there is indeed a middle ground between these two extremes. Fortunately, nothing important is lost by the realization that truth is not an absolute notion. It doesn't really matter that we can't see the world through God's Eyes; for we can see the world through shared, public eyes that are given to us by our embodiment, our history, our culture, our language, our institutions, etc. This does not mean, of course, that we are obliged to be happy with our present knowledge limitations. But it does mean that we can know that we are partially in touch with reality, not in the "one correct way" but in one or more of the possible ways in which Nature can be described. Thus, we can still preserve a notion of truth-as-correspondence, as long as it is contextually situated.

Some philosophers have tried to salvage Objectivism by granting that knowledge and truth are relative to standards dependent upon our purposes, while yet insisting that there is, in fact, *one supreme purpose* served by all structures of knowledge, namely, the "accurate description of reality." But this misses the point. "Accurately describing reality" is not a single, homogeneous purpose on a par with a purpose like making one's bed. "Describing accurately how things are" is a shorthand for "finding descriptions of reality that work more or less well given our purposes in framing descriptions of reality." You cannot eliminate the evaluative element from our notion of truth. Truth is always truth relative to a basic description and relative to standards of adequacy determined by our human purposes and the nature of our interactions with our environment. Truth is always relative to this embodied understanding. Even if we aren't looking through God's Eyes, we will still have the same standards and criteria of scientific progress that we have always had. We can go about our attempts to gain knowledge in the same way as before, since neither our purposes, our organism, nor our environment will have changed in a significant fashion.

Finally, we can still have a reasonable notion of "objectivity." Putnam gives an account of objectivity in terms of both *coherence* and *fit*.

What makes a statement, or a whole system of statements—a theory or a conceptual scheme—rationally acceptable is, in large part, its coherence and fit; coherence of "theoretical" or less experiential beliefs with one another and with more experiential beliefs, and also coherence of experiential beliefs with theoretical beliefs. Our conceptions of coherence and acceptability are . . . deeply interwoven with our psychology. They depend upon our biology and our culture; they are by no means "value free." But they *are* our conceptions, and they are conceptions of something real. They define a kind of objectivity, *objectivity for us,* even if it is not the metaphysical objectivity of the God's Eye view.[22]

It is important to see that objectivity is not merely a matter of the coherence of our beliefs with those of others. It is also a matter of *fit with our experiential beliefs.* These latter beliefs, of course, are framed within a system of meaning and description; but, as we have seen, they are nonetheless tied to reality because of that. Moreover, I would go beyond Putnam's focus on *beliefs* to stress the obvious importance of structures of embodied understanding, as shared structures that play a role in what a community regards as "objective."

Objectivity consists, then, in taking up an appropriate publicly shared understanding or point of view. This involves rising above our personal prejudices, idiosyncratic views, and subjective representations. On the account I have sketched, objectivity is thus made possible by the public nature of image-schematic and basic-level structures of understanding, and the metaphoric and metonymic projections based upon them. Objectivity does not require taking up God's perspective, which is impossible; rather, it requires taking up appropriately shared human perspectives that are tied to reality through our embodied imaginative understanding.

Notes

PREFACE

1. Hilary Putnam, *Reason, Truth and History* (Cambridge: Cambridge University Press, 1981). For an extension of Putnam's argument to formalist semantics in general see George Lakoff, *Women, Fire, and Dangerous Things: What Categories Reveal about the Mind* (Chicago: University of Chicago Press, 1987), chaps. 15–16. A brief summary of Lakoff's appropriation of Putnam's arguments can be found in George Lakoff, "Cognitive Semantics," in Umberto Eco (ed.), *Meaning and Mental Representation* (in press).

2. Important work on categorization includes: Eleanor Rosch, "Natural Categories," *Cognitive Psychology* 4 (1973), 328–350; Eleanor Rosch, "Cognitive Reference Points," *Cognitive Psychology* 7 (1975), 532–547; Eleanor Rosch, "Cognitive Representations of Semantic Categories," *Journal of Experimental Psychology* 104 (1975), 192–233; Eleanor Rosch and B. B. Lloyd (eds.), *Cognition and Categorization* (Hillsdale, N.J.: Lawrence Erlbaum, 1978); Edward Smith and Douglas Medin, *Categories and Concepts* (Cambridge, Mass.: Harvard University Press, 1981); Lakoff, *Women, Fire, and Dangerous Things;* Paul Kay and Chad McDaniel, "The Linguistic Significance of the Meanings of Basic Color Terms," *Language* 54, no. 3 (1978), 610–646; Brent Berlin, Dennis Breedlove, and Peter Raven, *Principles of Tzeltal Plant Classification* (New York: Academic Press, 1974); Lawrence Barsalou, "Determinants of Graded Structure in Categories" (unpubl. mss., Psychology Dept., Emory University, 1984); Floyd Lounsbury, "A Formal Account of the Crow- and Omaha-Type Kinship Terminologies," in W. H. Goodenough (ed.), *Explorations in Cultural Anthropology* (New York: McGraw-Hill, 1964); Barbara Tversky, "Components of Categories," in C. Craig (ed.), *Categorization and Noun Classification* (Philadelphia: Benjamins North America, 1985); R. M. W. Dixon, "Noun

Classes," *Lingua* 21 (1968), 104–125; Willett Kempton, *The Folk Classification of Ceramics: A Study of Cognitive Prototypes* (New York: Academic Press, 1981).

3. See, for instance, Charles Fillmore, "The Case for Case," in E. Bach and R. Harms (eds.), *Universals in Linguistic Theory* (New York: Holt, Rinehart and Winston, 1968); Charles Fillmore, "An Alternative to Checklist Theories of Meaning," *Proceedings of the First Annual Meeting of the Berkeley Linguistics Society* (1975); Charles Fillmore, "Topics in Lexical Semantics," in P. Cole (ed.), *Current Issues in Linguistic Theory* (Bloomington: Indiana University Press, 1976); Charles Fillmore, "The Organization of Semantic Information in the Lexicon," *Chicago Linguistic Society Parasession on the Lexicon* (1978), 138–147; Charles Fillmore, "Towards a Descriptive Framework for Spatial Deixis," in Robert Jarvella and Wolfgang Klein (eds.), *Speech, Place, and Action* (London: John Wiley, 1982); Charles Fillmore, "Frame Semantics," in Linguistic Society of Korea (ed.), *Linguistics in the Morning Calm* (Seoul: Hanshin, 1982); Charles Fillmore, "Frames and the Semantics of Understanding" (unpubl. mss., Dept. of Linguistics, University of California, Berkeley, 1984); Paul Kay, "Linguistic Competence and Folk Theories of Language: Two English Hedges," in *Proceedings of the Ninth Annual Meeting of the Berkeley Linguistics Society* (1983), 128–137; Eve Sweetser, "The Definition of *Lie:* An Examination of the Folk Theories Underlying a Semantic Prototype," in D. Holland and N. Quinn (eds.), *Folk Models in Language and Thought* (Cambridge: Cambridge University Press, 1985).

4. George Lakoff and Mark Johnson, *Metaphors We Live By* (Chicago: University of Chicago Press, 1980); Dedre Gentner and Donald Gentner, "Flowing Waters or Teeming Crowds: Mental Models of Elecrtricity," in D. Gentner and A. L. Stevens (eds.), *Mental Models* (Hillsdale, N.J.: Lawrence Erlbaum, 1982); Naomi Quinn, "Marriage as a Do-It-Yourself Project: The Organization of Marital Goals," *Proceedings of the Third Annual Conference of the Cognitive Science Society* (1981); Donald Schon, "Generative Metaphors: A Perspective on Problem-setting in Social Policy," in A. Ortony (ed.), *Metaphor and Thought* (Cambridge: Cambridge University Press, 1979), 254–283; Michael Reddy, "The Conduit Metaphor—a Case of Frame Conflict in Our Language about Language," in A. Ortony (ed.), *Metaphor and Thought* (Cambridge: Cambridge University Press, 1979), 284–324; Mark Turner, "Kinship Metaphors" (Ph.D. diss., Dept. of English, University of California, Berkeley, 1983).

5. Cf. Susan Lindner, "A Lexico-Semantic Analysis of Verb-Particle Constructions with UP and OUT" (Ph.D. diss., Dept. of Linguistics, University of California, San Diego, 1981), available from the Indiana University Linguistics Club; Claudia Brugman, "Story of Over" (M.A. thesis, Dept. of Linguistics, University of California, Berkeley, 1981), available from the Indiana University Linguistics Club; Claudia Brugman, "The Use of Body-Part Terms as Locative in Chalcatongo Mixtec," University of California, Berkeley, report no. 4 of the Survey of California and Other Indian Languages, 1983;

Laura Janda, "A Semantic Analysis of the Russian Verbal Prefixes ZA-, PERE-, DO-, and OT-" (Ph.D. diss., University of California, Los Angeles, 1984); Ronald Langacker, *Foundations of Cognitive Grammar*, vol. 1 (Palo Alto: Stanford University Press, 1986); Giles Fauconnier, *Mental Spaces* (Cambridge, Mass.: MIT Press, 1985).

6. See, for example, Michel Breal, *Semantics: Studies in the Science of Meaning* (New York: Henry Holt and Co., 1900; reprinted, New York: Dover, 1964).

7. Eve Sweetser, *From Etymology to Pragmatics: The Mind-As-Body Metaphor in Semantic Structure and Semantic Change* (in Press).

8. Leonard Talmy, "Semantic Structures in English and Atsugewi" (Ph.D. diss., University of California, Berkeley, 1972); Eugene Casad, "Cora Locationals and Structured Imagery" (Ph.D. diss., Dept. of Linguistics, University of California, San Diego, 1982); Ronald Langacker and Eugene Casad, "'Inside' and 'Outside' in Cora Grammar," *International Journal of American Linguistics* 51, no. 3 (1985), 247–281; Claudia Brugman, "The Use of Body-Part Terms as Locatives in Chalcatongo Mixtec"; Claudia Brugman, "Metaphor in the Elaboration of Grammatical Categories in Mixtec" (unpubl. mss., 1984); see also Lakoff, *Women, Fire, and Dangerous Things,* chapter on "Relativism."

9. Thomas Kuhn, *The Structure of Scientific Revolutions*, 2d ed., (Chicago: University of Chicago Press, 1970); Carl Hempel, *Aspects of Scientific Explanation* (New York: Free Press, 1965); Frederick Suppe, *The Structure of Scientific Theories*, 2d ed. (Urbana: University of Illinois Press, 1977); Harold I. Brown, *Perception, Theory and Commitment* (Chicago: University of Chicago Press, 1979); Paul Feyerabend, *Against Method* (London: New Left Books, 1975); N. R. Hanson, *Patterns of Discovery* (Cambridge: Cambridge University Press, 1958); W. V. O. Quine, *From a Logical Point of View* (New York: Harper Torchbooks, 1961); Hilary Putnam, *Reason, Truth and History* (Cambridge: Cambridge University Press, 1981).

INTRODUCTION

1. For a detailed account of the most significant philosophical assumptions and developments behind Objectivism see Richard Rorty, *Philosophy and the Mirror of Nature* (Princeton: Princeton University Press, 1979).

2. Rene Descartes, *Rules for the Direction of the Mind* (1628), in E. Haldane and G. T. R. Ross (eds.), *The Philosophical Works of Rene Descartes* (Cambridge: Cambridge University Press, 1911).

3. Gottlob Frege, "On Sense and Reference," in Peter Geach and Max Black (eds.), *Translations from the Philosophical Writings of Gottlob Frege* (Oxford: Basil Blackwell, 1966).

4. Ibid., p. 59.

5. For an excellent statement of the model-theoretic position, see David Dowty, Robert Wall, and Stanley Peters, *Introduction to Montague Semantics* (Dordrecht: D. Reidel, 1981). Concerning the metaphysical assumptions just

mentioned, for example, they explain that "as a first approximation let us simply assume that the world contains various sorts of objects—call them "entities"—and that in a particular state-of-affairs these entities have certain properties and stand in certain relations to each other" (p. 7).

6. Dowty, Wall, and Peters summarize: "A truth-conditional theory of semantics is one which adheres to the following dictum: To know the meaning of a (declarative) sentence is to know what the world would have to be like for the sentence to be true. Put another way, to give the meaning of a sentence is to specify its truth conditions, i.e., to give necessary and sufficient conditions for the truth of that sentence" (p. 4).

7. David Lewis, "General Semantics," in Donald Davidson and Gilbert Harman (eds.), *Semantics of Natural Language* (Dordrecht: D. Reidel, 1972), 170.

8. Jon Barwise and John Perry, *Situations and Attitudes* (Cambridge, Mass.: MIT Press, 1983), 19.

9. Ibid., p. 4.

10. Ibid., p. 17.

11. Ibid., p. 42.

12. Donald Davidson, "Truth and Meaning," *Synthese* 17 (1967), 310.

13. Donald Davidson, "Semantics for Natural Languages," in D. Davidson and G. Harman (eds.), *The Logic of Grammar* (Encino, Calif.: Dickenson, 1975), 18.

CHAPTER ONE

1. Zenon Pylyshyn, "The Imagery Debate: Analogue Media vs. Tacit Knowledge," *Psychological Review* 88, no. 1 (1981), 16–45.

2. Tim Beneke, *Men on Rape* (New York: St. Martin's, 1982), 43–44.

3. The following analysis was worked out with George Lakoff for our essay, "Metaphor and Communication," Linguistic Agency, University of Trier, ser. A, paper no. 97, December 1982.

4. See, for example, John Searle, "Literal Meaning," in his *Expression and Meaning* (Cambridge: Cambridge University Press, 1979), 30–57, for an account of some of the assumptions necessary for interpreting the simple literal expression, "The cat is on the mat." Searle gives a further analysis of "background" in his *Intentionality* (Cambridge: Cambridge University Press, 1983), chap. 5.

5. John Searle, "Metaphor," in *Expression and Meaning*, pp. 76–116; Donald Davidson, "What Metaphors Mean," *Critical Inquiry* 5, no. 1 (1978), 31–47; George Lakoff and Mark Johnson, *Metaphors We Live By* (Chicago: University of Chicago Press, 1980).

6. Richard Nisbett and Lee D. Ross, *Human Inference: Strategies and Shortcomings* (Englewood Cliffs, N.J.: Prentice-Hall, 1980).

7. Alvin Goldman, "Epistemics: The Regulative Theory of Cognition," *Journal of Philosophy* 75, no. 10 (1978), 509–523.

CHAPTER TWO

1. Perry W. Thorndyke, "Applications of Schema Theory in Cognitive Research," in John Anderson and Stephen Kosslyn (eds.), *Tutorials in Learning and Memory: Essays in Honor of Gordon Bower* (San Francisco: W. H. Freeman, 1984), 167–192.

2. David Rumelhart, *Introduction to Human Information Processing* (New York: John Wiley and Sons, 1977), 165.

3. Roger Schank and Robert Abelson, *Scripts, Plans, Goals and Understanding* (Hillsdale, N.J.: Lawrence Erlbaum, 1977).

4. Ibid., p. 41.

5. Ulric Neisser, *Cognition and Reality* (San Francisco: W. H. Freeman, 1976), 54.

6. Ibid., p. 56.

7. George Lakoff and Mark Johnson, *Metaphors We Live By* (Chicago: University of Chicago Press, 1980), chaps. 15–18.

8. Immanuel Kant, *Critique of Pure Reason,* trans. Norman Kemp Smith (New York: St. Martin's, 1965), A141/B180.

9. John R. Anderson, *Cognitive Psychology and Its Implications* (San Francisco: W. H. Freeman, 1980), chap. 3.

10. L. Brooks, "Spatial and Verbal Components of the Act of Recall," *Canadian Journal of Psychology* 22 (1968), 349–368.

11. For example, Gloria Marmor and Larry Zabeck, "Mental Rotation by the Blind: Does Mental Rotation Depend on Visual Imagery?" *Journal of Experimental Psychology: Human Perception and Performance* 2, no. 4 (1976), 515–521; Nancy Kerr, "The Role of Vision in 'Visual Imagery' Experiments: Evidence from the Congenitally Blind," *Journal of Experimental Psychology: General* 112, no. 2 (1983), 265–277.

12. R. Shepard and J. Metzler, "Mental Rotation of Three-dimensional Objects," *Science* 171 (1971), 701–703.

13. L. A. Cooper and R. Shepard, "Chronometric Studies of the Rotation of Mental Images," in W. G. Chase (ed.), *Visual Information Processing* (New York: Academic Press, 1973).

14. George Lakoff, *Women, Fire, and Dangerous Things: What Our Categories Reveal about the Mind* (Chicago: University of Chicago Press, 1987), case study 2.

15. L. Carmichael, H. Hogan, and A. Walter, "An Experimental Study of the Effect of Language on the Reproduction of Visually Perceived Form," *Journal of Experimental Psychology* 15 (1932), 76–83.

16. This issue is discussed in P. N. Johnson-Laird, *Mental Models: Towards a Cognitive Science of Language, Inference, and Consciousness* (Cambridge, Mass.: Harvard University Press, 1983), chap. 7.

17. Zenon Pylyshyn, "The Imagery Debate: Analogue Media vs. Tacit Knowledge," *Psychological Review* 88, no. 1 (1981), 16–45.

18. Lakoff, *Women, Fire, and Dangerous Things*.

19. As I mentioned earlier, John Searle *(Intentionality* [Cambridge: Cambridge University Press, 1983]) has devoted considerable attention to showing how every meaningful utterance presupposes a vast network of propositions and a massive background of nonpropositional, preintentional capacities, attitudes, and orientations. In Chapter 7 below I discuss the merits of Searle's view and my disagreements with him about the nature of meaning.

20. See, for example, Susan Lindner, "A Lexico-Semantic Analysis of Verb-Particle Constructions with UP and OUT" (Ph.D. diss., University of California, San Diego, 1981); Ronald Langacker, *Foundations of Cognitive Grammar*, vol. 1 (Palo Alto: Stanford University Press, 1986); Lakoff, *Women, Fire, and Dangerous Things;* Claudia Brugman, "Story of Over" (M.A. thesis, Dept. of Linguistics, University of California, Berkeley, 1981), available from the Indiana University Linguistics Club; Eve Sweetser, *Semantic Structure and Semantic Change: A Cognitive Linguistic Study of Modality, Perception, Speech Acts, and Logical Relations* (Cambridge: Cambridge University Press, forthcoming); Leonard Talmy, "Force Dynamics in Language and Thought," *Chicago Linguistics Society 21, Pt. 2: Parasession on Causatives and Agentivity* (1985), 293–337.

21. Lindner.

22. See George Lakoff and Mark Johnson *(Metaphors We Live By)* for an analysis of the ARGUMENT IS A CONTAINER metaphor and its relations to other central metaphors for rational argument.

23. See Leonard Talmy, "How Language Structures Space," in H. Pick and L. Acredolo (eds.), *Spatial Orientation: Theory, Research, and Application* (New York: Plenum Press, 1983) for a treatment of this notion of "viewpoint."

24. There is an interesting linguistic construction that supports this analysis of negation. If I say, "I pitched all day with*out* hitting Bill," I mean that I pitched all day and did *not* hit Bill. The event of hitting Bill is understood metaphorically as a container. But if I do *not* hit Bill, then I am *outside of* (or *without*) that event-container (in which Bill is hit). Likewise, if I keep the pitcher *from* hitting Bill, I keep him *away from* (i.e., outside of) that same event-container (in which Bill is hit).

CHAPTER THREE

1. Eve Sweetser, *From Etymology to Pragmatics: The Mind-as-Body Metaphor in Semantic Structure and Semantic Change* (in Press).

2. Ibid., pp. 58–59.

3. See John Lyons, *Semantics* (Cambridge: Cambridge University Press, 1977).

4. Leonard Talmy, "Force Dynamics in Language and Thought," *Chicago Linguistics Society 21, Pt. 2: Parasession on Causatives and Agentivity* (1985), 293–337.

5. My debt to Eve Sweetser will be obvious to anyone familiar with her work. I follow the structure of her study, selecting out whatever suits my purposes; and I rely on her analyses of particular examples in most cases.

6. Sweetser, p. 63.

7. George Lakoff and Mark Johnson, *Metaphors We Live By* (Chicago: University of Chicago, 1980).

8. Sweetser, p. 74.

9. The present analysis of epistemic *may* appears to restrict the notion of reasoning fairly narrowly to a movement from premises to a conclusion. A more adequate, comprehensive treatment would have to include richer conceptions of reasoning, such as dialectical reasoning, scientific problem-solving, and what I shall later describe as metaphorical entailments. For the present, it is sufficient to demonstrate that a widely presupposed conception of reasoning manifests the structures described herein.

10. There is a large and mushrooming body of literature that calls into question the adequacy of a rigid semantics/pragmatics dichotomy. My point is only that we ought not merely assume such a distinction a priori without seeing whether it can actually be maintained in real cases. See, for example, Paul Kay, "Linguistic Competence and Folk Theories of Language: Two English Hedges," *Berkeley Linguistics Society* 9 (1983), 128–137; Ronald Langacker, *Foundations of Cognitive Grammar,* vol. 1 (Palo Alto: Stanford University Press, 1986).

11. J. L. Austin, *How to do Things with Words,* 2d ed. (Cambridge, Mass.: Harvard University Press, 1975).

12. John Searle, *Speech Acts* (Cambridge: Cambridge University Press, 1969).

13. John Searle, "A Taxonomy of Illocutionary Acts," in his *Expression and Meaning* (Cambridge: Cambridge University Press, 1979).

14. Michael Reddy, "The Conduit Metaphor," in A. Ortony (ed.), *Metaphor and Thought* (Cambridge: Cambridge University Press, 1979).

15. Austin was the first to work out the range of these possible "infelicities" and "misfires" that prevent the successful performance of a speech act (*How to Do Things with Words*).

16. Sweetser, p. 91.

CHAPTER FOUR

1. Notable exceptions, as we shall see later, include I. A. Richards, *The Philosophy of Rhetoric* (Oxford: Oxford University Press, 1936); and Philip Wheelwright, *Metaphor and Reality* (Bloomington: Indiana University Press, 1962).

2. The recognition of metaphor as a central epistemological and semantic problem is obvious in more recent treatments of figurative language. See, for example, A. Ortony, *Metaphor and Thought* (Cambridge: Cambridge University Press, 1979); R. Hoffman and R. Honeck, *Cognition and Figurative Language* (Hillsdale, N.J.: Lawrence Erlbaum, 1980); and M. Johnson, *Philosophi-*

cal Perspectives on Metaphor (Minneapolis: University of Minnesota Press, 1981).

3. The *comparison* theory has been omnipresent in treatments of metaphor in the Western tradition. For a survey of its most prominent manifestations, see my introduction to *Philosophical Perspectives on Metaphor.*

4. S. T. Coleridge, *Biographia Literaria* (1817), chap. 13, ed. J. Shawcross (Oxford: Oxford University Press, 1907).

5. From Coleridge's lectures on Shakespeare, in T. M. Raysor (ed.), *Coleridge's Shakespearean Criticism,* 2 vols. (Cambridge, Mass.: Harvard University Press, 1930), 1: 212–213.

6. Coleridge, *Biographia Literaria,* chap. 13.

7. I. A. Richards, *The Philosophy of Rhetoric* (Oxford: Oxford University Press, 1936), 108–109.

8. Max Black, "Metaphor," *Proceedings of the Aristotelian Society,* n.s. 55 (1954–1955), 273–294.

9. Ibid., pp. 284–285.

10. Max Black, "More about Metaphor," *Dialectica* 31, nos. 3–4 (1977), 431–457.

11. Ibid., p. 454.

12. Ibid, p. 454.

13. Ibid., p. 446.

14. Donald Davidson, "What Metaphors Mean," *Critical Inquiry* 5, no. 1 (1978), 47.

15. John Searle, "Metaphor," in his *Expression and Meaning* (Cambridge: Cambridge University Press, 1979), 76–116.

16. Ibid., pp. 107–108.

17. John Searle, "The Background," chap. 5 in his *Intentionality* (Cambridge: Cambridge University Press, 1983), 149.

18. To my knowledge only a handful of theorists have ever embraced this strong constitutive view of metaphor. Besides Coleridge, Nietzsche is one of the first to take such a stance. See, for instance, Lawrence Hinman, "Nietzsche, Metaphor, and Truth," *Philosophy and Phenomenological Research* 43, no. 2 (1982), 179–199. I have already discussed I. A. Richards's contribution to this position. Paul Ricoeur, *The Rule of Metaphor* (Toronto: University of Toronto Press, 1977), also grants metaphor a special ontological status, especially in Study 7. George Lakoff and I, in *Metaphors We Live By* (Chicago: University of Chicago Press, 1980), treat certain kinds of metaphorical structure as experientially basic. See also Robert Verbrugge, "Transformations in Knowing: A Realist View of Metaphor," in R. Hoffman and R. Honeck (eds.), *Cognition and Figurative Language* (Hillsdale, N.J.: Lawrence Erlbaum, 1980), 87–126.

19. Michael Polanyi, *Personal Knowledge* (New York: Harper and Row, 1964).

20. Rudolf Arnheim, *Art and Visual Perception: The Psychology of the Crea-*

tive Eye, rev. ed. (Berkeley: University of California, 1974). Figs. 1–4 are taken from chap. 1, "Balance."

21. Ibid., pp. 13–14.

22. Ibid., pp. 18–19.

23. In Chapters 5 and 7 I argue for this broad conception of understanding, as our way of "being situated in" or "having" a world. Understanding exists both as reflective activity *and* experiential orientation or situatedness, in this sense.

24. Wassily Kandinsky, *Point and Line to Plane* (New York: Guggenheim, 1946), 92.

25. Wassily Kandinsky, *Concerning the Spiritual in Art* (New York: Wittenborn Art Books, 1947), 57.

26. David Katz, *The World of Color* (London: Kegan Paul, Trench, Trubner, 1935).

27. Quoted from an essay by Kandinsky in *Cahiers d'Art* 10, nos. 1–4 (1935), 54, in Paul Overy, *Kandinsky: The Language of the Eye* (London: Paul Elek, 1969), 96.

28. George Lakoff and Zoltan Kovecses, "The Cognitive Model of Anger Inherent in American English," Berkeley Cognitive Science Report no. 10, May 1983.

29. Jaime Carbonell, "Towards a Computational Model of Metaphor in Common Sense Reasoning" (unpubl. mss., 1982).

30. Ibid., p. 2.

31. Lakoff and Johnson in their chap. 1 provide an analysis of the ARGUMENT IS WAR metaphor.

CHAPTER FIVE

1. Relevant evidence is summarized in John R. Anderson, *Cognitive Psychology and Its Implications* (San Francisco: W. H. Freeman, 1980), chap. 3.

2. The literature on metaphorical systems is large and mushrooming. Representative studies include: Naomi Quinn, "Marriage as a Do-It-Yourself Project: The Organization of Marital Goals," *Proceedings of the Third Annual Conference of the Cognitive Science Society,* Berkeley, Calif., 1981; Donald Schon, "Generative Metaphor: A Perspective on Problem-setting in Social Policy," in A. Ortony, *Metaphor and Thought* (Cambridge: Cambridge University Press, 1979), 254–283; Michael Reddy, "The Conduit Metaphor—a Case of Frame Conflict in Our Language about Language," in Ortony, pp. 284–324.

3. George Lakoff and Mark Johnson, *Metaphors We Live By* (Chicago: University of Chicago Press, 1980), 52–55.

4. See especially, Ronald Langacker, *Foundations of Cognitive Grammar,* vol. 1 (Palo Alto: Stanford University, 1986); Susan Lindner, "A Lexico-Semantic Analysis of Verb-Particle Constructions with UP and OUT" (Ph.D. diss., Dep. of Linguistics, University of California, San Diego, 1981), avail-

able from the Indiana University Linguistics Club; Claudia Brugman, "The Use of Body-Part Terms as Locatives in Chalcatongo Mixtec," University of California, Berkeley, report no. 4 of the Survey in California and Other Indian Languages, 1983.

5. Eve Sweetser, *Semantic Structure and Semantic Change: A Cognitive Linguistic Study of Modality, Perception, Speech Acts, and Logical Relations* (Cambridge: Cambridge University Press, in press).

6. Ibid., p. 26.

7. Dedre Gentner and Donald Gentner, "Flowing Water or Teeming Crowds: Mental Models of Electricity," in Dedre Gentner and Albert Stevens (eds.), *Mental Models* (Hillsdale, N.J.: Lawrence Erlbaum, 1983), 99–129.

8. The following analysis and the treatment of the PATH schema was worked out in collaboration with George Lakoff. Part of our analysis appears in his *Women, Fire, and Dangerous Things: What Our Categories Reveal about the Mind* (Chicago: University of Chicago Press, 1987).

9. Eviatar Zerubavel, *Patterns of Time in Hospital Life* (Chicago: University of Chicago Press, 1979); Eviatar Zerubavel, *Hidden Rhythms* (Chicago: University of Chicago Press, 1981); and Eviatar Zerubavel, *The Seven Day Circle* (New York: Free Press, 1985).

10. F. Michael Connelly and D. Jean Clandinin, "The Cyclic Temporal Structure of Schooling" (paper delivered at Symposium on Classroom Studies of Teachers' Personal Knowledge, Ontario Institute for Studies in Education, December 9–11, 1985).

11. See Hans Georg Gadamer, *Truth and Method* (New York: Crossroad, 1975), for an interpretation of the horizonal character of all human understanding.

12. C. Alexander, S. Ishikawa, and M. Silverstein, *A Pattern Language* (New York: Oxford University Press, 1977); C. Alexander, *The Timeless Way of Building* (New York: Oxford University Press, 1979).

13. C. Alexander, *The Timeless Way of Building,* p. 181.

14. The following analysis of Selye's work is adapted from an essay coauthored with Nancy Tuana entitled, "The Rationality of Creativity in Science," in Diana DeLuca (ed.), *Essays on Creativity and Science* (Honolulu: Hawaii Council of Teachers of English, 1986), 225–235. Our joint analysis was worked out in ongoing conversation with our colleague, George McClure.

15. Hans Selye, "A Syndrome Produced by Diverse Nocuous Agents," *Nature* 138 (1936), 32.

16. For an account of this story see Hans Selye, *The Stress of Life* (New York: McGraw-Hill, 1956).

17. Ibid., pp. 25–26.

18. With the decline of vitalism in the early nineteenth century, medical science returned to the view prevalent in the iatrophysical and iatrochemical theories of disease which regarded the body as a machine. Medical science in the nineteenth century, especially the German schools, had reacted against the

"metaphysical" systems of eighteenth-century vitalism and turned toward an analytic method, based on physics and chemistry, which led to a purely materialistic concept of vital phenomena. A good example of this trend is Jacques Loeb's exposition of a mechanistic theory of life in his *The Organism as a Whole* (New York: G. P. Putnam's Sons, 1916).

19. Walter B. Cannon, *The Wisdom of the Body* (New York: W. W. Norton & Co., 1932).

20. Robert McCauley has noted that Seyle seems to have fallen prey to the "adaptationalist fallacy," in which every response is regarded as serving some specific function. However problematic this assumption may be, it does appear to represent Selye's understanding at that time.

21. Selye, *The Stress of Life,* p. 26.

22. We should remember that the concept of feedback did not exist then, even though some feedback devices were widely used, for example, governors on steam engines.

23. Selye, *The Stress of Life,* p. 26.

24. Ibid., p. 26.

25. Ibid., p. 12.

26. Ibid., p. 12.

27. Ibid., p. 217.

28. Ibid., p. 221.

29. Ibid., p. 243.

30. Ibid., p. 245.

CHAPTER SIX

1. For a very brief treatment of the history of imagination, see Harold Osborne, *Aesthetics and Art Theory* (New York: E. P. Dutton, 1970), 208–224. My survey draws heavily on his work. Other more specific historical developments are treated in R. L. Brett, *Fancy and Imagination* (London: Metheun, 1969); Mary Warnock, *Imagination* (Berkeley: University of California Press, 1978); and James Engell, *The Creative Imagination: Enlightenment to Romanticism* (Cambridge, Mass.: Harvard University Press, 1981).

2. Osborne, p. 208.

3. See, for example, Robert Hahn, *Did Plato Schematize the Forms?* (Ph.D. diss., Dept. of Philosophy, Yale University, 1976).

4. My diagram is based upon one provided by Robert Hahn, "A Note on Plato's Divided Line," *Journal of the History of Philosophy* 21, no. 2 (1983), 235–237.

5. John Herman Randall, *Aristotle* (New York: Columbia University Press, 1960), 95.

6. Cited in Osborne, p. 217.

7. Ibid., p. 219.

8. Thomas Hobbes, *Leviathan* (pt. 1, chap. 1), (1651; Indianapolis: Bobbs-Merrill, 1968), p. 25.

9. Ibid., (pt. 1, chap. 2), p. 27 in 1968 ed.

10. Thomas Hobbes, *Answer to D'Avenant* (1650), cited in R. L. Brett, *Fancy and Imagination* (London: Metheun, 1969).

11. Hobbes, *Leviathan* (pt. 1, chap. 8).

12. I follow the standard notation of Kant's works by referring to the Academy edition pagination in parentheses. Works cited are Immanuel Kant, *Critique of Pure Reason,* trans. Norman Kemp Smith (New York: St. Martin's Press, 1965); and Immanuel Kant, *Critique of Judgment,* trans. James Haden (New York: Hafner, 1968). *Critique of Judgment* citations are given by section number.

13. David Hume, *A Treatist of Human Nature,* ed. L. A. Selby-Bigge (Oxford: Oxford University Press, 1888), bk. 1, sec. iv.

14. The rejection by modern physics of the a priori, pure, and univocal nature of time does not effect the conclusions we are drawing about the nature of imagination.

15. Immanuel Kant, *First Introduction to the Critique of Judgment,* trans. James Haden (Indianapolis: Bobbs-Merrill, 1965), sec. 5, p. 16.

16. Mark Johnson, "Kant's Unified Theory of Beauty," *Journal of Aesthetics and Art Criticism* 38, no. 2 (1979), 167–178.

17. *Critique of Judgment,* sec. 43 (§43); hereafter, *CJ,* followed by the section number.

18. Hans Georg Gadamer, *Truth and Method* (New York: Crossroad Publishing, 1975).

19. See Kant's *Anthropology,* sec. 38. Kant's reasons for regarding symbolic presentations as insufficient for theoretical understanding are elaborated in Thomas Wilson, "Kant's Philosophy of Language" (Ph.D. diss., Dept. of Philosophy, Southern Illinois University, Carbondale, 1985), chap. 1.

20. The arguments for such a move are too well-known to need restatement here. The literature on the topic is immense. One focus of the debate has been W. V. O. Quine, "Two Dogmas of Empiricism," in his *From a Logical Point of View* (Cambridge, Mass.: Harvard University Press, 1953).

21. From Frege's review of Husserl's *Philosophie der Arithmetik,* extracted in Peter Geach and Max Black (eds.), *Translations from the Philosophical Writings of Gottlob Frege* (Oxford: Basil Blackwell, 1966), 79.

22. I have in mind here a theory of the sort elaborated by George Lakoff in *Women, Fire, and Dangerous Things: What Categories Reveal about the Mind* (Chicago: University of Chicago Press, 1987). See also the citation to the section on categorization in my Preface to the present volume.

23. By an inquiry into the structures of narrative unity, I have in mind explorations of the sort found in Alasdair McIntyre, *After Virtue: Study in Moral Theory* (Notre Dame: University of Notre Dame Press, 1981); and Paul Ricoeur, *Time and Narrative* (Chicago: University of Chicago Press, 1984).

CHAPTER SEVEN

1. Rudolf Carnap, *Meaning and Necessity* (Chicago: University of Chicago Press, 1947), p. 10.

2. This apt phrase is taken from Charles Fillmore, "Frames and the Semantics of Understanding" (unpubl. mss., Dept. of Linguistics, University of California, Berkeley, 1984). Fillmore gives an eloquent account of the nature and importance of such a "semantics of understanding" as complementing a "semantics of truth."

3. A brief description of cognitive semantics, which is another name for the view I am urging, can be found in George Lakoff, "Cognitive Semantics," in Umberto Eco (ed.), *Meaning and Mental Representation* (in press).

4. Jon Barwise and John Perry, *Situations and Attitudes* (Cambridge Mass.: MIT Press, 1983), are a notable exception to this tradition, but they still hold an Objectivist orientation on this issue central to the present study.

5. John Searle, *Speech Acts* (Cambridge: Cambridge University Press, 1969), 12.

6. In Searle's earlier work, he claims that the basic speech act theory must give an account only for *literal* utterances (*Speech Acts,* pp. 20–21). He assumes, then, a literal core or base of language, such that all other nonliteral uses are to be understood as functions of, or as derivative from, that literal base. I shall suggest later that this assumption gets him into trouble in important ways.

7. Ibid., chap. 2, sec. 6, pp. 42–50.

8. H. P. Grice, "Meaning," *Philosophical Review* (1957), 377–388.

9. John Searle, *Intentionality* (Cambridge: Cambridge University Press, 1983).

10. Ibid., p. 1.

11. Ibid., p. 164.

12. The major arguments for this view are presented in chap. 5 ("The Background") of *Intentionality* and in chap. 5 ("Literal Meaning") in *Expression and Meaning* (Cambridge: Cambridge University Press, 1979).

13. John Searle, "Literal Meaning." 117–136.

14. Searle, *Intentionality,* p. 145.

15. Searle, "Metaphor," in his *Expression and Meaning,* pp. 76–116.

16. Recall that principle 4 states that "it is a fact about our sensibility, whether culturally or naturally determined, that we just do perceive a connection, so that P is associated in our minds with R properties" (p. 108). As I interpret this claim, it says nothing more than that there is some basis for the metaphor, though we can't say what it is—it must lie in the Background.

17. Searle, *Intentionality,* pp. 148–149.

18. Ibid., p. 149.

19. George Lakoff and Zoltan Kovecses, "The Cognitive Model of Anger Inherent in American English," Berleley Cognitive Science Report, no. 10, May 1983.

20. Searle, *Intentionality,* p. 28.

21. Ibid., p. 151.

22. David Dowty, Robert Wall, and Stanley Peters, *Introduction to Montague Semantics* (Dordrecht: D. Reidel, 1981), p. 4.

23. See George Lakoff, *Women, Fire, and Dangerous Things: What Categories Reveal about the Mind* (Chicago: University of Chicago Press, 1987), for an account of kinds of categorical structure.

24. See Lakoff; also see George Lakoff and Mark Johnson, *Metaphors We Live By* (Chicago: University of Chicago Press, 1980), chap. 8.

CHAPTER EIGHT

1. For lively discussions of this issue see Richard Rorty, *The Consequences of Pragmatism* (Minneapolis: University of Minnesota Press, 1982); Hilary Putnam, *Reason, Truth, and History* (Cambridge: Cambridge University Press, 1981); Richard Bernstein, *Beyond Objectivism and Relativism* (Philadelphia: University of Pennsylvania, 1983); and Harold Brown, *Perception, Theory, and Commitment* (Chicago: University of Chicago Press, 1979).

2. Bernstein, p. 8.

3. Richard Rorty, *Philosophy and the Mirror of Nature* (Princeton: Princeton University Press, 1979).

4. Ibid., pp. 8–9.

5. Bernstein, p. 8.

6. See Thomas Kuhn, *The Structure of Scientific Revolutions*, 2d ed. (Chicago: University of Chicago Press, 1970); Frederick Suppe, *The Structure of Scientific Theories*, 2d ed. (Urbana: University of Illinois Press, 1977); Harold Brown; Richard Rorty; Richard Rorty, *Consequences of Pragmatism;* Paul Feyerabend, *Against Method* (London: New Left Books, 1975); and Hilary Putnam.

7. See Carl Hempel, *Aspects of Scientific Explanation* (New York: Free Press, 1965); Suppe.

8. Carl Hempel, "Empiricist Criteria of Cognitive Significance," in *Aspects of Scientific Explanation* (New York: Free Press, 1965), 101–119.

9. W. V. O. Quine, "Two Dogmas of Empiricism," in *From a Logical Point of View* (New York: Harper Torchbooks, 1961), 41.

10. The most influential arguments are given in Kuhn; Feyerabend; N. R. Hanson, *Patterns of Discovery* (Cambridge: Cambridge University Press, 1958); Richard Rorty, *Philosophy and the Mirror of Nature*, chap. 4.

11. Brown, p. 10.

12. Richard Rorty, *Consequences of Pragmatism*, xxiii.

13. Putnam, p. 49.

14. Ibid., p. 52.

15. It is often claimed by philosophers in the Anglo-American "Analytic" tradition that certain European philosophers really are antirealist, even to the point of denying the existence of physical things. It is often said, for example, that Derrida and his disciples really do believe that there are nothing in the world but *texts*. I do not wish to enter into this heated and angry debate, but it does seem perfectly clear that these people do agree that there are hunks of matter outside language. What they claim, however, is that matter is only *meaningful and comprehensible* by us insofar as it is grasped via "language." And

"language" here is used in a broad sense to include all structures of meaning and not just those that involve words. Whatever one's view is on these issues, it is clear that both Rorty and Putnam grant the existence of an "external world."

16. Robert McCauley, "Concepts, Theories, and Truth," *Emory Cognition Project Report #8* (November 1985), impugns this false dichotomy and argues for a realism falling in the middle ground between these extremes.

17. Putnam, p. 54.

18. Rorty, p. xxix.

19. John Searle, *Intentionality* (Cambridge: Cambridge University Press, 1983), 158–159.

20. R. Levins and R. Lewontin, *The Dialectical Biologist* (Cambridge, Mass.: Harvard University Press, 1985), 89.

21. For an explanation of this notion and a survey of the relevant literature, see Robert McCauley; and George Lakoff, *Women, Fire, and Dangerous Things: What Our Categories Reveal about the Mind* (Chicago: University of Chicago Press, 1987).

22. Putnam, pp. 54–55.

Index